398.8 Knapp, Mary, 1931–
KNA
　　One potato, two
　　potato ..

AUG　1974

APR　1977　　JUL　1978

APR 1977	DATE	1977	
APR 79			

MAR 7

One Potato, Two Potato . . .

One Potato,

Two Potato...

THE SECRET EDUCATION OF

AMERICAN CHILDREN

BY

MARY AND HERBERT KNAPP

W · W · NORTON & COMPANY · INC ·
New York

ACKNOWLEDGMENTS

Dylan Thomas: "Fern Hill," from *The Poems of Dylan Thomas.* Copyright 1946 by New Directions Publishing Corporation. Reprinted by permission of New Directions Publishing Corporation. *Collected Poems of Dylan Thomas.* Reprinted by permission of J. M. Dent & Sons, Ltd., publishers, and the Trustees for the Copyrights of the late Dylan Thomas.

Selections from "Jews and Jewishness in the Street Rhymes of American Children" by Nathan Hurvitz, *Jewish Social Studies*, 16 (1954), reprinted by permission of the Conference on Jewish Social Studies, Inc.

"Playmate," copyright 1939 by Santly-Joy Music Inc.; copyright renewed; all rights reserved, used by permission of Chappell & Company, Inc.

This book was designed by Jacques Chazaud. Typefaces used are Deepdene and Fairfield, set by Fuller Typesetting of Lancaster. Printing and binding were done by Haddon Craftsmen, Inc.

Library of Congress Cataloging in Publication Data

Knapp, Mary
    One potato, two potato . . .

    Includes bibliographies.
    1. Folk-lore—United States.   2. Folk-lore of children.   I. Knapp, Herbert, joint author.   II. Title.
GR105.K38   1976   398.8'0973   76–16571
ISBN 0–393–08745–X

First Edition

1 2 3 4 5 6 7 8 9 0

For Elly and Sarah

Contents

CONTENTS

Contents

CHAPTER 4—COPING WITH THE HERE AND NOW

CHAPTER 5—COPING WITH THE UNKNOWN

CONTENTS

Preface

Traditional childlore has never attracted the attention it deserves. Most adults simply assume that today's children don't play traditional games any more. Even those observant parents who perceive that traditional games and rhymes are still a part of childhood don't generally realize how important they are. Nor do most parents realize the great number of rhymes, games, and traditions that still exist.

Psychologists and sociologists who write about play and games usually discuss traditional lore as if it were a minor aspect of imaginative play or of organized sports. Actually, it differs from both, and it has been proving its functional importance to children for hundreds of years.

Unless otherwise noted, all the items in this book were collected during the sixties and seventies and were obtained from more than one state. Those found only once are followed by a notation specifying the year they were collected or published and the state in which they were found.

The material in this book is not comprehensive. A comprehensive collection of American childlore would run to several volumes. Our material is, however, representative and serves to illustrate how traditional lore functions in the lives of contemporary children from kindergarten through the sixth grade.

Of course, in reporting what children sometimes say about products, people and the world around them, it has been clear to the authors that such statements often bear no relation to reality or even to the attitudes of the children themselves.

... Under the new made clouds and happy as the heart
    was long,
        In the sun born over and over,
            I ran my heedless ways,
        My wishes raced through the house high hay
And nothing I cared, at my sky blue trades, that time allows
In all his tuneful turning so few and such morning songs
        Before the children green and golden
            Follow him out of grace. . . .

—DYLAN THOMAS, "Fern Hill"

One Potato, Two Potato . . .

1 | The Folk Curriculum

Who Needs It?

Some children spend practically every waking moment engaged in activities which are supervised, organized, or at the very least conceived by adults. During the school year, teachers decide how children spend most of the day. After school and during the summer, parents, often at considerable emotional and financial expense to themselves, schedule their children's time. And where parents leave off, television takes over.

But the best-laid plans of adults can never accomplish for children what children can accomplish for themselves, if given a chance. Few adults realize this, because not many have the opportunity, patience, or curiosity to observe children at unsupervised play for any length of time. When they do, they are unlikely to keep from interfering. It is the rare adult who can refrain from offering assistance when children have difficulty or who can keep his mouth shut when they begin to argue. But when the locus of authority is shifted—ever so slightly—from the children themselves to adult supervisors, the delicate machinery of their natural social relationships is thrown out of kilter. Left to work of its own accord, it functions in a remarkable way. Unsupervised children playing together learn how to govern themselves according to a system of rules. They learn how to deal with cheaters and crybabies and how to make sophisticated juridical distinctions that strike a fine balance between the self-interest of individuals and the good of the group.

They are competitive, but winning is not their goal. They come together voluntarily for a good game. Thus they learn the joy of team play and group solidarity without suffering from the depersonalization and bitterness that mark fiercely competitive, supervised contests where the goal has been reduced to mere victory.

They let off steam, releasing tensions created by the repressive atmosphere of the school. They mock the larger culture, distancing themselves from the intrusive demands of advertising. They play with the emotion of fear, thus becoming less fearful.

In all this, they are guided by their folk tradition, which includes games played in Roman times, expressions popular in the Middle Ages, and parodies of the latest television commercial. It provides them with the timeworn rituals for sharing secrets or foreseeing the future and time-tested ways of defending their self-esteem or dealing with social problems like farting or having a girl friend.

Folklore and the Folk

Many parents whom we talked to while gathering material for this book thought folklore survived only in out-of-the-way places like the Ozarks. That their own children knew all kinds of folklore was a curious, even disturbing, discovery.

But folklore flourishes in families that dress in factory-spun fabrics as well as those wearing homespun, and it is known to adults as well as to children. Passed on orally, it is nearly always anonymous in origin. It includes customs like "showering" the bride-to-be, lighting candles on a birthday cake, and taking food to a bereaved family; and superstitions like wishing on a falling star and walking around a ladder instead of under it. Folk ideas—the idea, for example, that in the United States nothing is impossible—are also part of our folk tradition; they are expressed in sayings like "Sky's the limit," "Go for broke," "Where there's a will, there's a way." So are traditional insults ("He's so tight he hums in a high wind," "Shut the door, were you born in a barn?") and cures—especially for ailments that defy modern medicine, like the common cold and the hangover.

There are also, of course, stories which are told over and over in assorted versions—and they don't all have to do with cowboys or backwoodsmen. Periodically, for example, a story circulates that a cigarette company will donate an iron lung or a kidney machine to a dying child if people will send in a million empty cigarette wrappers. The story is believed by those who tell it, but it is a legend which in this case has no basis in reality. It is part of our urban folklore tradition.

There are traditional jokes ("Did you hear about the little moron who . . . ?"), riddles ("What's black and white and read all over?"), and gestures (thumbs up and thumbing your nose).

Bearers ,of folk tradition live in mountain cabins, yes, but in tenements, split-levels, and high-rises as well. The folk are all of us.

And folklore plays a vital but unappreciated role in holding together the frayed, factory-made fabric of our lives. Whether it be useful or silly, true or false, folklore connects us to the past and to each other, because it requires face-to-face contact. It exists when people share an identity, when they recognize themselves as members of a group united by race, nationality, occupation, class, geography, or age; and since all of us once belonged to that group of human beings we call children, the folklore of childhood brings together all of us.

ONE POTATO, TWO POTATO...

The Formulaic Nature of Children's Lore

Children's verbal lore, like all verbal folklore, is largely formulaic; it consists of stylized, unoriginal expressions or patterns of expression—"commonplaces"—which are part of a special vocabulary used in special situations and in response mainly to other children. No child taunts an adult with:

> Roses are red, violets are black,
> You'd look good with a knife in your back.

The set phrases of childlore resemble the set phrases of the traditional ballad singers, who, in ballad after ballad, sing of a maiden with "gold-yellow hair" and "lily-white hands." Homer, too, used a special vocabulary of stock phrases when he composed the *Iliad* and the *Odyssey*. He referred to the "rosy-fingered dawn" and the "wine-dark sea" over and over again, not because he couldn't think of anything original, but because, like the ballad singers, he drew his material from an oral tradition that was developed in a preliterate society. Such a society, having no files, books, or data banks, depended on memorization to preserve its cultural heritage. Originality was not a virtue; familiarity was. Grade-school children, in their largely preliterate world, also prize the familiarity of formulaic verbal lore, and they have an oral tradition that can be traced back for centuries.

The Historical Background of Children's Lore

Some modern games are pale versions of earlier practices. Kickball, football, and soccer in Great Britain and America are descended from a game called the Dane's Head, in which a ball, or maybe an actual head, was kicked back and forth between Anglo-Saxon villages. And because bridge builders once felt obliged to sacrifice someone to propitiate the water spirit whose domain was being defiled by the bridge, some folklorists believe that the game London Bridge has a shadowy

origin in rites of human sacrifice. A popular rhyme employed
to decide who's It in a tag game may also echo sacrificial rites:

> Eeny, meeny, miney, moe,
> Catch a tiger [or "nigger," "baby," "lion," "rabbit"] by
> his toe.
> If he hollers, let him go.
> My mother told me to choose this ver-ry one.
> O-u-t spells out goes he,
> Right in the middle of the deep, blue sea.

There are many versions of this rhyme. One from Britain
goes:

> Eena, meena, mona, mite,
> Basca, lora, hora, bite.
> Hugga, bucca, bau;
> Eggs, butter, cheese, bread,
> Stick, stock, stone dead, o-u-t!

The Reverend Charles Francis Potter points out that when the
Romans decided to wipe out Druidism in England around
61 A.D., they sent troops over the Menai Strait to cut down
the sacred trees on the island of Mona, now Anglesea. The
words *lora* and *hora* in the rhyme mean "binding straps"
and "hour" in Latin. *Bucca* means "goblin" in Cornish. The
foods mentioned are traditionally associated with magic, and
"eeny" stands for "one" in an ancient counting jargon used
by shepherds in West England.

No one can say for sure what to make of all this, but the
Druids, the Celtic priests, did sacrifice people by burning
them in wicker cages or baskets. Possibly a rhyme similar to
this one was used to pick the It at a sacrifice.

The reference to the deep, blue sea in the first version of
"Eeny, Meeny" is linked to the past in a different way. Potter
suggests that it echoes Sunday-school lessons about Jonah: ". . .
the lot fell upon Jonah," and eventually they "cast him forth
into the sea."

Another folklorist, Sister Mary Jeremy, notes that the word

"O'Leary," which appears in several ball-bounce rhymes, goes back to the 1300's. "O'Leary" may rhyme with "Wallace Beery" or with "Mary." In the rhymes of West Indian children in Panama, it has become "ol' lady." Perhaps the most common version goes:

> One, two, three O'Leary,
> Four, five, six O'Leary,
> Seven, eight, nine O'Leary,
> Ten O'Leary, the postman.
> [or "Ten O'Leary, I made it!"]

On each "O'Leary," the ball-bouncer bends her left knee, lifts her right foot, bounces the ball under her leg, and swings her leg wide or brings it down crossed over her other one, depending on whether she is bouncing the ball from left to right or from right to left. "O'Leary," spelled "a-lery," is found in a 1370 manuscript of *Piers Plowman*. When Piers goes to check on those who are helping him plow his half acre, he finds them loafing about, pretending to be crippled: *Somme liede here leggis a-lery, as such losellis cunne.* (Some made their legs crooked, as such losers will.") Today the word "a-lery," referring to lame-looking legs, exists only in ball-bounce rhymes, and although children obviously use it correctly, not one of them can say what it means.

We have only begun to suggest the wealth of curious connections between present-day children's games and rhymes and the past. Paintings in Egyptian tombs show children playing ball. Girls were participating in a game similar to jacks well before the birth of Christ. Plato speaks of Greek boys playing Blind Man's Bluff, Hide and Seek, and other games. A hopscotch diagram can still be seen on the pavement of the Roman Forum, and Ovid mentions Roman children using polished nuts in a game similar to marbles.

Connections between the games children play today and those they played centuries ago are fascinating, but they may mislead us in two ways. First, a children's game that resembles an ancient religious ceremony isn't necessarily a degenerate form of the ceremony. Roger Caillois remarks that it is more likely that the game and the ceremony existed at the same time on different levels of seriousness, just as today children's marriage games and doctor games exist side by side with real marriages and visits to the doctor. Second, we should not assume, because certain games are very old, that childlore itself goes back to the pre-Christian era. The folklore of children could not develop until childhood became a distinct period of life; and, surprisingly, for centuries childhood, as we think of it, did not exist.

Throughout most of history, children began to blend into adult society as soon as they left infancy. Boys and girls as young as three or four enjoyed, to the best of their ability, the same games—tennis, hockey, Hide and Seek, gambling, marbles, tag—that adults enjoyed.

But roughly between the settlement at Jamestown in 1607 and the American Revolution in 1776, new ideas about childhood took hold. Teachers began objecting to having nine-year-olds and teen-agers in the same class, and during the nineteenth century, it gradually became customary for school classes to be limited to students of approximately the same age. Early in the nineteenth century, churches instituted Sunday schools, recognizing that children had special religious needs. People also came to believe that certain games were children's games and were inappropriate for adults, while others—gambling games, for instance—should be reserved for adults only.

The emergence of childhood as a distinct period did not mean, however, that the lives of children became completely different from those of adults, and all through the nineteenth century, young adults and children played many of the same games. A French etiquette book that was reprinted in the United States in 1833 and in 1841 recommended circle games and kissing games for businessmen. After the Civil War, the pre-eminent folk game for boys and young men was

7

baseball. There were no standard rules. Teams got together before a game to decide how it would be played. Some, for instance, used ten men on defense or believed a batter was entitled to four strikes or a pitcher to an unlimited number of balls.

In frontier areas, young adults borrowed children's songs and portions of children's chasing and kissing games, which they combined with movements from the square dance and verses from popular songs to create the play-party, also known as the flang-party or the bounce-around. The participants swung their partners by the hand instead of the waist and sang their own accompaniment, thus evading religious objections to dancing and to instrumental music.

To some extent, the folklore of children has always involved the imitation of adult behavior. The fact that today adults rarely amuse themselves by playing folk games has contributed to a decline in the popularity of some folk games among children. The players who serve as models for children today are often professionals. And the games that adults organize for children are imitations of those of professional players. This is especially true of the games played by boys, and as a result, boys today know fewer folk games than they once did.

Ironically, the school, which was instrumental in segregating the world of children from the world of adults and thus providing the necessary condition for the development of a childlore tradition, today acts as a strong force against the perpetuation of that tradition.

The School

In our country, schools have assumed tremendous importance in the lives of children, for the success of the American experiment is seen to depend on an enlightened citizenry. Our reverence for a formal education (if not for intellectuals) is so great that we are not content to offer it as a right; we require it. At least, we require that all children attend school.

For children, this dual right/obligation has traditionally meant submitting to a rigidly structured environment where a teacher supervises and directs their learning. It is generally assumed that all knowledge is "passed down" from an experienced adult to an innocent child. (A corollary bit of wishful thinking which everyone denies accepting but which has greatly influenced our attitudes toward the school is that children can't find out anything that adults don't teach them.) Even children's play has been brought into the rigidities of the official curriculum, so that in many elementary schools, recess—with the freedom and respite the word connotes—has given way to the physical-education period or to supervised recreation, as if children cannot even play without instruction.

We are so preoccupied with what we have to offer children that we overlook the education that they can offer one another; yet in the unsupervised nooks and crannies of their lives, where they perpetuate centuries-old folk traditions, children learn what no one can teach them.

The Transmission of Children's Lore

Childlore is usually passed on from one child to another, without the mediation or even the knowledge of adults. But sometimes parents, grandparents, teen-age brothers and sisters, even books, help tie together the forever unraveling strands of children's lore. One mother, for example, taught her children the following rhyme, which she remembered from her own childhood in the thirties:

> Eeny, meeny, miney, moe,
> Crackafeeny, finey, foe,
> Alma nujer, papa tujer,
> Rif, bif, bam, bo.

This rhyme appears in a late-nineteenth-century collection, and somewhere may have been continuously transmitted from child to child from that time to this; but in at least one neighborhood in Indiana where it was unknown, it was re-introduced into childlore by an adult.

Teen-age brothers and sisters also reintroduce material into childlore. A joke—"What does a virgin have for breakfast?" "I don't know." "I didn't think you would"—may drop out of the repertoire of fifth- and sixth-graders for a time, but it is soon reintroduced by more sophisticated older children.

Books, too, help keep folklore alive. Since folklore is, by definition, an oral tradition, the role books play in its transmission has always been a problem for folklorists. But folklorists themselves put material from oral tradition into books, where it is read and then again passed on orally. Children's books of traditional games, rhymes, songs, and riddles are widely available today. A child may read a rhyme in a book and recite it to some playmates; they, in turn, may pass it on to others. It's still folklore as long as it is learned orally somewhere and exists in different versions.

Children do not just repeat old favorites. They often admit new verses or songs from the larger culture into their oral tradition. But such material undergoes a sea change as it is passed from one child to another. Look at what happens to "Kookaburra," a song regularly taught at Campfire Girl and Girl Scout meetings and at school. Here are the official verses:

> Kookaburra sits on an old gum tree,
> Merry, merry king of the bush is he,
> Laugh, Kookaburra, laugh, Kookaburra,
> Gay your life must be.

> Kookaburra sits in an old gum tree,
> Eatin' all the gum drops he can see,
> Stop, Kookaburra, stop, Kookaburra,
> Save some there for me.

> Kookabura sits in an old gum tree,
> Counting all the monkeys he can see,
> Stop, Kookaburra, stop, Kookaburra,
> That's no monkey, that's me!

In Eugene, Oregon, Robert Atkinson found that children who sang this song outside of class changed the lines so that they would sound more natural, make more sense, and be more dramatic. Line 4 became more natural as "How gay your life must be"; so did line 8 as "Just save some for me." Line 6 made no sense to a girl who had never heard of gum drops, so she changed it to "Eating all the old gums . . . ," meaning chewing gums. More important, in line 10 another girl changed "counting" monkeys to "shooting" them.

The preference of the folk for dramatic action is even more apparent in the unofficial stanzas that Atkinson collected:

> Kookaburra sits in a rocking chair,
> Along comes a bear and pulls his hair,
> Poor Kookaburra, poor Kookaburra,
> How bald your life must be.
>
> Kookaburra sits on a country road,
> Sits right down on a horny toad,
> Poor Kookaburra, poor Kookaburra,
> Bloody his life must be.
>
> Kookaburra sits on an old rail track,
> Along comes a train and knocks him flat,
> Poor Kookaburra, poor Kookaburra,
> Dead your life must be.

The kookaburra, incidentally, is an Australian bird, not a creature American children are likely to know about. We collected one version in which Kookaburra is transformed into an American "Cocoa Burro."

A child's desire for a rhyme to make sense, sound natural, be up-to-date or exciting, and last long enough for his purposes, along with his attempts to fill the gaps in his memory, tends to result in changes as he casually transmits his stock of folklore to others. On the other hand, his gang's regular repetition of songs and games fosters stability. Paradoxically, a child's desire to repeat a song just as he heard it may promote either change or stability—depending on how accurately he heard it in the first place. The jeer "Liar, liar, pants on fire!" sometimes becomes "Liar, liar, pacifier!"—actually a more profound commentary than the original. And the line from the children's version of "Battle Hymn of the Republic" that goes, "I hid behind the door with a loaded forty-four," may be sung, "I hid behind the door with a load of four-o-four." If that's what a child hears, that's what he sings.

The Distribution of Children's Lore

A great deal of childlore is international in scope. Versions of the same games are found in many countries. For instance, Kick the Can has been reported from the English-speaking countries and from Italy (where it is called *Barattolo*), France (*La boîte*), Germany (*Stäbchenversteck, Ballversteck, Russisch Versteck*), Holland (*Buske Stamp*), and Panama (*La lata*). Parallels of the Ladybird (or "Ladybug") rhyme,

> Ladybird, ladybird, fly away home,
> Your house is on fire
> And your children alone,

are found in France, Germany, Switzerland, Denmark, and Sweden. The nicknames of this insect in Hindu, Russian, English ("Our Lady's Bird"), and other Indo-European languages indicate that it has often been associated with things sacred. Even today, children feel it's unlucky to kill a ladybird.

Other childlore has more limited distribution. In America, when two children say the same word at the same time they often shout "Jinks!" One might expect this custom to be found in other English-speaking nations, but it has so far been reported only from the United States and U.S. bases overseas.

And while it is clear that ethnic and regional childlore exists, not enough of it has been collected for us to describe it with assurance. Readers from the West and Middle West probably won't recognize the game Ring-a-levio, which is popular in the East and in parts of the South. However,

Buck-buck (Johnny on a Pony), which is often called a New York game, has been reported to us by children as far south as Georgia and as far west as Idaho. And while there are distinctive elements in the childlore of some blacks, Catholics, Chicanos, and Jews, many children from these groups seem to share their childlore not only with one another but—in large part—with the children of the rest of the population.

Nor has much work been done toward describing the class distribution of children's games and rhymes. People sometimes assume that rough games like Ring-a-levio are not played by middle-class children. (In Ring-a-levio one team tries to capture the members of another team. Each capture may involve a fight. Captured players are put in the "pot"; their teammates try to rescue them.) Or people take it for granted that only "neglected" children still know traditional games. Certainly games vary in popularity from one neighborhood to another, and the children in some neighborhoods play more roughly than those in others. However, few games seem to be restricted to any one social class.

Some children absorb much more lore than others. Some know more than they will tell. We have repeatedly interviewed children who seemed honestly to believe they knew nothing of childlore, but who, when we observed them with their play group, turned out to know a great deal. And while we suspect that certain rhymes and jokes are more familiar to working-class children than to others, we have been impressed by the uniformity of American childlore.

The Organization of This Book

In organizing the material for this book, we have kept uppermost in our minds the way the folklore of childhood functions in the lives of children. Our purpose is to show how children use their traditional lore to cope with the stresses of their lives and to learn what it means to be a member of a human society.

13

ONE POTATO, TWO POTATO...

We have divided their lore into categories, but actually children's lore defies tidy categories. Children adapt particular items of their lore to a variety of needs and situations. An example comes readily to mind. One gray, cold, winter morning we observed a group of what appeared to be first- or second-graders waiting for a bus in Austin, Texas. A teacher stood nearby, her hands in her pockets, her collar turned up, a scarf wrapped around her ears. Dozens of dour adults intent on future goals strode past. Soon the children began chanting:

> I love coffee, I love tea.
> I love the boys and the boys love me.
> Yes. No. May-be so.

As the chant, with repetition, grew louder, the children, facing in all directions, began jumping in place. They were grinning gleefully.

Now, "I Love Coffee" is widely reported as a traditional jump-rope rhyme, and jump-rope is a game that tests the skill and endurance of girls. This group, however, was composed of both boys and girls. The children were using the rhyme to assert their fellowship and their presence in a world in which nobody was having any fun and which was ignoring them. They were using it to pass the time until the bus came, and certainly they were using it to help keep themselves warm. But they were clearly not using it as a part of a game of skill. For in this particular instance, although the children were chanting what we call a jump-rope rhyme, and were indeed jumping, there was no rope.

We hope that the reader will keep in mind that while children are remarkably conservative in preserving their traditions for generations, they are also very flexible in adapting their lore to present concerns.

NOTES

Folklore and the Folk

Alan Dundes describes "Folk Ideas as Units of Worldview," in *Toward New Perspectives in Folklore,* edited by Américo Paredes and Richard Bauman (Austin: University of Texas Press, 1972), pp. 93–103.

The Historical Background of Children's Lore

For a history of football, see David Riesman and Reuel Denney, "Football in America: A Study in Culture Diffusion," in *Sport, Culture, and Society,* edited by John W. Loy, Jr., and Gerald S. Kenyon (New York: Macmillan, 1969), pp. 306–19. Alice Bertha Gomme argues that London Bridge has its origins in sacrificial rites in *The Traditional Games of England, Scotland, and Ireland,* 2 vols. (1894; reprint ed., New York: Dover Publications, 1964), Vol. I, pp. 346–48. The history of "Eeny, Meeny" is traced by Charles Francis Potter, "Eeny, Meeny, Miny, Mo," in *Funk & Wagnalls Standard Dictionary of Folklore, Mythology and Legend,* 2 vols. (New York: Funk & Wagnalls, 1949), Vol. I; and that of "O'Leary, the Postman" by Sister Mary Jeremy, " 'Leggis A-lery,' *Piers Plowman* A VII, 114," *English Language Notes,* 1 (1964), 250–51. Roger Caillois' remark is found on p. 62 of *Man, Play, and Games,* translated by Meyer Barash (New York: The Free Press, 1961). The best book about the development of the idea of childhood is still Philippe Ariès, *Centuries of Childhood: A Social History of Family Life,* translated by Robert Baldick (New York: Alfred A. Knopf, 1962). The French etiquette book is described in William Wells Newell, *Games and Songs of American Children* (second ed., 1903; reprint ed., New York: Dover Publications, 1963), p. 6. B. A. Botkin describes the play-party in *The American Play-Party Song* (1937; reprint ed., New York: Frederick Ungar, 1963).

The Transmission of Children's Lore

The "Crackafeeny" rhyme is No. 608 in Henry Carrington Bolton, *The Counting-Out Rhymes of Children* (1888; reprint ed., Detroit: Singing Tree Press, 1969). The transmission and transformations of "Kookaburra" are recorded in Robert M. Atkinson,

ONE POTATO, TWO POTATO...

"Songs Little Girls Sing: An Orderly Invitation to Violence," *Northwest Folklore*, 2 (1967), 2–8.

The Distribution of Children's Lore

Iona and Peter Opie discuss the distribution of Kick the Can in *Children's Games in Street and Playground* (Oxford: Clarendon Press, 1969), pp. 167–68, and that of "Ladybird" in *The Oxford Dictionary of Nursery Rhymes* (Oxford: Clarendon Press, 1952), p. 263. "Jinks" is discussed by Mary and Herbert Knapp, "Tradition and Change in American Playground Language," *Journal of American Folklore*, 86 (1973), 137–41. A book about the regional childlore of a rural black girl who grew up in the South in the early years of this century is *Step It Down*, by Bessie Jones and Bess Lomax Hawes (New York: Harper & Row, 1972). Stanley Aronowitz speculates about the functions of the childlore of the working class in *False Promises: The Shaping of the American Working Class* (New York: McGraw-Hill, 1974), p. 65.

2 | The Games Children Play

GAMES AS LEGISLATURES AND COURTS OF LAW

The Nature of Folk Games

Not all the things children do to amuse themselves are traditional games. Take playing dolls, for instance. It's traditional, but it's not a game; there are no rules for playing dolls. Modern football, on the other hand, is a game, but it's not traditional; its rules are written down in a book and enforced by referees. The distinguishing characteristic of a traditional folk game is that although it has rules, they are not written down. Nobody knows exactly what they are. The players have a tradition to guide them, but must settle among themselves the details of how to play a particular game.

As they argue about rules, add new ones, agree to exceptions, and censure a playmate who is cheating, they are exploring how necessary rules are, how they are made, and what degree of consensus is needed to make them effective. They are also learning something about the relationship of personality to power and of fairness to order.

Perhaps even more important, while playing a folk game, children are also learning to play with roles, with feelings, with the rules of the game itself. In 1823, during a game of British football—something like soccer—William Webb Ellis astonished his friends by picking up the ball and running with it. They were, after all, playing "football." But on second thought, many players liked the idea of running with the ball. There was no convention of athletic directors, no meeting of a rules committee. Running with the ball simply caught on in one locality after another. Later, the British set up a stone to honor Ellis:

THIS STONE

COMMEMORATES THE EXPLOIT OF

WILLIAM WEBB ELLIS

WHO WITH A FINE DISREGARD FOR THE RULES OF

FOOTBALL, AS PLAYED IN HIS TIME,

FIRST TOOK THE BALL IN HIS ARMS AND RAN WITH IT,

THUS ORIGINATING THE DISTINCTIVE FEATURE OF

THE RUGBY GAME

A.D. 1823

In the creative mixture of organization and chaos, of law and disorder, that characterizes folk games, "mistakes" like Ellis' are not unusual, but can you imagine what would happen to a Little League player who introduced a similar innovation?

Unlike the players of supervised games, who are specialists —halfbacks, second basemen, forwards—the players of folk games have multiple roles. Each is a competitor, referee, spectator, and scorekeeper, all at the same time, and, in addition, may be acting out fantasies, experimenting with social ploys, testing friendships, and looking after a little brother. Because of their multiple roles, the children who play folk games have ideas about what's fun, what's cheating, and what's going on that are not at all what an adult might suppose.

Pregame Ceremonies

Children can start a game with magical suddenness. One second they are just talking; the next, a game is on. At other times, however, they go through elaborate pregame ceremonies that are wildly irritating to score-oriented adults, who see the interminable preparations as a sign that the kids need help getting started. Such adults don't know the score. They think folk games are about points instead of about law and order.

One pregame ceremony consists of chanting a rhyme that "legally" restricts the number of players to those present when it is recited:

> Tick tock, the game is locked,
> Nobody else can play.
> And if they do, we'll take their shoe,
> And we'll beat them black and blue ["and purple, too" may be added].

"Crisscross, double-cross" may be substituted for the first line. Sometimes the last line goes, "And we won't give it back for a week or two!" A variant from Maryland changes the last two lines:

> If you try, I'll hit you in the eye,
> And then I'll run away!

Latecomers sometimes hear, "Too late, too late, we've already locked the gate!"

Gestures often accompany the locking rhyme. Children may form a circle, join hands, and swing their arms as they recite it. A girl in Indiana says that she makes a circle with her fingers and everyone else puts one finger in the hole; then they chant the rhyme. Girls in Oregon stack their hands together and bounce them up and down as they say, "This game is locked. L-o-c-k-e-d!" On *d* they throw their hands high. Jump-rope players may do a kind of *entrechat* as they chant the locking rhyme. If a newcomer joins the chant before it's over, she can participate in the game.

This locking rhyme has become popular only since World War II, but children have chanted its last two lines in other contexts for over a hundred years. They were recited during traditional dialogue games—little playlets, really—like Old Mother Tipsy Toe and Old Witch. These games are forgotten or known only in abbreviated forms today. In the first, the mother warned her children to behave, but they continued to be impertinent until she chased them. Whomever she caught was out of the game. In the second, the disobedient children were captured by an old witch and rescued by the mother. (Contemporary versions of Old Witch are described in the section on "Scaries" in Chapter 5.) Possibly another ancestor of the locking rhyme is a work rhyme once recited by British farm boys whose first job was to scare birds away from the fields at planting time:

> Away, birds, away.
> Take a little, leave a little,
> And do not come again;
> For if you do,
> I will shoot you through,
> And there is an end of you.

Participation in games is also limited in other ways. In Hawaii in 1972, girls limited the number of players in their games of jacks by making V signs with their fingers, stacking the V's on top of each other, and inviting a newcomer to poke her finger down the center of the stack. If she could touch the ground, she could play.

Starting games that have sides is complicated because the players may range in age from four to fifteen. The older children often disdain leadership roles and affect only casual interest, but they take part just the same. A group may include a child with a foot in a cast, a boy wearing his good clothes, a girl whose mother has told her she can play for only five minutes, a spoiled brat, a wallflower, a little dictator, a clown—whoever is available. The players of folk games get some experience with the diversity of society, experience they do not get in the classroom, where they are segregated by age, or in supervised sports, where they are segregated by age, size, skill, and, usually, sex.

One good player is worth two or three poor ones. Fairness requires merciless public evaluations. The lame, the awkward, and the small are chosen last, often with howls of protest from their teammates. Inadequacies are not politely glossed over, but, on the other hand, nobody is left out either.

To start an It game like Hide and Seek or tag, a child may simply yell, "Let's-play-tag-Not-It!" all in one breath, or "Last-one-to-the-tree-is-It!" as he gets off to a two-step lead. Often shouts of "No fair!" go up on every side.

There are several things children can do next. They can draw straws or flip a "nick" (nickel). Younger children may hold hands and surround a player who stands with his eyes closed, one arm extended, one finger pointing. He turns in one direction; those around him move in the other, and as they do, they sing:

> Round and round and round she goes,
> And where she stops, nobody knows.
> Point to the east, point to the west,
> Point to the one you love the best.

This song combines two lines from the spiel of a midway barker and two lines from the old ring game Rise, Sally, Rise (see the section on "Singing Games" in Chapter 3). At some point, someone in the ring shouts "Stop!" Whoever the person in the center is pointing to is It.

But more often than not, when an argument about who's It can't be settled quickly, some child calls, "Let's play Eeny, Meeny." He means, "Let's count out."

Children who count out are repeating a ceremony that is hundreds of years old, and found in many different countries. In the 1880's, Henry Carrington Bolton collected 873 counting-out rhymes in English, German, Platt-Deutsch, Swedish, Dutch, French, Italian, Spanish, Portuguese, Bulgarian, Greek, Romany, Marathi (a language of western India), Basque, Arabic, Turkish, Armenian, Malagasy, Japanese, Hawaiian, and Penobscot (an American Indian language). He was fascinated by the similarities among the verses, noting especially, for instance, the similarity in the rhythms of his examples. More recently, Robbins Burling found that children's verses in Chinese, Arabic, Yoruba, English, and many other dissimilar languages have a four-beat line that disregards unaccented syllables. Burling suggests that this may be among the universal linguistic patterns that are narrowed and shaped by the rules and restrictions of particular languages.

Bolton believed that there was another significant similarity in his examples. He noted that words approximating "eeny meeny" appeared in the first lines of rhymes in French, Spanish, Italian, Swedish, German, Dutch, Platt-Deutsch, English, and Bulgarian. He also remarked that "Eeny, Meeny" was apparently the favorite verse of American children.

Almost a hundred years later, it is still one of their favorites. And we have collected German and Dutch rhymes from foreign students in American schools that are almost identical to rhymes that Bolton collected in the 1880's.

> *Iene miene mutten,*
> *Tien pond grutten,*
> *Tien pond kass,*
> *Iene miene mutten is de baas.*
>   (Dutch, Bolton, No. 101)

> *Ene mene mu,*
> *Müller's Kuh,*
> *Müller's Esel*
> *Das bist du.*
>   (German, Bolton, No. 302)

Moreover, we have found in Panama several versions of a Spanish counting-out rhyme which could be added to Bolton's list and which would lend additional support to his observation that rhymes containing an approximation of "eeny

meeny" in the first line are widely distributed. A favorite
of Panamanian children is:

Tin marín [pronounced "teen mareen"] de dos pingüé,
Cúcara mácara títiri fué,
El hijo del rey,
Pasó por aquí,
Comiendo maní;
A todos les dió,
Menos a mí.
Palos y palos,
Para los caballos,
Tústurustus,
Para que salgas tú.

Bolton concluded that the wide distribution of such first
lines made it reasonable to assume that they had a common
origin in antiquity. His citation of rhymes from Slavic, Ro-
mance, and Germanic languages suggests that the common
origin he had in mind was proto-Indo-European, and that he
believed the "eeny meeny" sounds had been preserved inde-
pendently in the counting-out rhymes of different languages.

There is, however, another possibility that may in part account for the wide distribution of these sounds. Children
borrow words and rhymes from foreign languages, perhaps
more often than most adults would think. The Opies cite a
case in which Danish children borrowed the rhyme "Jack
and Jill" from British occupation troops during the Napoleonic
wars and recited it as a nonsense verse. And two English
words have become part of the regulatory language of the
playground in Panama. Both are regarded by Panamanian
children as nonsense words. One is *fitting,* which is apparently
derived from "feeding." It entered Panamanian culture
through the children of West Indian immigrants who speak
English and Spanish and is used the way an American child
would use "Bites." An American child who doesn't want to
share his candy bar must say "No bites" before a hungry friend
can stake a claim to it by saying "Bites." The second word is

machin (pronounced "mahtcheen"). This word is part of a truce term and is the equivalent of "Kings X" or "Times." ("Times," incidentally, is also used as a truce term by Panamanian children.) When a Panamanian child wishes to declare himself "safe," he seizes something immovable and says *"Machin candado."* *Candado* means "lock" in Spanish. *Machin* is a nonsense word apparently derived from the English "machine." A child who uses this phrase is declaring himself protected by a machine or time lock, though he doesn't know it.

A high-school student from the village of Vav, in the Surat district in the state of Gujarat, India, told us that when children there select the It for Hide and Seek, the first step is to form a group of three; each of the three swings his arms and chants, *"Een, meen, sahri, mahri, teen,"* and on *"teen"* slaps either the palm or the back of one hand against the palm of the other hand. The odd man is out, and a new player joins the group. When only two players are left, a third is drawn from those who have already been eliminated. Finally, one of the last two is the odd man. The remaining player is It. *Een, meen, sahri, mahri, teen* seems to be a version of the numbers one through five in the Anglo-Cymric score, a counting system related to Welsh, and once widely known in rural Britain. Over fifty versions of it have been collected there. Others have been found in the United States:

> ENGLAND: Een tean tether mether pimp.
> ENGLAND: Eina peina paira puttera pith.
> IRELAND: Eina mina pera peppera pinn.
> UNITED STATES: Een teen tuther futher fip.

English settlers taught a version of this counting jargon to the Plymouth Indians, who in turn taught it to other colonists who had not known it, and who called it "Indian Counting." English soldiers or children in India may have passed on another version to the Gujarat Indians.

Although American children may call counting-out "playing Eeny, Meeny," they use many different rhymes; currently the most popular is:

> One potato, two potato, three potato, four,
> Five potato, six potato, seven potato, or.

It is so popular that some children refer to the child who does the counting as the Potato Man or the Potato Masher no matter what rhyme is used.

Before the Potato Masher begins to chant, each player places both fists in the center of a circle. As the rhyme is chanted, the Masher keeps time by tapping the fists of the players with his own fist. When he comes around the circle to himself, he hits himself on the left hand and then on his chin—in lieu of the fist he is using to keep time. The fist tapped as the rhyme comes to an end is withdrawn. When both of a child's fists have been withdrawn, he is out of the circle. As the number of remaining players diminishes, the excitement grows. If four children are playing, the Potato Man has to say the rhyme seven times. The last child left in is It. Sometimes each child places one foot in the center of the circle, and the counter taps the feet as he says the rhyme. This is a quicker method of counting-out.

The counter is almost always a dominant personality in the group. But if two children vie for this position and hold up the game by arguing about which one of them will count out, the group may move to one side and count out without them. Quiet children who never get to be counter while among their contemporaries may have the opportunity when they play with younger children. Different children get a chance to play leadership roles on different occasions because the group that gathers for a folk game varies in size and composition from one time to the next.

Choosing an It is not only a preliminary to another game, but a game in itself, and more complicated than it sounds. The process involves a mixture of show business, roulette, and chicanery, and not all players understand it the same way.

Some children see it as mainly show business. We watched one counter, a boy, whose prestige in the group was related to the size of his repertoire:

> My mother and your mother
> Were hanging out clothes.
> My mother hit your mother
> Right on the nose.
> What color blood came out?
> [The child on whom the word "out" lands shouts the
>   name of a color, and the Potato Man continues.]
> G-r-e-e-n! And you are *out*.

> Dog shit, you're it. *Out!*

> Aka, baka, soda cracker,
> Aka, baka, boo.
> If your father chews tobacco,
> *Out* goes you.

> Engine, engine, number nine
> Goin' down Chicago Line,
> If the train should jump the track,
> Do you want your money back?
> ["Yes" or "No" is the response.]
> Y-e-s spells yes, and you are Not It!

> Monkey, monkey, bottle of pop,
> On which monkey do we stop?
> One, two, three,
> *Out* goes he.

Most children use one or two favorites over and over, one of the following, perhaps:

> Superman, Superman, fly around,
> Around, around *out*.

> Bubble gum, bubble gum in a dish,
> How many pieces do you wish?
> [A number is specified.]
> T-w-o and you are Not It.

26

Boys are rotten, made of cotton,
Girls are dandy, made of candy,
Pick a pack of soda crackers
Out goes you.
                    (Hawaii, 1973)

Mickey Mouse built a house,
How many windows [or "nails," "sticks"] did he need?

I lit a candle and it went *out*.

Pennies, pennies in a fountain,
How many pennies make a mountain?

Three horses in a stable,
One runs *out*.

Tarzan, Tarzan in a tree,
Tarzan fell *out*.

Mr. Brown went to the store to buy a bucket of paint,
What color did he buy?

Eeny, meeny, choo cha leeny,
I buy gumbaleeny,
Achee, pachee, liverachee,
Out you go!

Piggie on the railroad
Picking up stones,
Along come an engine
And break piggie's bones.
"Oh," cried piggie, "that's not fair."
"Oh," cried the engineer, "I don't care."
                    (Montana, 1975)

Blue shoe, blue shoe,
How old are you?

The element of chance in counting-out makes it similar to roulette. In both, the winners and losers seem to be chosen by fate. Thus, counting-out seems to many children to be a fair, impartial way of choosing.

But as folklorist Kenneth Goldstein has shown, for some

27

children, counting-out is not a game of chance at all. It is a game of strategy, like chess. A strategically minded counter can eliminate whomever he wishes by thinking ahead and extending or shortening the rhyme. He can add single words or whole lines in order to make the rhyme come out "right." He can vary the relationship of his beat to the syllables of his chant. "Eeny, meeny, miney, moe," for example, can be four beats or seven. The counter may silently count around the circle ahead of time and select a rhyme with a particular number of stresses. He may skip people as he counts, or declare that the first person the count ends on is It instead of being out. He may change his own or another child's position in the circle. In some play groups, a child who sees that the rhyme is going to end on him may call it off once by shouting a formulaic, magic word. And children in all play groups will sneak their fists in or out of the circle, depending on whether or not they want to be It. Often children want to be It, and the group has to count out because there are too many volunteers for the job.

But aren't the strategists sometimes detected and charged with cheating? Yes, but the word "cheating" doesn't always mean the same thing to a child that it does to an adult. What it means to children is bound up with their general attitude toward rules and rule-making.

Rule-making in Chasing and Hiding Games

Children playing a chasing and hiding game sometimes spend more time arguing over the rules than they do playing the game—but the arguments are actually an important part of the game. Folk games often involve verbal as well as physical competition. Some players have more prestige than others, but no player has complete authority.

Arguments obviously interrupt the physical competition and threaten the unity of the group, but they are also appeals for order, and signify the players' concern for a degree of con-

formity to the rules. The players understand that the consequence of complete lawlessness is the dissolution of the game.
One function of arguments is to publicize the rules.

Usually, before beginning a game the players agree only
on the identity of the It (or the composition of the sides),
the placement of the boundaries, and the prohibition of hiding places. Most rules are established *ad hoc*. An It suddenly
remembers or invents a rule about the length of time a person
can stay on base. He may shout, "One, two, three,/Get off
my father's apple tree!" a rhyme that some say requires a
base-hugger to leave the base. Or the It may demand a re-
definition of the boundaries. If a Not-It in a game with
several Its observes a whispered conference between two Its,
he may shout, "No teams!" and halt the game until the group
decides if the Its can conspire together. A player may rule
himself "free" after he has been named in a game of Kick
the Can if he feels that the It is a "can-sticker": "You've got to
go past the green car or it's no fair!"

If children cross their fingers and call "Times!" they can
temporarily remove themselves from a game. You call "Times"
when you need to go to the bathroom, catch your breath, or
tie your shoe. But if a person calls "Times" too often (how
often is that?) or claims that crossed toes, hairs, or shoelaces
are as good as crossed fingers, someone will shout, "Bee, bee,
bumblebee,/Everybody come in free," or, in other dialects,
"Allie, allie in come free," "Allie, allie oxen free," "Allie,
allie in-fan-tree." When the players assemble, parliament comes
to disorder and the debate is on.

And either the It or the Not-Its may demand a definition of
"tagging." Does it include touching hair or a flapping shirt? Or
does it mean touching a solid part of the body? "Elbow and
knee/Always go free!" was the rule in 1883.

What if a player who has ahold of the base shouts, "Electricity!" and reaches out for a friend who is hotly pursued by
an It? Is touching a person who is touching the base the same
as touching the base? The Not-Its will argue that "electricity"

29

or "safety" passes from the base through the body of anyone touching it.

But keeping the group together and the game alive is more important to children than establishing and enforcing an ideal set of rules. If an obstinate player insists on having his own way, he may get it—if the group decides that getting on with the game is more important than enforcing strict fairness.

Small children learn the game mainly by imitating the big ones, but if a little kid does something really bad, he gets a brief but intense lesson about the rules from his more able playmates. We saw a child who persistently hid out-of-bounds temporarily banned from the game—"You can't play any more ever!" And when a four-year-old who was the guard in a game of Ring-a-levio walked absentmindedly through the "pot," thus freeing all the prisoners, she was instructed in stentorian shouts about her proper duties. But soon the older kids gave up on her. They declared her a Butterfingers. In that play group whatever a Butterfingers did, didn't count unless it was good. It's humiliating to be a Butterfingers, but you get to keep on playing, and that's the main thing.

Sometimes good players lend a little kid a hand. Watching a game of tag in Kansas, we saw a star player stealthily show a four-year-old how to tag an artful dodger who was preoccupied with the other good players. When she got him, the game broke up for a couple of minutes while everyone laughed, to the immense satisfaction of the four-year-old.

The rules are not relaxed for the lame, the weak, or the awkward, however. A child is expected to do his damnedest. On the other hand, it is understood that there won't be a good game if the best players start off by picking on the worst. That's a way to win but not a way to have fun.

The consideration of the older children and the better athletes for the less able is dictated by self-interest. A play group needs players, and no one can be expected to play if he's not having a fairly good time. Also, in the background lies the wrath of Mother. If she hears Junior squalling and learns that big sister hasn't been looking out for him, she is likely to spoil everyone's fun. Parents play an important if invisible role in their children's folk games.

The number of rules that best serves the group varies from one folk game to another. In tag games, which are often played by large groups, numerous, clearly defined rules would be difficult to establish. And there is no need for them, since children do not win or lose in these games in the sense that one wins or loses in marble games or in organized sports.

In the first place, there is no official score. In the second, each player brings a different degree of commitment to the game. Growing bored, two players may stop and talk and when tagged announce, "Oh, we aren't playing any more."

And different players have different aims. Some are seeking to display their physical skill; others, to show their tactical genius. Each one strives to achieve a self-defined goal—to outrun, outdodge, outhide, or outargue someone, actually or in his imagination. This child may use the game as an opportunity to tease a friend or bait an enemy, while that one may simply seek to hold the center of the stage for a while. (In a street game a child can do this without being able to excel in any way; he can appoint himself the group's car-watcher and be the first to warn, "Car! Car! C-a-r! Stick your head in a jelly jar!") Traditional games provide more scope for inner direction than do organized sports.

Cheating versus Testing the Rules

This scope for inner direction promotes both morality (as opposed to mere obedience) and "cheating." What for lack of a better word is called cheating occurs because in folk games children play *with* as well as *by* the rules, and part of the game is to define what is permissible and to discover what one can get away with.

A girl explained to her mother, "It's against the rules to hide in the house, but it's okay if you don't get caught." Her mother was appalled: "That's cheating." But the issue isn't that simple. Each player in his role as referee is alert for violations committed by others, but a trickster in his role as referee can justify his behavior to himself, and if caught, will try to justify it to others.

Cheating in the adult sense occurs when rules are well-defined and impossible to amend. That situation doesn't exist in chasing games. A player caught out-of-bounds can argue like a sophistical lawyer that he understood the boundaries differently or that they need to be revised. Perhaps the green car marking one boundary has been driven away. Obviously, a legal question exists about the line's location, but a clever player who sees the car leave won't mention that it's missing. He will interpret the boundary to his own advantage until another player demands an accounting.

This is not to say that anything goes. Whatever ruins the game, like regularly stepping over the line in dodgeball or running off with the can in Kick the Can, is immediately labeled "No fair!" And if a player continues to break a rule, some children will refuse to play with him. What happens next depends. If the rule-breaker is small or not especially popular, he will have to sit out a few games, until he learns to honor the customs and procedures of the group. But if he has some prestige within the group, there won't be enough of a consensus to exclude him, so some angry players will quit, thereby diminishing the excitement of the game for everyone. At this point, other players will act as honest brokers, putting pressure on the rule-breaker to promise to behave, soothing the feelings of those who have quit, pulling the group together again. They are usually aided in their ministrations by the desire of everyone to keep the game going. But no one wants to lose face. Children on such occasions behave with a kind of "wild civility."

These experiences of pressuring, compromising, demanding, denying, backing down, confusing the issue, accommodating various temperaments, and so on, are every bit as important as

"Two plus two is four" or "Columbus discovered America," but these important experiences cannot be "designed" and presented to children in gradable units. They can occur only when children play together free from the shadow of adult coercion.

In folk games children demystify their ideas of rules and fairness. They learn that rules are not made by God or the teacher, and that fairness is an imperfect balance of competing interests. When an older child breaks a rule, he is defying his comrades, not some authoritarian deity. And his purpose is not exactly to win the game, though that could be the result of his "cheating." His purpose is to test his friends' alertness, to test the rule's strength and clarity, and to test his own cleverness. His "cheating" does not ruin the game; it is part of the game.

For example, a sixth-grader who long ago realized that counting-out was not always an honest game of chance told us, "It's your fault if you let him [the Potato Man] cheat, but sometimes you don't care." Her remark is illuminating. First, it's *your* fault. If you are outsmarted, you have no one to blame but yourself. Second, "sometimes you don't care." Children could insist that the one doing the counting use a cheat-proof rhyme; for instance, he might begin:

> Eachy, peachy, pear, plum,
> Tell me when your birthday comes.

At this point, the child who had been reached would name a month, and the counter would then proceed on the basis of that unpredictable answer, counting around the circle from January to the birthday month, or spelling the month, with a letter assigned to each child in turn. But such rhymes are not popular. Children prefer "One Potato" or "Eeny, Meeny," rhymes that are easy for the counter to manipulate. Impatience to get on with the game and curiosity about whether a trick will work may outweigh the desire for absolute fairness. In fact, the group's idea of fairness has more to do with keeping everyone happy than with obeying rules. If, on the basis of completely fair counts, the same individual is repeatedly chosen to be It, the players will at some point declare the count unfair. They believe in leaving the choice of the It up to Fate, but they also believe that Fate shouldn't choose the same victim too often. Hence, they often ask the oracle for a recount.

The same children who told us that sometimes they don't care if the count is fixed also told us that sometimes they do care a lot! If they sense something fishy going on, they may shout their objections. But while they refer to the strategist whose ploy has been discovered as a "cheater," they don't ostracize him, nor is he ashamed of what he has tried to do.

What we need is two different words, one for the cheating that is despicable—the kind that ruins a game—and another for the cheating that is just a teasing and testing among friends.

This teasing and testing takes many forms. The players who hide in Kick the Can may trade shirts or hats and then expose themselves, hoping the It will shout, "One-two-three for Jerry behind the trashcan," when he really sees George, wearing Jerry's shirt. And the young politicians who play Ring-a-levio know that what happens often depends on what people say happens. To realize this is at least as important as to idealize objective truth. If the captives in Ring-a-levio can lure or tug their guard anywhere near the "pot," they may unanimously declare, "He touched!" and run away. The unhappy guard is left to reflect that men in responsible positions not only must obey the rules but must avoid even the appearance of impropriety.

And what of the children who succeed in outthinking or outtalking their playmates? In her book *Where Nothing Is Long Ago: Memories of a Mormon Childhood,* Virginia Sorensen describes one child's reaction. Tagged, but just barely, by a boy she admired so much that she was unable to acknowledge defeat at his hands, she argued convincingly that he had missed and that she was "in free." Elated, she went home, only to confront her guilt as she lay in bed remembering. There is no measurable result of such experiences, no way to separate them from the totality of the influences that shape our childhoods. But surely they contribute to our capacity to understand and evaluate the behavior of ourselves and others in more serious situations. We have tasted desperation, have glimpsed the power of words, and have known the confusion that follows a triumphant deception, all within the context of a game, which in spite of the intensity it generates is a privileged area, where we can explore moral questions without fear of being damned by some authority if we make a wrong move.

When rules lose their sacredness, however, children can abuse them as badly as adults. An eleven-year-old told us that when she grew tired of including her younger brother in the games she played with her friends, she would interpret the rules in ways designed to frustrate him. When he was thoroughly unhappy, she would present him to her mother and say that because he was so little he couldn't understand the rules and was ruining the game for everyone. Her mother would accept this explanation and take the boy inside the house. The girl thought this a great joke.

There are many analogies in adult life to the "cheating" that goes on during children's folk games. When we fill out our income-tax forms we come close to playing as children do. Where is the line between tax avoidance and tax evasion? Neither we nor the I.R.S. knows for sure. As a result, both sides attempt to score in a game with poorly defined rules, and neither side is eager to refer matters to the courts. (No one wants to call in Mother to settle things.)

Stock-car racing, which evolved from a folk sport as recently as the fifties, provides another example. Slam-bam on the track, it is also an arcane, quiet game of wits. Each racing team is out to artfully modify its car in violation of the rules. The team's first opponents are the inspectors, not the other racing teams. Everybody knows this and enjoys the situation. "Cheat neat," advises Richard Petty, a top driver. Clearly, what is going on is not "cheating" in the sense that the word is used at West

35

Point, nor as it is used by bridge players, or golfers. In these games a cheater is held in contempt. There is a scandal when he is caught.

But the mechanic who adds a hidden gas tank to his team's stock car suffers no disgrace if he is caught. He is "cheating" all right, but it's part of the game. Everyone expects this behavior of him—and it doesn't follow that to be consistent he must approve of breaking and entering. Nor will children who "cheat" in Hide and Seek necessarily cheat on a test at school. Hide and Seek and school are different games, and they involve different kinds of cheating.

The highly publicized cheating during the 1973 Soap Box Derby offers an instructive contrast to the cheating at stock-car races. The atmosphere that surrounded the Derby was a lot like the atmosphere at a stock-car race. There was, however, one big difference. At the Derby, the official myth was that the rules were being strictly obeyed. That pretense was what made the cheating that went on reprehensible instead of a fudgin' an' foolin' among friends.

Folk Games as Social Events

All too often, an adult who wants to write up a folk game calls a group of children together, and like Miss Havisham in *Great Expectations,* says, "Play." He sees only half of what goes on when a folk game is played in a natural setting. He sees the competition in isolation, not as part of a social occasion.

The game provides a framework within which children gossip, play tricks on one another, make plans for the morrow, and expand or revise their circle of friends. Equals seek each other out. In his autobiography, *If School Keeps,* Phil Stong describes a game of Blackman that he and his friends played shortly after the turn of the century. When a small boy was It, he would have to tag other small boys, until together the Lilliputians could mob a Gulliver. The best player was the last one caught and the next It. But as the It, he would ignore the weaker players and deign to chase only those with skill comparable to his own. The small players could for a while race near the It with nervous impunity. To be chased was an honor, a sign of social election. We found a similar pattern in the games we observed.

The fact that folk games are social occasions often makes them better as games than they would be if they were played with complete concentration. A Kansas City group plays a game called Batman. In a pregame huddle which excludes the It, each of the other players chooses the name of a character in the Batman television series. The children line up facing the It, who calls out the name of a character without knowing which of his playmates he is designating. That player dashes toward a distant baseline, while the It tries to tag him. As tagged players join the It, the odds against the runner increase, to the point where he would be unable to take a single step without being tagged if the Its pursued him single-mindedly. However, in the two games we watched, the Its kept themselves scattered—talking to friends, teasing one another, chasing a dog—and thereby gave the last few runners a sporting chance to show their skill.

Ending a Chasing or Hiding Game

There is no final whistle, no last out. A mother calls for one player. Another remembers that a good television show is on. Some players get tired and go inside. Others may tease the It for a while—"I quit, I quit, Itters can't quit!"—but soon the tailenders are sitting on the curb, telling scary stories.

Rule-making in Marble Games: A Question of Property

Though many men take it for granted that theirs was the last generation to draw the ring and knuckle down, marbles is alive and flourishing. The best study of the functions of marble games was written by Jean Piaget. He and a group of other psychologists studied marble players in Geneva during the early thirties, and although this work was done over forty years ago, our recent observations and interviews suggest that Piaget's conclusions are still valid.

In *The Moral Judgment of the Child,* Piaget asserts:

> Now, the rules of the game of marbles are handed down, just like so-called moral realities, from one generation to another, and are preserved solely by the respect that is felt for them by individuals. . . . The little boys . . . are gradually trained by the older ones in respect for the law; and in any case they aspire from their hearts to the virtue, supremely characteristic of human dignity, which consists in making a correct use of the customary practices of a game. As to the older ones, it is in their power to alter the rules. If this is not "morality," then where does morality begin?

Piaget notes that boys stop playing marbles in early adolescence, so eleven- to thirteen-year-old marble players have no seniors. They are the wise old men of their society; beyond them is no appeal. Not for years will they enjoy such a role again.

Girls also play marbles, but Piaget says that girls are mainly interested in dexterity and not in the "splendid codification and complicated jurisprudence of the game of marbles." He suggests that the legal sense is less developed in girls than it is in boys. The girls we watched play marbles were indeed relatively uninterested in arguing about the rules. They focused on marbles as a game of skill and were sometimes better shooters than the boys. Their attitude toward the game may reflect the fact that in our culture girls are more strongly discouraged from gambling than boys are.

And certainly marbles is a form of gambling. Boys show off their lucky marbles; they shout magic words like "Jinks!" They cross their fingers when it's their turn to shoot, or shake their lucky marble and blow on it and kiss it—"Just like dice." And in spite of Sunday-school lessons about not coveting "anything that is thy neighbor's," boys covet their neighbor's aggies and cat's-eyes. Hence, the need for elaborate sets of rules. A teenager, recalling his heyday as a sharpshooter, remarked, "The more rules you knew the better. And if you didn't know them —you'd better watch out!"

Possibly, it is because boys are freer than girls to accept the fact that playing marbles is a form of gambling involving the transfer of real property that they are also freer to develop the "splendid codification and complicated jurisprudence" that will govern the transfer of that property. By discouraging girls from gambling, we may also discourage them from developing a certain kind of legal sense.

For boys, the value of marbles often transcends their use in a game. Boys speculate in marbles, trading two for one, in hope of making a profit later on. They use marbles to buy comic books from each other—or baseball cards, or popguns. They even use marbles as chips in poker games.

Some boys forget all about marbles as a game and simply devote themselves to acquiring more and more marbles, any way they can. Such a boy was William Allen White. Back in 1877 he devised a scheme—he called it a "bank"—whereby he placed a valuable marble at a "hazardous distance" and charged boys two or three less valuable marbles for a shot at it. His father discovered his son's glassy wealth one day and told him that while playing for keeps was okay, running a con game was not. (Mrs. White never learned that her son played for keeps. She would not have approved, but the two men in the family knew that playing for keeps was something that real men had to do.)

Mr. White called the marbles that Willie had won by enticing his friends to take hazardous shots "dirty marbles" and told his son to give them back.

ONE POTATO, TWO POTATO...

Taking risks is a man's business, but enticement produces "dirty" profits. A man must "play the game." It seems to us that marble games mirror many of the complexities of our commercial society. They also mirror the increasing officialization of our society.

Since 1922 there has been a National Marbles Tournament and, heaven help us, statistical records: won–lost percentages, best-inning averages, the works. The rules are all down in a book. Referees and official scorers are required. Adult supervisors wield standardized marble gauges, offer trophies, and promote the motto "All championship marble shooters play for fair," meaning "according to the book." Five will get you ten that at least some of the adults who sponsor these tournaments go home afterward and complain about how the federal bureaucracy is taking over the country.

Marble games are especially popular in the spring and early summer, but kids play them all year round, indoors and out. They carry their precious cat's-eyes, clearies, tradies, aggies, and the rest in tin fruitcake cans, in the tops of hair-spray cans, in store-bought drawstring bags, or in one of Dad's old socks. And they play many different games:

POISON: Holes are dug in three of the corners of a ten-foot square. Each player tries to put his marble around the course, sinking it in each hole. When a marble gets back "home" it is "poison" and can "kill" the other marbles. Killed marbles belong to the player who kills them.

POTS, or the RING GAME: Each player puts the marbles he bets in the "pot," a circle drawn on the ground. The shooter keeps all the marbles he knocks from the circle. If his marble stays in, he gets another shot. Sometimes kids draw a triangle instead of a circle.

BOMBSIES: Like the Ring Game, but marbles are dropped from above instead of being shot in from the side. A player gets only one shot at each turn.

MARBLE SHOE: The players take turns pitching marbles at a

shoe. A player whose marble lands inside the shoe is paid one marble by each of the other players.

CHASE: Each player has one marble and tries to hit one of the others. He keeps any marble he hits.

A NAMELESS GAME: One player shoots out a marble. Another tries to hit it. If he misses, another player tries to hit either of them, and so on. When someone hits a marble he keeps all those that are on the ground.

LINE: Shooters try to make their marbles stop as close to a line as possible. The owner of the marble closest to the line keeps all the others. Sometimes this game is used to decide who gets first shot in a ring game.

CHINESE: Like Line, but each player tries to shoot his marble closest to the center of a circle.

And as boys match themselves against one another in their shooting skill, they also match themselves in their knowledge of the law. If a player calls "Spans" before someone thinks to say "No spans," he has the right to move his marble a hand's length closer to the target. "Bombs" gives him the right to try a drop shot. Slippery legal sharks call "Changies" and substitute a ball bearing for a target marble or a "boulder" for a regular-size shooter. If you're called for "hunching" (moving your hand forward while shooting), you have to take the shot over. And experienced players outlaw backstopping with your hand if they think of it in time—that is, before someone shouts "Cages!"

Players quarrel about attempts to apply different rules to the same situations. And they debate such questions as, Do "bouncies" count? Is there a limit to how hard you can shoot? Do "fudgies" (mistakes) count? How about "slippants" (when your shooting finger slips)? Another common point of dispute is whether a loser gets to pay off in old marbles or must use "good" marbles.

Without these arguments and legalistic ambushes, marbles loses its glamor; a marble player is reduced to a mere machine for projecting a round piece of glass a certain distance. He now strives to become not a clever folk hero, but a perfect shooter.

This is what happens when marbles is made an "organized" sport.

Folklore, Organized Sports, and Manufactured Games

Baseball, which got started around 1850, has gone the whole route from folk game to factory product. Its folk roots nourished it and helped make it our national game. But baseball traditions and legends never received much house from baseball executives, and as the game became more and more of a business, its folklore lost its roots in particular communities. Baseball lore does exist today, but mainly as a form of occupational lore.

However, some folk characteristics still influence the way baseball is played. For instance, among the professional sports in the United States, baseball is the only one in which photographs of an unsportsmanlike manager nose to nose with an umpire are an accepted part of the game's iconography. These arguments hark back to the days when the rules weren't standardized and at least part of the crowd was close enough to hear what was being said. Enjoying the argument was part of enjoying the game—as it always is in folk games.

Adults like to promote organized sports for children, and in some cases have been tremendously successful. Over 600,000 boys between eight and twelve are involved in Little League baseball alone. But kids still find time for scrub and other pickup games of folk baseball. We watched a neighborhood group play baseball every day one summer. Sunday mornings were the only times during daylight when there wasn't a game. The players ranged in age from seven to fourteen, and included both boys and girls. Of course the pitcher didn't zing the ball past the seven-year-old. He helped her all he could to get a hit. Hits were what the game was all about. All the players, incidentally, believed that if you hit the ball with the trademark on the bat, the bat would crack. Three of them swore that they'd seen it happen.

Not only do folk versions of professional sports continue to flourish but cheerful folk taunts continue to be shouted during supervised games, in spite of the efforts of intense adults to teach children that such fun is unsportsmanlike:

> We want a pitcher, not a belly itcher.

> Batter up, pitcher down!
> Who's that monkey on the mound?

> Pitcher in a hole, ten feet deep;
> Can't get out so he's pitchin' with his feet!

> Regurgitate, regurgitate,
> Throw up all the food you ate!
> Vomit, Vomit, Vomit!

> The pitcher has a girl friend!
> He's all shook up!

> Three-six-nine! Pitcher looks like Frankenstein!

Folk football can accommodate both big and little players almost as well as folk baseball. Some of its versions are quite simple. In Murder Ball, or Smear the Queer, a player kicks or lobs the ball high into the air and everyone pursues whoever catches it. In more sophisticated games on city streets, downs may be measured by the lengths of parked cars. The defense has to count to three before charging, and the idea is to hold, not to block. (Some boys call bricks or cobblestones "natural turf" and asphalt "artificial turf.")

Few grade-schoolers play folk basketball, but slightly older boys do. It is a half-court game, and the rules vary. In some neighborhoods, rebounds recovered by the defense must be "taken out" before a player can score. In others, it's "Everything up!": if a player misses, anyone can tip the ball in and score. On some playgrounds, it's "Make it and take it": the scoring side retains possession if it can. On others, the scoring side gives up the ball. If there aren't enough players for sides, boys may play Follow the Leader, each player trying to match the successful shots of the leader, or they may play a game in which two boys defend against a third, who tries to score. The one who gets the ball becomes the offensive player. The first to score twenty-one points wins.

Folk elements even find a place in the play of the manufactured board game Monopoly, and may account for its remarkable popularity. Though Monopoly is Parker Brothers' all-time best seller, the current president of the company still considers it an imperfect game. He says that it takes too long to play, and objects to the fact that it eliminates players before it's over.

But what's the first thing that happens when a family buys a Monopoly set? They lose the rule book and half the money. As players start creating money and arguing about the rules, Monopoly turns into something very like a folk game, and no one is eliminated until he is ready to quit. Often nobody really wins either, but that's true of most folk games.

How Folk Games Blend into the Daily Lives of Children

Adult sports have a special place, a special time, and special rules that take precedence over the rules of ordinary life. Unlike adult players, children do not draw a line between games and life. They play Cooties in the classroom under the nose of their teacher—and still manage to listen to part of what she has to say. They play Poison as they walk along the sidewalk or down a tiled hallway—and still get to where they're going, eventually. (If you step off a crack or on a crack, in some cases—you're "poison.") This mixing of games and life means that some game rules carry over into life, and some nongame situations become very much like games.

The best-known rule in childlore is that you are safe if you call "Times!" and cross your fingers. You call "Times" during a game in order to get a drink or when you are about to be tagged. You call "Times" outside of a game when you have insulted somebody bigger than you are—and he's gaining.

"Times" is both a truce term and a sign of submission—though not as humiliating as "I give." So the insulted child is satisfied to make threatening noises and gestures. He didn't really want to fight anyway. "You both get out of it," one child told us.

If you are forty or over, you may not remember "Times." In the thirties and forties, and as far back as anyone knows, the main truce term on the playground was "Kings!" or "Kings X!" (pronounced "Kings Ex"), accompanied by crossed fingers, and sometimes crossed legs, arms, and even eyes, if the other guy was really angry. Today "Times," a term borrowed from organized sports, has almost completely replaced "Kings X," but the practice of crossing fingers has carried over.

Other aspects of children's lives are also governed by folk law. If a child sees something that he wants but it's out of reach, he claims it by shouting "Dibbs!" or "Dubbs on it!" Some New Yorkers say, "I hock it." In Battle Creek, Michigan, some use the old truce term "Kings," while in parts of southern Illinois, "Sooks" declares your claim.

Another sort of claim is declared by "Finders keepers, losers weepers!"

A person who changes his mind after making a trade is an Indian Giver, an Indian Trader, or an Indian Traitor. To seal a trade, a child asserts, "Black, black, no trades back!" a cry which parallels the game rule "Black, black, no tags back!"

Folk rules also apply to one's behavior while standing in line. "Butts!" shouts the child who wants the right to crowd in. "No butts!" (or "Buttsies!" "Cuts!" "Ups!") shout children who see a well-known Butter approaching. "Chinese cuts" or "Double cuts" means that you let a friend in in front of you, then he lets you in in front of him. A child who leaves the line says, "Save my place," or "I call my place," if he expects to return to the place he left.

The venerable oath,

> Cross my heart and hope to die,
> Stick a needle in my eye,

still certifies truthfulness among the natives of the playground. Secretly crossed fingers invalidate this oath, however, so interested parties may shout, "No crossies or black magic counted!"

Our modern reverence for sincerity and authenticity often inspires children to add to "Cross my heart" phrases that, paradoxically, are best described as formulaic personal touches. They add lines like, "And eat red ants," or "In a cellar full of rats." Sometimes the formula is almost lost amid the protestations of sincerity: "Honest to God. Cross my heart and hope to die. Really, man, that's the truth!" or

> Cross my heart and hope to die,
> Step on a cat and spit in his eye,
> And I hate animal haters!

Traditional versions of the second line include: "May God strike me dead if I tell a lie!" and "I hate God if I tell a lie!" Another second line is, "Lick my thumb or be a bum," which faintly echoes a British rhyme:

> Wet my thumb and wipe it dry,
> Cut my throat if I tell a lie.

Alternatives to "Cross my heart . . ." are "I swear on the Bible" (or ". . . on a stack of Bibles ten feet high") and "Scout's honor," which children who have never been Scouts use freely. Some children invent oaths: "I promise, and if I break it I'll throw away my football."

To protect his candy bar at lunch time, a child proclaims, "No gives, no takes." To get a bite of someone else's candy bar, he says, "Munchies!" "Bites!" or "Hey, kick down!" Another dietary law is "First come, first served."

Only a few children these days still say, "Two against one, nigger's fun," when outnumbered in a jeering match or a fight. But almost all children, even "tattletales," obey the command "Pass it on," when a note is crossing the classroom. Pass It On is also a spontaneous game, usually played while children are waiting in a line. A boy will slug another on the shoulder and command, "Pass it on."

The formula for excluding oneself from impromptu games like Pass It On is "Not included!" It's important to know this. Otherwise, a child may find himself paying a penalty in a game he didn't ever intend to join.

Adults always want to know how effective these "laws" are, and they nod cynically when we explain that they are often ignored. But children's folk laws are not contemptible because they are not always honored; they are admirable because they are so often voluntarily obeyed.

Children's folk laws have a generally unappreciated civilizing function. H. L. Mencken noted in his autobiography that under "boys' law," in the Baltimore of his youth, a top branded with a red-hot nail would not be stolen. This, he says, impressed him, gave him "a sense of the majesty of the law" which sustained him later in his life. He added, with characteristic irony, ". . . and I always take off my hat when I meet a judge —if, of course, it is in any place where a judge is not afraid to have his office known." Mencken's jaundiced view of adult authority does not invalidate his admiration for boys' law. His admiration for boys' law, however, may account in part for his jaundiced view of adult authority. The folk laws of children give us a blurred glimpse of a prelapsarian world in which laws are based on custom and tradition and observed by common consent.

Folk Games and Democracy

Some adults object that the slam-bang bargaining and raucous politicking that goes on during Monopoly or Kick the Can isn't very democratic. Their idea of democracy is a meeting at which no one raises his voice and everyone observes Robert's Rules of Order. But they are confusing democracy with gentility. The two have never had much in common.

ONE POTATO, TWO POTATO...

The argumentative mixture of seriousness and silliness that characterizes folk games reminds us of descriptions of the meetings of Americans who came together in wagon trains, mining camps, Actual Settlers' Associations, Claim Clubs, and town meetings (often held before there was a town). They made laws to suit their special needs, protected themselves "legally" against land speculators, and maintained order without waiting for the slow-moving authorities—the experts—to do it for them. The historian Daniel J. Boorstin remarks, "Among the transients, in the mining camp, the law was everybody's—to understand, to defend, to enforce." And so it is in children's folk games.

We aren't suggesting that if children play folk games, nations will adopt democratic governments. Games are but one of many influences upon the life of an individual or a nation. Moreover, the democratic ambience of folk games is not philosophical but accidental. It depends on a rough balance of power: to perpetuate itself, a play group has to secure its members' voluntary participation, but a bully or a clique can (as in ancient Athens, some mining camps, and some modern "democracies") exert extraordinary influence, at least for a while. And in isolated villages, the folk tradition itself becomes a kind of tyrant. Some of the concern for rules and rule-making on the part of contemporary American children is undoubtedly the result of the American wanderlust, which prevents the development of strong local traditions. When parents move, children enter new play groups; games are not played exactly the way they were back home, and there is a lot of explaining and compromising—a lot of legislating—to do.

Folk games, then, do not represent some sort of instinctive, primitive wisdom on the part of children who are meant to lead us to the promised land. They simply represent an alternative to gym classes and organized sports. We must consider which kind of activity will benefit our children most.

While organized sports provide some of the character-building discipline of work in an age when meaningful household chores are less and less available, it's only fair to recall that no one has ever been charged with swallowing pep pills to play a faster game of Ring-a-levio, taking diet pills to stay in a certain weight division of Red Rover, or conniving with gamblers to throw a game of hopscotch. No distraught adults stand around shouting, "Smash them!" or "Kill them!" to the players of folk games.

We hesitate to say it in an age that nods approvingly at the "wisdom" of professional "game" players who snarl, "Nice guys finish last," "Winning isn't everything; it's the only thing," and "Losing is like dying," but the value of folk games still lies not in whether you win or lose but in how you play the game.

And if the function of games is to "prepare children for life" in a modern, competitive society, then it seems to us that folk games, which involve verbal competition and individual judgment, are a more useful map of the territory ahead than organized sports, which emphasize physical competition and submission to authority.

There are, though, dangerous aspects to folk games. A child we know hid in a washing machine while playing Hide and Seek. The fire department had to extricate her. And no parent can watch his child playing British Bulldog without a twinge of anxiety as the mob hoots and jeers, waiting for him to cross the line. Even in games that aren't so rough, children must develop their own strategies for dealing with bullies and spoilers. They can't appeal to authority and avoid responsibility and danger.

But that, of course, is why folk games are important.

GAMES AS STAGES
OR LABORATORIES

The Theater

One of the best things about traditional games is that while they are social events, governed by rules, they also encourage self-expression. Some serve as stages for a disciplined kind of self-expression; others encourage a wild emotional release.

Lemonade is an acting game. The two teams line up on opposite sides of a lawn. One team approaches the center and begins the dialogue:

> "Here we come."
> "Where you from?"
> "New Orleans."
> "What's your trade?"
> "Lemonade."
> "Show us some if you're not afraid."

The first team then acts out a scene showing people at work at a particular task—a mother serving dinner, a doctor operating, or the like. When the second team—the audience—guesses what is being acted out, the actors must run to a predetermined base. Those in the audience try to catch as many actors as they can. Anyone caught must join the team that caught him. Next time, the second team, augmented by its new members, marches to the middle of the lawn and puts on the show.

In Lemonade, the dramatic performance is public. More often children put on private dramatic performances within the framework of a game ostensibly devoted to something else. Hide and Seek and its variants, for instance, provide several metaphors—the terrible It, the hide-outs, the possibility of being caught or lost—which can mean whatever a child wants them to mean. He can act out his feelings about parents or teachers as he challenges the It. He can dramatize his freedom and independence as he hides beneath the spiraea and is all at once alone and preternaturally aware of the stars, the lightning bugs, and the little noises of the night. There is no sure way to tell when a child is only playing a game and when he is playing out some private drama as well. The absence of intense competition in folk games makes it easy for a child to play a game in his head as well as one in the yard with his friends.

The Laboratory

The screams that punctuate some folk games frighten adults. So does the way children sometimes behave as if they were possessed. "Stop being silly!" adults command. "Calm down; you're getting hysterical!"

Some folk games emphasize order—marbles, for instance, and in a different way, clapping games; others satisfy a child's craving for unruliness and disorder. Most games, of course, have both orderly and unruly aspects. Hide and Seek is relatively structured, but children can get pretty wild, racing for home base, leaping from porches, trampling flower beds, knocking down smaller children who are in the way.

Compared to Statues or King of the Hill, however, Hide and Seek looks positively dignified. Take Statues. The largest player swings each of the others around, letting go unexpectedly. The child reels drunkenly, then freezes in a crazy posture. Children say that the "winner" is the most grotesque "statue," but there is no winner because there is no judge. Everybody wins.

In a more elaborate variant of Statues, the child being swung calls "Pepper" or "Salt," indicating whether he wants to be swung fast or slow. When everyone is disposed, a Buyer asks a Seller if the statues are for sale.

"Of course, come in."

"Thank you. I'll take that one."

"All right, that's one of our best; I'll just turn it on for you."

The Seller pantomimes turning on the statue. How it behaves when it comes to life depends on what it is. Sometimes the Seller tells the statue in a whisper what it is; sometimes each child decides for himself. But the Buyer doesn't know. It may be a princess who will do a pirouette. It may be a gorilla or a Frankenstein monster which will chase the Buyer away and break all the statues in a fine dramatic frenzy.

51

ONE POTATO, TWO POTATO...

King of the Hill is just a name for a jolly fight. A boy takes a position atop a steep slope, declares himself King of the hill, and pushes down anyone who tries to join him. The point of the game is to displace the King, but the fun of the game is to roll down the hill as dramatically as possible and with great sound effects.

Less obviously unruly is Sardines. It may be a cozy game, but it may reproduce—with pleasurable faintness—the panic of those locked in the Black Hole of Calcutta. Which it is depends on how small the hide-out is. The It hides. The others search for him. Whoever finds the It quietly joins him in his hide-out. As the hide-out fills up, it becomes easier to find: it's where the gasps, groans, and strangled screams are coming from.

Then there's Doctor, sometimes called Rattlesnake. In New York City, children join hands and their leader leads them around and between one another, in and out until they become a tangled, living knot. While this is going on, they chant, "R-a-t t-l-e s-n-a-k-e spells Rattlesnake!" In Montana and in the Canal Zone, children play the same game but don't chant, and once entangled, they call for the Doctor to come and untie them.

Any tag game involves a large measure of disorderliness, but some are wilder than others. Hospital Tag (one of its several names) requires each player to hang on to the spot on his body where he has been tagged. Players lurch crazily about. In Marco Polo, which is played in swimming pools, the It must blunder about with his eyes shut. Each time he shouts "Marco," the others must reply "Polo." The It then churns through the water, trying to tag the owner of the nearest voice.

In tag games, children are caught by someone who chases them. In another kind of "catch" game, the leader tries to "catch" his playmates disobeying his instructions. Such games offer both ruly and unruly pleasures. The most orderly is Mother, May I. The Mother gets to behave like a tyrant: "You may take two baby steps and one scissor step." The only fun the other players have is to get caught for forgetting to ask,

52

"Mother, may I?" But getting caught is a wilder and more exciting experience that one might think.

We watched four first-graders play a catch game for forty minutes before school. They never tired of it. "Get ready, get set . . . ," announced the starter. The other three boys crouched. But as often as not, the starter hollered, *"Stop!"* or *"Evel Knievel!"* instead of *"Go!"* Even when he said, *"Go!"* there was no race. The boys were testing themselves—seeing if they could catch themselves starting when they should stop or stopping when they should start. They "won" whether or not they were fooled, laughing at or with themselves. On another level, they were also learning to obey their teachers' sometimes confusing directions by playing a game that mimicked and mocked the idea of following orders.

Red Light, Green Light, involving as it does real sneakiness, is one of the more unruly catch games. A slick player will try to steal a step forward while the light is red and the It is busy arguing with another player whom he claims to have caught. If the It sees such an attempt, his outrage will, of course, be doubled—and while his anger blinds him, another cool player will steal a step forward.

The game of Chinese School comes right out and encourages disorder. The rhyme that starts it was once a sectarian taunt:

> Quaker meeting has begun,
> No more laughing, no more talking,
> No more chewing chewing gum.

Today it goes like this:

> Chinese school has just begun,
> No more laughing, no more fun.
> If you show your teeth or tongue,
> There will be a penalty done!

That's asking for it. The child who is It makes faces and plays the fool, trying to raise a laugh. Children who spend the day in strictly controlled classrooms are well served by Chinese School. They have learned to fear spontaneous outbursts of emotion.

Chinese School recreates the tensions of their classrooms, then sends them on a joyous, long-suppressed emotional binge.

Truth or Dare fits in here, too. Some children eagerly choose Dare and revel in the attention that they get, but most know that sooner or later they will be dared to do something they won't want to do, or asked to tell something they don't want to tell. Playing Truth or Dare is a way of tempting Fate.

Theoretically it could be a dangerous game. But most of the dares are things like, "Tell the name of your boy friend," or "Run through old man Schuster's yard." Often, too, a child will refuse to take a dare or answer a question. This sets off a flurry of teasing, but the pressure to conform is pretty mild— nowhere near as great as it is in a game supervised by adults who roar for every boy to go "all out" or be disgraced forever.

Sometimes a child who accepts a dare gets more than he bargained for, but that's something he needs to learn can happen. A neighbor boy was dared to stop the next car that came along and sing "A Spoonful of Sugar" to the driver. The boy waved the car down, stepped into the glare of its headlights, and sang his song, underlining its message with exaggerated gestures. Then he bowed. The car door opened, and a uniformed policeman got out.

Almost any game can be transformed into something wild and unruly if children happen to be in the mood. Look what happens in Red Rover when the players decide to invite a whole side to "come over" at once. There's an instant carnival —a wild celebration of just being alive.

And, of course, children cultivate disorder in nongame situations, too. They spin until they drop, walk along curbs with their eyes shut, or walk all the way home from school backward.

All this is fun: staggering about, laughing uncontrollably, whooping, falling in a heap, tempting Fate, enjoying the jitter of being caught. Adults, too, think this kind of behavior is fun, but they have to get drunk to make it socially acceptable.

A young child must be watched when he plays an unruly

game because he may abandon himself to it too completely. But as he grows older he no longer abandons himself. He is sometimes unintentionally destructive, but he is no Dionysian reveler. He is only playing a game, a game that permits him to run wild within limits.

There is another kind of limit that he must observe as well. Folk games have no official courts or special fields. They are played in places not designed for games at all. A child soon learns that he must not fall in the flower bed, run into the street without looking, or hurdle Mrs. So-and-So's hedge—if he wants to keep on playing. So he plays at being out of control, while at the same time standing apart, as it were, to observe the limits imposed by the game and by its context.

NOTES

GAMES AS LEGISLATURES AND COURTS OF LAW

The Nature of Folk Games

Ellis' exploit is described by David Riesman and Reuel Denney, "Football in America: A Study in Culture Diffusion," in *Sport, Culture, and Society,* edited by John W. Loy, Jr., and Gerald S. Kenyon (New York: Macmillan, 1969), p. 308.

Pregame Ceremonies

The locking rhyme is discussed by Mary and Herbert Knapp, "Childlore: Locking a Game," *Western Folklore,* 34 (1975), 55–57. The farm boys' rhyme is in Iona and Peter Opie, *The Oxford Dictionary of Nursery Rhymes* (Oxford: Clarendon Press, 1952), p. 83. Versions of "Eeny, Meeny" from many languages are in Henry Carrington Bolton's invaluable *The Counting-Out Rhymes of Children* (1888; reprint ed., Detroit: Singing Tree Press, 1969), pp. 45–48. The rhythm of children's verse is discussed by Peter Farb, *Word Play* (New York: Alfred A. Knopf, 1974), pp. 133–36; and by Robbins Burling, "The Metrics of Children's Verse: A Cross-Linguistic Study," *American Anthropologist,* 68 (1966), 1418–41. The Opies tell about the Danish version of "Jack and Jill" in their *Dictionary of Nursery Rhymes,* p. 11, and cite examples of the Anglo-Cymric score on p. 13. Other examples of this score are in William Wells Newell, *Games and Songs of American Children* (second ed., 1903; reprint ed., New York: Dover Publications, 1963), pp. 200–201. Kenneth S. Goldstein talks about "Strategy in Counting Out: An Ethnographic Folklore Field Study" in *The Study of Games,* edited by Elliott M. Avedon and Brian Sutton-Smith (New York: John Wiley & Sons, 1971), pp. 167–78.

Rule-making in Chasing and Hiding Games

"Elbow and Knee" is in *Games and Songs of American Children,* p. 161.

Cheating versus Testing the Rules

Our ideas about children's attitudes toward cheating benefited from the description of Hide and Seek in Virginia Sorensen, *Where Nothing Is Long Ago: Memories of a Mormon Childhood* (New York: Harcourt, Brace & World, 1955), pp. 177–78; and from Richard Woodley, "How to Win the Soap Box Derby," *Harper's,* 249 (August 1974), 62–69; and John S. Radosta, "Stock-car Streaking," *The New York Times Magazine,* June 16, 1974, pp. 22–29.

Folk Games as Social Events

Phil Stong's account of a game of Blackman in his autobiography, *If School Keeps* (New York: Frederick A. Stokes, 1940), p. 8, directed our attention to the social aspect of folk games.

Rule-making in Marble Games: A Question of Property

The statement by Jean Piaget on morality in marble games is from *The Moral Judgment of the Child,* translated by Marjorie Gabain (New York: The Free Press, 1966), p. 14. He discusses the role of older marble players on p. 76 and the attitudes of girl marble players on p. 77. William Allen White's "bank" is described in *The Autobiography* (New York: Macmillan, 1946), pp. 46–47. Our information about the National Marbles Tournament comes from Fred Ferretti, *The Great American Marble Book* (New York: Workman, 1973), pp. 137 ff.; Mark Kram, "Ring of Bright Marbles," *Sports Illustrated,* 41 (July 8, 1974), 24–26; and Dorothy Howard, "Marble Games of Australian Children" in *The Study of Games,* pp. 179–93.

Folklore, Organized Sports, and Manufactured Games

Robert Cochran discussed "Folk Elements in a Non-Folk Game: The Example of Basketball" in a paper delivered at the 1974 meeting of the American Folklore Society in Portland, Oregon. James F. Fixx in "The Game Game," *Saturday Review*, 55 (Dec. 9, 1972), 62–66, reports the attitude of the president of Parker Brothers toward Monopoly.

How Folk Games Blend into the Daily Lives of Children

"Times" and "Kings X" are in Mary and Herbert Knapp, "Tradition and Change in American Playground Language," *Journal of American Folklore*, 86 (1973), 131–41. The synonyms for "Dibbs!" are from the archives of the Folklore Institute of Indiana University. The quotation from H. L. Mencken is from his *Happy Days: 1880–1892* (New York: Alfred A. Knopf, 1940), p. 160. The quotation from Daniel J. Boorstin is from *The Americans: The National Experience* (New York: Random House, 1965), p. 84.

GAMES AS STAGES OR LABORATORIES

The Laboratory

The verse "Quaker Meeting" is described by Iona and Peter Opie, *The Lore and Language of Schoolchildren* (Oxford: Clarendon Press, 1959), p. 346.

3 Prestige and Power

JEERS

Common Insults and Comebacks

Jeers are usually loud, often vulgar, and may sound like the prelude to a fight. For the sake of propriety, parents and teachers feel obliged to suppress them. But even when jeers show real animosity—as they often do—they do not usually lead to a fight. On the contrary, a jeering contest often takes the place of physical combat.

And insulting jeers may be shouted by good friends who have established a jeering partnership. Their friendship is masked by hostility, which gives them a chance to advertise their wit and intimacy. What would be insulting coming from anyone else is sport coming from a friend.

As for the vulgar jeers, most of them are designed to promote propriety, not to violate it. They are meant to shame a child who is not conforming to accepted standards of behavior. When an adult sees a little girl unwittingly display her underwear as she bends over, he says nothing because he assumes that when she is older she will be more careful. If she is, it may be because in the back of her mind she can still hear some delighted boy crowing:

I see London, I see France,
I see *Laura's* underpants.
They ain't black, they ain't white,
Oh, my God, they're dynamite!

Jeering helps keep people in line in many societies, and has been particularly important in stateless societies like those of the Tonga of Zambia, the Tangu of New Guinea, the Eskimo, and American Indian tribes like the Cheyenne and Crow. In these societies, jeering takes the place of written law and is often restricted to those who have special obligations toward one another. It is also therapeutic, and provides entertainment for the community.

In our own society, too, jeering has social functions. Political jeers provide an important safety valve during hard-fought campaigns. We jeer at relatives or friends, sometimes to shame them, but as often to attest to the closeness of our relationship. And we enjoy jeering as an art form. Comedians include strings of jeers in their skits, each man trying to top the other.

But jeering does not play as important a role in our large, impersonal, literate society as in smaller, preliterate ones. Even in the semiliterate subsociety of American children, jeering does not function as formally as it does among the Tonga or the Eskimo. Informally, however, it serves a variety of purposes. Besides helping to establish a sense of decorum, formulaic jeers provide the linguistically immature child with something simple and appropriate to say when he is angry or flustered. They enable children to partly control situations that would otherwise be almost unbearably frustrating. In a rough and tumble way, children are learning about rhetoric as they trade traditional jeers—and their behavior is closer to that of some togaed Greek and Roman orators than many people might suppose.

Traditional jeers include epithets, bathroom jeers, jeers about cheaters and teacher's pets, clever comebacks, sexual and racial jeers, and those reserved for sports events—or for the moment somebody farts. Most have as their targets other children, but there are two kinds that are aimed, usually from a distance, at authority: shockers and parodies. Jeers of these two kinds, and those reflecting racial and political attitudes, are discussed in the initial sections of Chapter 4.

When Phil hears Roger sing out, "Phil's in love with El-ly!" using the traditional melody of abuse:

what can Phil do? He can deny the charge like a mature adult: "No, I'm not." That is clearly unsatisfactory. Slightly better is the traditional "None of your beeswax!" But best of all is to counterattack with:

> Liar, liar, pants on fire!
> Nose as long as a telephone wire!
> [or "Hangin' on a telephone wire!"]

This belongs to the group of jeers that single out a defect in a child's character. Cheats hear, "Cheater, cheater, pumpkin eater!" or

> Copycatter, dirty ratter,
> Stick your face in monkey splatter!

> Copycatter, dirty ratter,
> Call your mother a baseball batter!

Crybabies are taunted with:

> Cry, baby, cry, put your finger in your eye,
> Tell your mother it wasn't I,

and with:

> Baby, baby, suck your thumb,
> Wash it out with bubble gum,

or "Let the baby have his bottle; it's sour anyway." Besides Crybaby, traditional names for such a child include Sissy, Leaky-faucet, Bawl-baby, and Water-bag. Children thought to be tattlers must endure:

> Tattletale, tattletale,
> Stick your head in ginger ale,

or

> Tattletale, tattletale,
> Hang your britches on a nail,
> Hang them high, hang them low,
> Hang them in a picture show.

or

> Tattletale, tattletale,
> Hang her [or "him"] on the post like a bull's ["pig's"] tail.

Sophisticated children sometimes shout, "Tattletale narc!"—a redundancy, really, but a curious one. "Nark" is venerable British slang for "informer." American children once associated the term specifically with "narcotics agent" but have now generalized it to refer, once again, to any informer.

Bathroom jeers belong to another group, though of course there is some overlap from one group to another.

> Fatty, Fatty, two-by-four,
> Couldn't get through the bathroom door,
> So he did it on the floor!

A related jeer from our childhood in the thirties is:

> Hasten, Jason, bring the basin.
> Urp! Slop! Too late. Bring the mop.

Bathroom jeers may be shouted at someone who has actually wet his pants in school. That does happen. But as a rule, they are used as all-purpose jeers and are not reserved for any particular occasion. Their frequency does serve to remind everyone of the perils of incontinence.

ONE POTATO, TWO POTATO...

Some bathroom jeers are directed obliquely at adult society as well as at another child. Surely the pleasure of playing with verbal taboo-boos accounts for the popularity of:

> Nanny, Nanny, boo-boo,
> Stick your head in doo-doo.

And the following from rural Indiana is almost pure giggle, though it could be used to taunt another child:

> Push the button, pull the chain,
> Out comes a little black choo-choo train.

Just because the design of toilets has changed is no reason to abandon a good rhyme.

Color rhymes—each beginning with the repetition of a color word—are another important kind of common jeer. Logically, the color should identify the target of the jeer. Blue might refer to a blue shirt; red, to red hair. Sometimes it does work that way, but no child holds back just because his enemy doesn't happen to be wearing the right color. He goes ahead and blasts him: "Blue, blue, you belong in a zoo!" Even if the target is wearing brown, he gets the idea.

> Blue, Blue, go catch the flu.
> I don't want to play with you.

> Blue, Blue, who are you?

> Blue, Blue, God hates you.

> Red, Red, wet your bed.
> Wipe it up with gingerbread.

> Red, Red, you look dead.

> Pink, Pink, you stink, you fink.

> Green, Green, you're a queen.
> Stick your head in gasoline.

> Green, Green, you aren't very clean.

Yellow, Yellow, kiss your fellow.
Go upstairs and eat some Jell-O.

Gold, Gold, you eat mold.

Brown, Brown, you're a clown.

Black, Black, step on a crack.
Hope you break your mother's back.

Black, Black, step on a tack.

Black, Black, you're cracked.

Black, Black, sat on a tack,
Rolling down the railroad track.

White, White, gonna get married tonight.

White, White, go fly a kite.
Fly it up your toilet pipe.

White, White, want to fight?

Color rhymes provide a traditional pattern for original expression. And the young poet uses rhyme, rhythm, and images more enthusiastically in his "flyting" sessions than he ever does in the classroom.

Mary, Mary, big fat fairy.

Marlene, Marlene, thinks she's keen.

Phil, Phil, is a pill.

Children have available formulaic rhymes that can be used to introduce a jeering note into almost any conversation:

Don't give me no lip, Potato Chip.

Shut up, Ketchup.

I'm the boss, Applesauce.

It's your fault, Garlic Salt.

Don't get wise, Bubble-eyes.

63

ONE POTATO, TWO POTATO...

You're cruisin' for a bruisin'.

Understand, Rubber Band?

Yes, I do, Tennis Shoe.

To send an unwanted child away, children may say:

Be like a banana and split.

Be like dandruff and flake off.

Be like a tree and leave.

Be like a ghost and vanish.

Be like a bee and buzz off.

Take a long walk off a short pier.

Or they may employ that old standby:

Go jump in the lake.

High-school and college students also use these formulas, but their repertoire includes more sophisticated comparisons, such as:

Be like a baby and head out.

Be like a hockey player. Get the puck out of here.

A grade-school child who wants to shout a more elaborate insult can insert the name of his enemy into the appropriate variant of this long-popular rhyme:

Jimmy, bum binny,
Tee aligo, Jimmy,
Tee leg-ged,
Tie leg-ged,
Bow leg-ged, Jimmy!

The sounds are altered to suit the subject's name; one says, fo example, "Sarah, bum bara," or Herby, bum berbie."

If a person quits a game before it's over, his friends may jeer:

> Every party needs a pooper,
> That's why we invited you!
> Party pooper! Party pooper!

A child who uses the word "so" in an ordinary conversation may hear suddenly dinned at him:

> So, so, suck your toe,
> All the way to Mexico.
> You were cut low, Cool-Joe.

Clearly jeers are not always shouted as part of a quarrel, but are part of the verbal texture of everyday relationships.

The phrase "cut low" is a taunt that means something like *touché*. A child shouts "Cut low!" to claim he has "scored," but it is also used as a sneering response, as if to say, "Big deal," or "So what?" Both the taunt and the response are derived from a kind of brag which is called a "cut-low." Children say, "I'm going to cut you so low that

if they stood a dime on edge, you'd need a parachute to get down."

you'll need an umbrella so the ants won't piss on you."

you'll have to pull down your socks to see out."

you'll need a pole vault to jump over a crack in the sidewalk."

you'll have to look up to see bottom."

you'll be too thin to fry."

you'll have to look up to look down."

you'll have to look up to tie your shoelaces."

Cut-lows are obviously too artful to be used by a child who is really angry.

> Cut you low, I must confess
> That in your mouth your tongue must rest.

Tone always contributes a great deal to the meaning of children's jeers. Their literal import, in fact, may not be very significant at all. The ever popular *"Tommy* * is It, had a fit, couldn't pass arithmetic!"* may be used to tease an It in a tag game or a person who has lost his temper, or it may be shouted at someone simply to get a rise out of him. But it is never, as far as we have been able to ascertain, directed at a student because he is poor in arithmetic.

Children have a reputation for the cruel way they tease their fellows, especially those who are different from themselves. They have a large repository of colorful epithets which they shout at each other—a practice that strikes adults as shockingly insensitive.

Just how hurtful a name is, however, depends on a number of things, including, of course, the disposition of the individual child to whom it is applied. Some children are reduced to tears if they are the target of one of the color rhymes previously mentioned. For instance, a girl we know weeps when her mother tries to dress her in pink, so sensitive is she to the stigma of "Pink, Pink, you stink." Generally speaking, however, the most hurtful thing a child can shout is a name—and the more infrequently that name is applied to others on the playground, the more hurtful it is. The cruelest epithets are those which are the most specific—for example, names used to point out relatively unusual habits or physical characteristics: Pipe-neck, Platypus, Fish-lips, Beaver-teeth, Mush-mouth, Bubble-head, Spider-legs, Candy-grabber, Buger-peeler. These are widely used but are not as common as the names applied to children who are different in more standard ways. Such individuals are called, among other things, Fatso, Hippo, Blubber, Bimbo, Skinny-minnie, Bag-a-bones, String-bean, Pip-squeak, Peewee, or Spaz (Spastic). Spaz is directed at a child who has done something awkward or who has accidentally slobbered a little while talking, not a child who is really spastic. Those who wear glasses may be called Four-eyes, Eye-blinker, or Glass-eyes. A

---

* Throughout, the use of italics for a proper name indicates that the child inserts whatever name he considers appropriate.

bad guy is a Rotten-egg. Snobs are Snot-noses. Redheads and those who wear braces on their teeth have an especially hard time. Redheads hear not only "Red, Red, wet your bed, . . ." but "Carrot-top" and "I'd rather be dead than red in the head," which echoes an adult political slogan of the fifties. Children wearing braces are dubbed Tin-grin, Metal-mouth, Railroad-tracks, Wire-head, Silver-mouth, Brace-face, or Tin-sel-teeth. How badly a name like Tin-grin hurts depends partly on how many Tin-grins there are around. If the name applies to more than one person, it loses some sting.

Actual profanity—Son-of-a-bitch, Mother-fucker, Shithead, Bastard, and so on—was relatively uncommon on middle-class playgrounds a few years ago. At that time, profanity was often a serious invitation to a fight. Today, in many localities, profanity is much more common—but far less serious.

Many names refer to a youngster's mental ability. Egghead, Smarty-pants, Smart-ass, Kiss-ass, Teacher's Pet, and Brown-nose apply to a child who is or who pretends to be more brainy than his friends. However, most jeers in this category refer to one whose behavior makes him seem intellectually inferior: Dumb-cluck, Dumbbell, Dumb-dumb, Dumbo, Dumb-bunny, Bird-brain, Dork, Kook, Nitwit, Dip, Numbskull, Freak, Fathead, Space-case, Dufus, Reject, Jerk, Dodo, Knuckle-head, Ding-a-ling, Nincompoop, and Retard. These are generally used in response to specific behavior that seems stupid, and are among the least offensive names children can use—unless the one at whom they are directed is really retarded. Perhaps their relative inoffensiveness reflects the importance we in the United States have traditionally given to character over cleverness. They are often very offensive to a child with a Latin-American background. In many Latin-American countries, *"estúpido"* is a serious insult.

Other names used in response to specific behavior include Nosey-nut, Tattletale, Fairy, Fruit, Fag, Garbage-mouth, Mighty-mouth, Sissy, and Chicken.

Taunts may make a play on a real name: Tricky Dick,

ONE POTATO, TWO POTATO...

Herby Knapp-crap, Clara Bare-a, Silly Billy, Eddy-spaghetti-your-meatballs-are-ready. Some children find epithets of this sort extremely offensive, while others are able to shrug them off.

No child can shrug them off, however, if he is singled out to be tormented day in and day out. Scapegoating is a serious problem which calls for the concerted intervention of parents and teachers to help the victim become less vulnerable and the tormentors to understand their motives. But the exhortations and instructions of adults would fall on deaf ears if the tormentors did not themselves know what it really means to be hurt by name calling.

To suggest that most of the time children benefit from verbal duels may strike the reader as sentimental or romantic. But the traditional ways children have devised for dealing with feelings of hostility are better than most of us realize.

And although cruel taunts and jeers are part of the tradition of childlore, so are formulaic responses to taunts and jeers. If a child were to ask a wise adult for advice about how to handle someone who was calling him names, he would be told, to report his tormentor to his teacher (he would rather die), to ignore him (impossible), or to fight him. Fighting is a possibility in this kind of situation, but a child will usually reject it unless the odds are overwhelmingly in his favor or unless he feels strongly that adults expect him to fight. (It's not just international wars that are declared by the old and fought by the young.) But while adults can't help the victim much, other children can help a great deal. From them a child can learn the traditional comebacks of the playground, snappy, decisive replies like:

> I'm rubber, you're glue;
> Whatever you say bounces off me
> And sticks to you!
>
> Twinkle, twinkle, little star,
> What you say is what you are!

[Or "Who the heck do you think you are?"
"Your mouth is bigger than my daddy's car!"]
And no returns forevermore!

Sticks and stones will break my bones
But words will never harm me!
[Sometimes, two additional lines follow:
"When I die, you shall cry
For all the names you've called me!"]

You call me this, you call me that,
You call yourself a dirty rat [or "a fraidy cat"].

Diamonds may shine but don't have to glisten;
You can talk, but I don't have to listen!
(Canal Zone, 1954)

With the *chutzpah* that transforms an insult into a compliment, a child can assert, "That's me, the one and only!" Or he can counter with, "That's my name; want my address?" or ". . . my biography?" A variant is, "That's my name; don't wear it out. I'll need it next year." A child may insist that both he and his opponent are tarred with the same brush: "Takes one to know one, and you know them all!" or "I was born this way. What's your excuse?" He may inquire sneeringly, "I know *you* are, but what am I?" or "Talking to yourself?" He may observe sympathetically, *"Danny, Danny,* don't be blue;/Frankenstein was ugly, too!" Other replies include: "I don't make trash; I burn it!" and "I'm fire; you're wood!" (It is understood that fire *"burns* wood *up."*) Another response based on an analogy is, "I'm a mirror; whatever you say to me, you're really saying to you!" A tough guy can snarl, "If you don't like it, you can lump it!" And in Louisiana in the early fifties, some kids responded to insults with the philosophical, "I'm one by name, but you're one by nature!"

Caught off guard, a child can always reply with, "You're ten times worse," or "Same to you but more of it!" These are fast-draw responses, useful but crude. Our favorite requires an expert sense of timing and presence. Holding his fire until there is a lull in his tormentor's attack, a child earnestly beseeches the name caller, "Consider the source."

Some jeers are designed for specific exchanges. When someone trumpets "Cut low!" bragging thereby that he has put a rival down, the latter replies, "I know *you* are; did you just find out?" To an opponent who sticks out his tongue, one responds aloofly, "No thanks, I use toilet paper." Anticipating an insult, one says:

> Don't say it,
> Your mother'll faint,
> Your father'll fall
> In a bucket of paint!
> (New York, 1965)

A girl called a "hog" or a "pig"—"You're a p-i-g! Dot, dot, dot and no erasing!"—can reply, "Yes, I'm an Honest, Obedient Girl, aren't I?" or "Thanks for calling me a Pretty Intelligent Girl." A child who is being mimicked says, "Monkey see, monkey do!"

To an established jeering partner, one can respond to an insult with:

> You call me names? My strength you doubt?
> Pardon me while I knock you out!

Partners also run through the routines that go:

> "What's your name?"
> "John Brown."
> "Pardon me while I knock you down,"

and

> "What's your name?"
> "Puddentaine. Ask me again and I'll tell you the same."

Actual strangers are never that flip with each other. ("Puddentaine," incidentally, seems to be a name used during the Renaissance for the devil.) Another friendly sort of insult is

I wish I were a grapefruit
And here's the reason why:
When you came to eat me,
I'd shoot you in the eye.

In more serious encounters, a tormentor may be trapped by
the apparently feeble reply, "Aw, shut up!" Overconfident, the
name caller taunts, "Come on, make me!" and is squelched by,
"You're already made but too dumb to know it!" Probably, by
the time he has figured that one out, the bell has rung, the
class has assembled, and everyone has shifted to a different
register of discourse. There are, however, two formulaic responses that the name caller could have used to counter "Shut
up," and both of them are powerhouses:

I don't shut up,
I grow up!
But when I see you,
I throw up!
["And you lick it up," may be added.]

Shuts don't go up,
Prices do.
Take my advice,
And you shut up, too!

A child who shouts, "You're queer!" at a playmate may be
flattened by the syllogistic response:

A queer is a drip,
A drip is a drop,
A drop is water,
Water's nature,
Nature's beautiful,
Thank you for the compliment!

With traditional jeers, a child not only instructs his enemies,
he delights himself. He experiences the aesthetic pleasure of
balancing phrases, of setting words off in antithesis, and of

71

linking them by alliteration and rhyme. Long after an argument is over, a child will jeer the empty air, savoring his language, as if the rhymes were snatches of melody remembered in passing:

> Tarzan, monkey man,
> Swinging on a rubber band!

Children do not learn to fear, enjoy, and respect words in the schoolroom the way they do on the playground. The triteness of the words in their textbooks, as Bruno Bettelheim has pointed out, "destroys any possibility that reading as such could be viewed as a worthwhile experience." It is easy to see why this is so. The language of first-grade primers has been castrated in the name of some dream of efficiency. It is an admirable language for teaching machines to read—should they ever want to do so. Consider, for instance:

> Janet and Mark.
> Come, Mark. Come, Mark, come.
> Come here, Mark.
> Come here, come here, Mark.

Textbook writers seem to assume that the students are without taste or passion, and such writers, by their own efforts, soon turn their assumption into a fact. (Dick and Jane, by the way, have gone to their reward. They have been replaced by Janet and Mark. This is called educational reform.)

If a first-grade child continues to love language after being forced to read his textbooks, part of the reason is his familiarity with the linguistic deliciousness of such first-grade jeers as "Kindergarten baby,/Stick your head in gravy!" On army posts an alternative version ends, "Born in the navy!" In the higher grades children read about Australian bauxite production in class while on the playground they are enjoying theologically provocative and artistically satisfying linguistic cartwheels like:

> God made mountains,
> God made lakes,

God made you,
But we all make mistakes!

Children do sometimes learn to fear and respect the language of a teacher, but hers is still a foreign language—grown-up talk. It is in dealing with his own kind that a child learns to evaluate the expression and the expresser on different scales and to appreciate the style of:

Teeter, totter,
Bread and water,
Stick your head in dirty water!

There she goes, there she goes,
All dressed up in her Sunday clothes!
Ain't she sweet, ain't she sweet,
All but the stink of her dirty feet!

The "Roses Are Red" series teaches a child to appreciate differences within a fixed form. (These rhymes are used mainly as autograph verses, but may also serve as jeers in verbal duels.)

Roses are red,
Peppers are green.
You'd look better
In a washing machine!

Roses are red,
Violets are blue.
Sugar is sweet,
And so are you.
But the roses are wilted,
The violets are dead.
The sugar is lumpy,
And so is your head!

Roses are red,
They grow in this region.
If I had your face,
I'd join the French Foreign Legion.

Roses are red,
Violets are blue.

ONE POTATO, TWO POTATO...

> Do you hate me
> As much as I hate you?

Or the quatrain may be concluded with one of the following:

> This sidewalk is cracked,
> And so are you!

> You fell on your head,
> That's a dumb thing to do!

> Lemons are sour,
> And so are you!

There seems to be no end to such examples:

> If I was your sweeetheart,
> I'd jump in a sewer!

> I kissed a cow,
> And I thought it was you!

We were glad to discover that a favorite of our childhood still survives. "Hot Squat!" we drawled in the thirties, meaning, "So, what's the big deal?" Today it is used in tag games for "I'm safe." We think the appeal of "Hot squat!" for us lay in its mysteriousness and in the repetition of the vowel sounds in the two monosyllables. We knew nothing of its use around 1900 as part of a longer jeer: "Hot? Squat. Stick your nose in a mustard pot!"

"Besides the jeers that are widely known and that have been around for many years, children also employ some that are never popular outside of one school or school district. For instance, at a school in the Canal Zone, "Yikki, ikki, high-ho!" repeated several times, was once felt to be a suitable way to taunt uppity children. And at several schools in the Zone, "Feel weak!" a command, often pronounced, "Few eak!" and accompanied by a wiggling of magic fingers pointed at one's enemy, was long used as both a jeer and a comeback, but we have never been able to collect it in the United States.

As a friend of ours listened to his children screech insults at

74

one another, he consoled himself with the thought that they would outgrow the practice. But not everyone does. We live in what Stephen Spender has called a "Shouting democracy," although in this age of television most of our "shouts" are printed on signs or bumper stickers: "Ford is an Edsel," "Impeach the Expletive Deleted!"

But adults do, of course, have an attitude toward jeers which is different from that of children, and nowhere has that difference been more clearly illustrated than during the student and police confrontations of the late sixties. The students were challenging the police to a jeering contest and presumed an unwarranted intimacy. They were treating the police not as strangers, but as playmates. The police, on the other hand, had an adult attitude toward jeers. Words were not playthings to them; students were not playmates. As adults they had only two choices—to stand mute or to fight.

Obviously, the jeering techniques of the playground won't work if the other side won't play. Nor is it a good idea to reduce serious matters to the level of a children's game. But we can't help fantasizing about a confrontation in which the police respond to cries of "Pig!" and "Fascist!" and worse with a disciplined, deep-voiced choral chant: "Twinkle, twinkle, little star,/What you say is what you are!"

The virtue of formulaic taunts and jeers is that they can turn serious quarrels into something close to sport—into verbal games, which can be intensely competitive without being violent.

Ambushes, Scapegoats, and Punishments

We envy the way children can lose themselves in whatever they are doing. It's a trait we hope they retain when they grow up—but as parents we also worry that our children aren't sufficiently aware of what's going on around them. One of our jobs is to snap them out of their self-absorption. We are aided in this by the children themselves as they play traditional ambush games. These games are always "on," and daydreamers always lose.

Ambush games test a child's alertness and punish him if he is caught napping. The punishment in turn tests his ability and willingness to be a good sport—to affirm his membership in the group. The punishment may be psychological, as in those versions of Cooties in which a particular child's name is repeatedly called out, or it may be physical, as in Jinks and Flinches. It is usually fairly mild, unless consistently directed at a scapegoat.

Some ambush games are popular in a school for a month or so, then vanish. The craze for suddenly twisting someone's T-shirt to leave "tit marks" is this sort of game, as is the fad for spotting cars that are worth a certain number of hits. Say a child sees a yellow Chevrolet. He shouts "Kings!" Then he counts until someone yells "Stops!" He adds the number of hits the car is worth to the number he reached in counting and begins punching everyone within reach on the shoulder. But a boy can protect himself by shouting "No Kings!" if he even senses that a pal is about to score by shouting "Kings!"

Other ambush games are popular all year long—games like Apple Core, for instance. First, a child eats an apple. Holding up the core, he says, "Apple core."

Someone replies, "Baltimore." By this time, wary children are ready to dodge.

"Who's your friend?" asks the first speaker.

The second one names somebody, and the first throws the apple core at the person named. Like good bureaucrats, they have blurred the question of who is responsible. The thrower didn't name the target; the person who named the target didn't throw anything.

Flinches is also popular throughout the year. You fake a punch or flick your fingers in a child's face. If he flinches, and he always does, you get to hit him ten times, but you must wipe off each hit. If you forget, he shouts, "One-two-three-contact!" and gets to hit you. He must wipe off his hits, though, and if he forgets. . . .

The two best-known and most popular ambush games are Jinks and Cooties. When two children say the same word at the same time—and it happens more often than you'd expect —that's the signal for the quickest one to say, "Jinks! One-two-three-four-five-six-seven-eight-nine-ten! Owe me a Coke!" Local variants include "Diddies" or "Dixies" for "Jinks" in the Canal Zone; "Pinch, poke, owe me a Coke!" in Smithville, Indiana; and "Jinks, Cokes, and hamburgers!" in Tacoma, Washington.

The child who fails to say the formula first doesn't really owe the other a Coke. But in some schools, the loser can't speak until someone says his full name. In others, the winner gets to slug the loser on the shoulder. Sometimes the first child to react draws an X on the other's shoulder, shouts "Jinks!" and counts until the loser shouts "Stops!" The number he has reached is the number of hits he is allowed. But if he gets excited and forgets to "wipe off" his hits after delivering them, the loser gets to hit the winner. Everyone has rights.

The word "jinks" doesn't come from "jinx," meaning a hoodoo. It's from High Jinks, an ancient drinking game in Scotland that involved paying a forfeit and playing the role of a mute.

Before World War II, children who said the same word at the same time didn't shout "Jinks"—at least not often. Sometimes one of them shouted "Shakespeare!" and the other replied "Longfellow!" They then linked little fingers, made a silent wish, and pulled until they broke their grip. A more popular reaction was for the children to link pinkies and recite the following parody of a fraternal society's recognition ritual:

"Needles."
"Pins."
"Triplets."
"Twins."
"When a man marries"

"His trouble begins."
"When a man dies"
"His trouble ends."
"What goes up the chimney?"
"Smoke."
"I wish this wish"
"May never be broke."

There are no supervised Cootie leagues, but more people in the United States have played Cooties than have played baseball, basketball, and football combined. It began to be popular sometime after World War I, and today it's our unofficial national game.

Cooties are "imaginary germs" or "contaminated bugs." All a child does to start a game is touch someone and say, "You've got cooties!" Or he may specify the source of the infection: "You've got *Larry's* cooties!" At that, everyone scatters, screaming in mock panic. The cootie carrier passes on the cooties and purifies himself by tagging another person and shouting, "You've got *Larry's* cooties!" He may add, "No tag backs." Children mimic immunization shots with ballpoint pens, or mark a magic X on their hands with an appropriately named Magic Marker. They write "C P" on their tennis shoes—for "Cootie Protection."

Cootie games take place in class as well as on the playground. A child goes to sharpen his pencil; he passes on *Larry's* cooties. A smart aleck will even give the teacher those cooties. The next person she touches gets them. Everyone in the room knows what's going on except her.

Cooties is often a boys-against-girls game. In one Georgia school, the girls had the cooties and chased the boys. A report from New Hampshire was that the boys had them and chased the girls. Even when an individual is singled out as the source of infection, Cooties is not necessarily a scapegoat game. As often as not it's a teasing game among friends, a way of taking a teacher's pet or a popular but conceited kid down a notch.

Sometimes, however, a child is permanently assigned the role of the cootie carrier, and Cooties then does become a scapegoat game. One school we know about had a Cootie Queen for over three years. At the cry, "Watch out, here comes the Cootie Queen!" children jumped off the sidewalk, if she was on the sidewalk, or off the grass, if she was on the grass. Anyone standing on the same surface as the Queen caught her cooties.

Slam Books can also be used for scapegoating, but that isn't their main purpose. Girls "keep" these books, but boys and girls alike write in them. To start one, a girl takes an ordinary spiral notebook and writes a different person's name at the top of each page, except the first. On the first page, she numbers each line. Those who wish to write comments about the individuals listed in the book must first sign in on page 1. The owner usually covers the earlier signatures. A child who signs on line 10 then writes "10" beside each of his comments. If a child who is writing comments in the book tries to sneak a look at page 1, the book's owner squeals and grabs the book. She is supported by those who want their names kept secret and opposed by those who want all the names revealed.

The comments in the books are usually pretty abstract: "Real nice" or "Ugh!" Occasionally criticism is sharp: "Shoots beavers at all the boys!" Most children get mixed reviews. Some receive unexpected compliments—"Sticks by her friends"—that are treasured. But sometimes one child turns out to be everyone's target. Here are the comments about one such person in a 1969 Slam Book: "Scago la vomit," "Stupid" (three times), "Gross" (twice), "Ugh!" (three times), "Not nice," "Show off," "Stinks," "Dumb Dope," "Scab," "Pu Pu," "Ugh boo."

This is scapegoating, and it is appalling. But Slam Books have redeeming features. Children who write in them discover that writing is good for something besides homework, and they learn a lot about the perils and pleasures of judging other people. They need to be surprised when they are misinterpreted, to be shocked as they discover what others think of them, and to find out all those complicated things one learns from quarrels and reconciliations, from secret agreements, treaties, and alliances.

Slam Books and Cooties are formal manifestations of our children's practice of making informal judgments about each other. Both can be used for scapegoating; certainly adults should intervene when this happens. But in a world where children are discouraged from making critical judgments about people—"If you can't say something nice about a person, don't say anything at all"—they keep their critical faculties intact by exercising them on each other in games like Cooties and customs like keeping Slam Books.

Not all games that test a child's ability and willingness to take punishment are ambush games. Some are formal games that each participant must consent to play. They are not, however, as popular as ambush games. One such punishment game is Club Fist. It is played in Arkansas, Kentucky, and other Southern States. Boys stack their fists, each holding the thumb of the fist below his own. The player whose fist is on the bottom is the leader. He keeps one hand free and asks, "Take it off or knock it off or let the crows pick it off?" If the boy whose fist is on top says, "Take it off," he removes his fist and is scorned by his playmates. The manly thing to do is to say "Knock it off," whereupon the leader batters the fist until it comes off the stack. If the reply is "Let the crows pick it off," the leader pinches the fist until it is removed. When only the leader's fist is left, the players ask him, "What have you got in that hole?"

He replies, "Bread and cheese."

The interrogation continues:

> "Where's my share?"
> "Mouse got it."
> "Where's the mouse?"
> "Cat got it."
> "Where's the cat?"
> "Hammer killed it."

"Where's the hammer?"
"Behind the old church house cracking hickory nuts."

The leader then tries to make his friends grin. The first to do so pays a forfeit of punches, pinches, or hair pulls.

All these are meant to hurt, but none of them is dangerous. Boys do trade information about how best to punch a friend on the shoulder. They all know that there is a sensitive spot in the middle of the upper arm, just below the shoulder proper. The best way to hold one's knuckles is a matter of dispute. But while the right sort of punch to the upper arm can be painful, few grade-school boys can deliver that kind of punch, and those who can are not consistent. Boys who play Flinches, Jinks, or Club Fist often go home with bruised shoulders, but they are never in danger of being seriously hurt.

However, in at least three games, children risk serious injury. One of these is Chicken. All our reports of this game came from boys growing up in various small towns in Idaho, but we doubt that the game is confined to one state. Chicken requires two players. They stand facing each other, their feet spread wide apart. The boy who has first turn throws a knife between the feet of his opponent, who moves one foot to the place where the knife entered the ground, removes the knife, and throws it between the feet of the other boy. The first to chicken—to refuse to continue—loses.

The other two games are punishment games in which one child hits others with a belt. We first collected these games from the children of West Indian workers in the Canal Zone and later found that at least one of them is also played in New York City. The first is a version of Drop the Handkerchief called I Drop the Letter. The It walks around the outside of the circle while everyone sings:

> I dropped a letter 'roun the ring,
> Someone pick it up
> An' won't give it up,
> It's a Bombay zapatilla all over.

81

She—for this is a girls' game—drops a belt behind another player and runs around the circle. The chosen player picks up the belt and chases the It. The object is to belt the It a few times before she can reach the vacant spot in the circle.

Another belting game is called Hot Bread and Butter in the Canal Zone and Hot Peas and Butter in New York City. The It hides a man's belt while the rest of the players stay on base, hiding their eyes. "Hot bread and butter, come for your supper," calls the It. Everyone hunts for the belt. The one who finds it conceals it behind his back until he can approach his friends; then he swings it against as many of his playmates as possible before they regain the base. This is an example of a game that is not played by many of today's middle-class children, though they may know it in a milder form, played with a towel and called Swatter Go Find, which at least one recreation leader recommends for schools and summer camps. The street version is not mild. A Puerto Rican boy from New York bragged to us about the size of the welts that he received playing the game. We asked if the game didn't lead to fights. "You know what you're getting into," said another boy, and shrugged.

Belting games may reduce the terror that children feel in families where the father is apt to "use the belt" as a means of correction—the child has learned from his play that he can "take it." And to some extent the child may be better able to ignore the hatred, fear, and confusion that go with a beating from one's father by relating it to a game.

The Battle of the Sexes

When the boy who lives down the street went off to kindergarten, the first rhyme he learned was the old dodgeball taunt, "Missed me, missed me, now you got to kiss me!" A terrible fate. By the time he reaches sixth grade, the amount of sex-related lore that he knows will have increased geometrically. Sex lore consists of prophecies, autograph rhymes, superstitions, jokes, shocking songs, and jump-rope soap operas, as well as of taunts and jeers, but it is the last two, and the games that may accompany them, that concern us here.

By the fifth or sixth grade, children find it necessary to get used to the idea that there is going to be a greater difference between girls and boys in the future than there has been in the past. Since at this time it is the girls who are doing the obvious differentiating, it is the boys who must respond to what's going on. Now, a grownup might object that boys don't need to respond, that they should go on about their business and ignore the fact that this girl needs a bra and that girl has one. But such an attitude is really not reasonable. If women's breasts didn't enlarge until they were thirty, adults would surely not just ignore their development; there would be some traditional way to recognize what was happening.

Children rely on tradition, too, and their traditions transform the whole embarrassing business into a game. Boys pretend to sneeze in front of a girl's chest, demonstrating thereby that they are allergic to foam rubber, the substance they believe all falsies are made of. (All girls wearing an over-the-shoulder-boulder-holder are said to be using falsies.) Or a boy may say, "I see you've brought your Band-Aids today."

Even normally demure girls have been known to chase such a wit with the intention of twisting the material of his T-shirt so that it looks as if he possesses tiny breasts or giant nipples. Twisting T-shirts can become a craze that sweeps through a school, affecting boys and girls alike. It becomes an ambush game—one that is always "on"—and anyone wearing a T-shirt must guard his chest lest even his best friend give him "tit marks."

Snapping bras is also an ambush game. A boy swoops out of hiding shouting, "Robin Hood! Robin Hood!" and *twack!* he snaps the girl's bra—his bow. Thus he acknowledges its mysterious presence, which bothers him as much as it does her, and proves his daring by touching the forbidden object. The girl may try to punch him or slap him, but she has received proof of her attractiveness and can console herself for her discomfort by meditating upon the immaturity of stupid little boys. Sometimes boys snap the bra and say, "Pop goes the weasel!" or "Pearl Harbor—sneak attack!"

Bra snappers may rely on traditional tricks. "Do you want to hear a snappy joke?" asks the boy. The gag line is, "I see you grew up overnight," accompanied by a snap. Another trick goes:

> "What's this?" [The speaker points to a girl's back.]
> "What?"
> "A snapping turtle!" [He snaps the bra.]

A variant is:

> "Are you a turtle?"
> "No."
> "How come you snap, then?"

Still another approach is to tap the girl's back while saying, "North, South, East, West—*Equator!*" and snap her bra upon reaching the last word. Twenty years ago, a popular trick was for a boy to ask a girl to play Radio. If she agreed, he put on a set of imaginary headphones, bent over her chest, and chanted, "Come in Tokyo; come in Tokyo," meanwhile pretending to turn her breasts as if they were dials. Then he ducked. This game may still be played in some areas, but our last report of it is from Minnesota in the fifties.

Since there are so many flat-chested girls in fifth and sixth grade, rhymes belittling them are rare. About the only common one of this type is a variation on "Roses Are Red" ending, "Pancakes are flat and so are you."

But flatness is undesirable, so little girls chant:

> We can, we can, we know we can,
> We can, we can, we must.
> We can, we can, we know we can,
> Increase the bust.

Or this more recent favorite:

We must, we must,
Increast our bust.
The bigger the better,
The tighter the sweater,
The boys like you better,
And so we must.

Before any women's liberationist goes tromping off to the playground to straighten the kids out, consider these rhymes in context. They are chanted on all sorts of occasions, but most often while the girls are doing calisthenics in gym class. The girls' tone is militant, though there is a strong note of mockery, too. They are proclaiming their new-found sexuality to all the world and getting used to it themselves—in an atmosphere of feminist solidarity. What's more, the pitter-pat of *b*'s and *t*'s in the second version is fun for its own sake. That's why they always say "increast" instead of "increase." There's more to those rhymes than meets the eye.

Mothers and older sisters sometimes recite these same lines in weight-reducing salons, a context only superficially similar to a school gym class. Adopted by adults, the rhymes change radically in tone. They lose their mocking quality and become work chants.

Little erotic folklore shows up in grade school. The extensive folklore of masturbation, contraception, and seduction is more commonly collected from students in junior high rather than from those still in grade school. But grade-school children have intimations of immorality, and these are not freely shared with inquisitive adult collectors. For instance, we stumbled across the existence of "greenies" by accident. We had given written interviews to several hundred fifth-graders in a county in Indiana, and as we were sorting our material, we found replies that didn't seem to make sense—enigmatic references to "the bases" and to children who "wouldn't go to the bases." We asked our sixth-grade daughter what it meant to say that a person wouldn't go to the bases.

To our surprise, she blushed. Shrugging, she said, "Oh, they're greenies."

"Who?"

"People who won't play the bases."

"But what are 'the bases'?" Her blush reappeared more extensively than before.

First base, we learned, was kissing. Third was. . . . We were told we must know what third was because, as our daughter pointed out, "You've got me."

"And what about home?"

"Oh, my goodness. You'd *never* guess!" As scholars we no doubt had a duty to pin down the exact meaning of second base and home, but as parents we felt that the implications were, after all, plain enough.

Many children in the county that we were investigating knew about the bases, but not all of them clearly understood what each base represented. We have the impression that for most of them, the territory after one rounded first was progressively more mysterious. Some understood the whole circuit but did not share their knowledge with just anybody. Not wanting to be thrown out of the schools where we were doing our research, we did not pursue this matter. One of the reasons for establishing public schools in the first place was to separate innocent children from corrupt adults.

We did ask children if they knew what a greenie was. Most of them did, but they often refused to tell us. They said, "That's for me to know and you to find out," a tried and true folkloric answer, or they said, "People say it all the time, but I won't give the meaning." Definitions we did receive included: "you aren't nasty if you're a greenie," "greenies are afraid to make out," "a person who has never been kissed by a boy," "someone who's shy in front of girls," "a stupid person," "someone scared to play the bases."

A greenie, we concluded, is a person who acts excessively bashful or fluttery around a particular member of the opposite sex. A child who is taunted as a greenie is not being teased for failing to be "nasty." That business about greenies being those who do not go to the bases is largely metaphorical and not an indication that orgies are taking place in the fifth and sixth grades, though a few sophisticates have been to first base. The greenie is being teased rather for failing to act grown-up. A mature person doesn't get giggly or show-offy around a potential boy friend or girl friend. And, of course, children like to play grown-up. It follows—somewhat circuitously, to be sure—that the "cool" (i.e., "grown-up") youngsters will childishly taunt their playmates who are so un-cool as to behave childishly.

The term "greenie" isn't popular everywhere. It was widely known in one Indiana county, but even there was much more important in some schools than in others. And in two of the fifteen schools we visited in that county, it wasn't known at all. But "greenie" isn't a local invention. College freshmen told us in 1974 that greenies and the bases were part of their grade-school and junior-high lore in Pennsylvania and Virginia. "Greening" and "greens" are British dialect terms that have been used to refer to a sexual craving or to intercourse for centuries. And "greenhorn" has applied to a recently initiated young man since at least 1680. Closer to home, Laura Ingalls Wilder, in the classic *Little Town on the Prairie,* described an episode occurring when she was almost fifteen, in 1881, in which a girl speaking to other girls referred to a young man as a "greeny," and his girl friend blushed.

Embarrassment is an almost constant hazard for children. There are so many things to learn, and some of them are contradictory. If you won't play the bases you are a greenie, but if you show that you like a member of the opposite sex, you hear:

> *Roger* and *Debbie,* sitting in a tree,
> K-i-s-s-i-n-g!
> First comes love, then comes marriage,
> Then comes *Debbie* pushin' a baby carriage.

Sometimes more lines are added:

ONE POTATO, TWO POTATO...

>Sucking on his bottle,
>Wetting in his pants,
>Doing the hula-hula dance.

Another variation is:

>Bring out the diapers,
>Bring out the pins.
>*Roger* and *Debbie* just had twins!

Heard somewhat less frequently is another rhyme of the same type:

>Cooties, cooties,
>She'll be your wife,
>And you'll be makin' booties
>All of your life!

Any of these rhymes may be accompanied by a gesture that means kissing: the tips of the index fingers pressing and twisting against each other. "That always makes 'em mad," a girl told us.

The most frequently used sexual jeers have to do with clothing. Any school-day morning, children all over America are likely to hear the banshee wail "X-Y-Zee-ee!" to which is sometimes added "P-D-Q-oo!" This means, "Examine Your Zipper, Pretty Darn Quick." All the exhortations of a mother to her absent-minded son are not as effective as "X-Y-Z." Embarrassed, the victim pulls himself together and goes hunting for a chance to shout the same taunt at one of his playmates.

Besides using the popular "X-Y-Z," the town criers announce that a playmate has an open fly by shouting:

>All the cows are leaving the barn.
>One cow, two cows, three—
>All the cows are coming to me!
>Better close the barn door.

Or they broadcast the less subtle:

Barn door's open.
The cock is running wild.

Jokes too are used to embarrass the unzipped child:

"What do airplanes do?"
"Fly."
"Ha-ha!"

"Do you own an airplane?"
"Huh?"
"Your hangar's open."

"Is somebody in your family dead?"
"No."
"Well, your flag's at half-mast."

A child may simply begin counting when he spots an open zipper. Others join him. Sometimes even the guilty party joins in. As the count gets higher and louder, everyone looks around to see who is at fault. Finally the boy with the unzipped fly discovers it. (The problem of forgetting to zip up is international. In Panama, a child may say, *"La farmacia está abierta y Don Pepe está en la puerta."* "The pharmacy is open and Don Pepe is in the doorway.")

To a girl whose slip is showing, boys shout, "S-O-S!" (Slip On Show!) or "It's snowing down south!" or "I'm dreaming of a white Christmas!" An American adult male has no expressions as slick as these for telling a woman her slip is hanging below her hem. He must ignore it or whisper the utilitarian but lifeless, "Dear, your slip shows." In Yiddish he could say it better: *"Dyan mitvoch iz langer vi dyan donershtik."* ("Your Wednesday is longer than your Thursday.")

Slips, however, aren't as exciting to boys as are a girl's panties. The two basic panties rhymes are:

Teacher, Teacher, I declare,
I see *Shirley's* underwear,

and

ONE POTATO, TWO POTATO...

I see London, I see France,
I see *Shirley's* underpants.

Various endings are attached to either of these:

Might be white, might be pink,
Boy, oh, boy [or "P.U."], sure do stink.

Not too big, not too small,
Just the size of a cannonball.

They aren't purple, they aren't white,
Oh, my God, they're dynamite!

Somewhat less popular are:

Oh my wonders, oh my stars,
I see *Nelly's* underdrawers!

It's raining, it's pouring,
Your underwear's showing!

Jesus, Jesus, in the air,
I see someone's underwear!

I like apples, I like pears,
I like *Mary's* underwears!

From swinging California comes a reply to such taunts.

Made you stare,
Made you stare,
Made you eat my underwear!

Some underwear taunts can be applied to either girls or
boys:

There goes *Betty* [or *"Johnny"*],
Walkin' down the Delaware,
Chewin' on her ["his"] underwear,
Can't afford another pair.
Ten days ["six months"] later,
Bitten by a grizzly bear ["polar bear"],
Poor grizzly bear.

[Sometimes, an additional line follows:
"That's the way the story goes."]

And a few underwear taunts are just for fun. Directed at no one, they are victimless rhymes:

> Tarzan, Tarzan, in the air;
> Tarzan lost his underwear;
> Tarzan say, "Me no care,
> Jane will make me another pair."
> Jane, Jane, in the air;
> Jane lost her underwear;
> Jane say, "Me no care,
> Cheetah make me another pair."
> Cheetah, Cheetah, in the air;
> Cheetah lost his underwear;
> Cheetah say, "Me no care,
> Cheetah need no underwear."

Children often ask simple questions like, "Where do babies come from?" or "When will I start growing fur, too?" But they aren't worldly or self-confident enough to ask, "How do I act around Joanne when she bends over and shows her pants? I want her to like me, but I don't want to be teased by the boys. Also, I want to look. Do I have an excuse? What can I do to make her notice me?" and so on. Their oral tradition provides answers to the questions children don't know how to ask. Moreover, the answers are not "thought-provoking." They are useful—and enable children to deal with the sexual aspects of a child's world in a child's way.

JOKES

Tricks and Wit

In one form or another, the trickster shows up in the folklore of many groups. In American Indian stories, he is a coyote or a raven; in the stories of rural blacks, Brer Rabbit or John, the clever slave. He is a bad man in the long, narrative toasts of urban blacks, a man crazy enough to do anything. Many of us hear about him in jokelore, where he is a crazy Polack or an elephant wearing tennis shoes. The trickster appears also in childlore—in jokes, in scary stories, but mainly in person. American playgrounds are full of tricksters.

> "Bet I can make you say an Indian word."
> "How?"

Tricksters may be malicious, innocent, or crazy, but always they are energetically lawless. "Spreading strife is my greatest joy," explains Edshu, a trickster-divinity from West Africa. As a spreader of strife, a trickster does more than play tricks; he plays the fool. He is the little moron who throws a clock out the window in order to see time fly.

Some folk tales tell of a trickster hero who outwits the unjust gods and steals fire or rain, whatever is necessary, to save mankind. But when a trickster isn't heroically duping the gods, he is unheroically duping his friends and neighbors:

> When somebody's sitting down where you want to sit, you tell them somebody wants them, and when they get up to leave, you sit down.

> Say you've got a secret, then yell in their ear.

> When they're about to sit, pull out the chair.

In folk tales, the trickster violates not just the laws of polite society, but the laws of nature as well, and people who tell stories about him do so partly to compensate for their own powerlessness against the gods, nature, or, in the case of slaves, their masters.

But our children, the tricksters of the playground, are not characters in folk tales. They're real, and they play tricks on one another, not on the gods, and not, as a rule, on their masters, though we know of one trickster who spit in his teacher's coffee while the man was out of the room. Sometimes tricks compensate a child for his powerlessness in the classroom, but most of the time he uses them to help establish his identity on the playground. He wants to be recognized, and a trick is an exploit that will make him known.

> Tell them, "Give me your hand"; then point and say, "Here's the barn, there's the hen house, here's the out-house, but—hey, where's the swimming pool?" And so you raise their hand up close to your face like you were looking for it; then you spit and say, "Oh, here it is."

His teachers may forget who he is, but his victim won't.

His victim is not particularly upset, however. Though in a sense lawless, the playground trickster is governed by tradi-tion, which grants him the right to violate social norms in certain ways and up to a certain point. As long as his tricks don't go beyond what is traditionally permissible, he doesn't risk ostracism.

> You hold up your hand and wiggle your fingers, see; then say, "The king is walking down the street! Want to see the king? Okay, I'll tell the people to bow down so you can see him." Then you fold back all your fingers but the middle one.

> What starts with f and ends with c-k?
> Firetruck, dummy, what'd you think it was?

> Tell them to say, "I'm not the sheet slitter, I'm the sheet slitter's son, but I'll slit your sheets till the sheet slitter comes."

> Say to some guy, "I hear if your hand's bigger than your face, you'll die at twenty." When they put their hand up to see, hit it so they smash themselves. Or you can do it by saying, "Did you know your hand smells like peanut butter?"

> Hey, dreamboat. Not you, shipwreck!

93

> Draw a *B* on their back, like a guessing game. You use
> your finger. Then you say, "What's that?" When they say
> what it is, you say, "A bee will sting you. I better kill it."
> Then you hit them on the back as hard as you can. If they
> know that one, make them say *J*. You say, "A jay will peck
> you!" and you poke them with your fingers stiff and you
> say, "Peck, peck, peck!"

It's easy to understand why the school disapproves of this sort
of thing. The school wants students to make names for themselves by seeking the approval of the faculty, not the recognition of their peers. And the school is prepared to grant distinc-
tion to only a small number of students—academic superstars
and favored collaborators. The rest are supposed to do their
homework, sit quietly, and be content to be invisible. The
teachers are not unkind; the children are warm, safe, and busy.
It's a good life. What more could they want?

What more? A life of excitement, adventure, and trouble.
A chance to be somebody. Thus tricksters go about spreading
strife by causing pain and embarrassment:

> Make them hold up their hand. Then count each finger
> while you say, "Super-man-never-says. . . ." Then pull back
> their little finger hard, and they'll say it.

> "Knock, knock."
> "Who's there?"
> "Little Boy Blue."
> "Little Boy Blue who?"
> "I don't know who he blew, do you?"

Homer called his trickster-hero Odysseus ("Bringer of Trouble," "Causer of Pain"). Odysseus troubled his family by leaving home to search for fame, and he caused someone trouble
wherever he went. Were he a child today, we can be sure he
would be called to account by his teacher for some crafty exploit on the playground. And his mother, if she were sum-
moned to a parent-teacher conference, would side with the

teacher. His mother's name was Antikleia ("Opposed to Fame").

Children seem to be aware of something that parents and teachers don't know, or at least don't feel they can admit—that there is no way to live a life of any scope without hurting and being hurt.

> Have them put their hand down on a piece of paper. Then take a pencil and trace around their fingers while you tell about the farmer who goes to town to get some meat: "And he went up the hill and through the valley, up the hill and through the valley. . . ." You just make up stuff he goes for and keep drawing lines until after a long time you say, "Oh, he forgot the salt. But he's so tired. I guess he'll take a short cut," and you run the pencil hard over their finger backs.
>
> "What does t-w-a spell?"
> "T-wa."
> "What does t-w-e spell?"
> "T-we."
> "What does t-w-o spell?"
> "T-wo."
> "What's the matter with you? T-w-o spells 'two.' "
>
> Make two dots on their hand and ask them, "What's the difference between these two rats?" When they give up, you take your pencil and draw a long line up their arm and say, "This one's got a longer tail."

A life without trouble is a shadow life. Yet—necessarily—it is the ideal life promoted by the school. For the school represents society and all the necessary restraints upon rampant individualism. But there is more to life than conformity and an absence of pain. The children's traditional playground tricks teach them something that the school by its very nature must omit from the curriculum. And if the school, with its naïve faith in its own omnipotence, takes over the playground and

95

begins "guiding" children through every moment of their day, it will be depriving them of important experiences.

Childen love the trickster and his tricks, in spite of the embarrassment and pain he causes them. They love him so much that they will play along even when they know the trick, or when they clearly sense that they are being set up.

"Do you feel like a cup of tea? Say Yes."
"Yes."
"Well, you look like one, too."

You imitate a cheerleader and say, "Hey, gimme a *D!*" and they all go, "D!" And you say, "Gimme a *U!*" and they go, "U!" And you go, "Gimme a *H!*" and they go "H!" and you go, "Okay, gang, whadawegot?" and they go, "Duh!"

"Okay, I'll tell a knock, knock joke. You start."
"Okay, knock, knock."
"Who's there?"
[The victim, not prepared with a joke, remains silent.]
"What'samatter, dum-dum?"

Hold your hand in a fist and say, "Raise the lid," and lift up your thumb. Then tell them to put in their finger and stir around. Then you put your thumb down and say, "Thanks for cleaning my toilet."

Tricks that aren't excessively painful are life-enhancing for both the trickster and his victim, which explains why tricksters both in folk tales and on the playground are so willing to play the role of the moron, the clown, the dumb-nut.

Rub a pencil lead around the rim of a quarter; then hold the quarter with two fingers in the middle and roll it over your face. It leaves this line, and everybody wonders about it.

A boy told us that the following trick was for suckers. But we watched him play it on a sucker, and it would be impossible to say which of them enjoyed it more. The trickster asked the sucker to write answers to a written set of questions (A) on a separate piece of lined tablet paper, just as if he were taking a test in school. The trickster then took the page of answers and lined it up with a second set of questions (B), which he only now produced, so that the sucker's answers applied to them.

A	B
1. What's your name?	What's your name?
2. Do you like dirt?	Are you sure?
3. Do you like cars?	Have you ever been kissed?
4. Name a girl [or "boy"].	By whom?
5. Write a number.	How many times?
6. Name a terrible food.	What did it taste like?
7. Write "Yes."	Did you enjoy it?
8. Do you like yourself?	Would you do it again?
9. Write a number.	How many times?
10. Do you like to go to the movies?	Are you going steady?
11. With whom?	With whom?
12. Name an animal.	What does she ["he"] look like?
13. Write a number.	How many teeth does she ["he"] have?
14. Write "No."	Is she ["he"] ugly?
15. Write "Yes."	Did you ever do anything?
16. Name a girl ["boy"].	With whom?
17. Where do you like to read?	Where at?
18. Do you like to eat?	Did you enjoy it?
19. Are you okay?	Aren't you ashamed?
20. Why do you go to school?	Why did you do it?

In his clownish mood, a trickster exuberantly turns language inside out:

> One dark day in the middle of the night,
> Two dead boys got up to fight.

ONE POTATO, TWO POTATO...

Back to back, they faced each other,
Drew their swords and shot each other.
A deaf policeman heard the noise,
Stood up and shot those two dead boys.
If you doubt this story's true,
Ask the blind man. He saw it, too.

Ladies and Germs [or "Geritols"],
I come before you to stand behind you
To tell you something I know nothing about.
Admission free; pay at the door.
Pull up a chair; sit on the floor.
Refreshments will be served in empty glasses.

This meeting will come to disorder.
We will discuss something we know nothing about
At the four corners of the round table.

(Wisconsin, 1975)

'Twas midnight on the ocean,
Not a streetcar was in sight,
The sun was shining brightly,
For it rained all day that night.
'Twas a summer day in winter,
And the snow was raining fast,
As a barefoot boy with shoes on
Stood sitting on the grass.

In another mood, a trickster exploits the innate trickiness of language itself—and teaches his victims an important lesson about what the school terms "language arts."

This plane crashes, see, in this river that's right between Mexico and Texas. It crashes right in the middle. So where do they bury the survivors?
Dummy, you don't bury survivors.

Are you smart? Okay, what's your name?
Okay, spell it.
Dummy, that's not how you spell "it."

They have to say the same thing each time, like "pea-green soup" or "rubber mountains." Then you start a lot of sentences and they finish them with those words; and then you say, "Before I go to bed, I . . ." or "Julie lets me . . . ," and they say . . .

"I'm a gold lock."
"I'm a gold key."
"I'm a silver lock."
"I'm a silver key."
"I'm a brass lock."
"I'm a brass key."
"I'm a monk lock."
"I'm a monk key."

"Guess what."
"What?"
"That's what!"

How many traditional tricks are in oral circulation is anybody's guess. They seem to go on forever.

See my finger? See my thumb? Gee, you're dumb.

Look up. Look down. Look all around.
Your pants are falling down!

Tell him to hold up five fingers. Then say, "Did you kill your sister, baby finger?" and fold it back. "Did you kill your sister, ring finger?" and fold it back. "Did you kill your sister, middle finger?" and fold it back. Then you ask him did he kill his sister, and when he says "No," you say, "What are you holding a gun for then?"

"Which hand do you eat with?"
"My right."
"You dirty kid. Why don't you use a spoon?"

Tell them to look down inside their shirts and spell "attic."

ONE POTATO, TWO POTATO...

"Say 'eighty.'"
"Eighty."
"Bald-headed baby!"

This last trick has some mysterious appeal to first-graders. They shout the last line exultantly, as if the child who said "eighty" had fallen into some carefully prepared trap.

The trickster is no antisocial grouch, nor is he an impassive schemer pulling strings behind the scenes. He is an adventurer and showman with unabashed pride in his work. If his tricks serve to educate, so be it, but their main purpose is to celebrate—himself.

Telephone Jokes

Telephone jokes are most popular in junior high, but children begin practicing them in the fifth and sixth grades. Sometimes they are motivated by feelings of hostility toward a particular person or toward the adult world in general, but more often they are not. While the pranks may be irritating and frustrating to those on the receiving end, youngsters generally play them in a spirit of merriment that is free from rancor.

Folklorist Norine Dresser, who made an extensive study of telephone pranks performed by junior-high students, has pointed out that children almost always play these jokes in groups, and that the reaction of the prankster's fellow conspirators is more important to him than the reaction of the person being called. A prankster may not even wait for the reaction at the other end of the line before hanging up. What counts is the admiration of his peers.

The telephone serves much the same function as a carnival mask. A child can use it to experiment with new roles, to pretend to be someone he isn't—or does not yet dare to be.

The jokes often require the child to assume the role of an adult, frequently an adult in an "official" capacity. In what is perhaps the most widely known prank, the child pretends to be employed by the power and light company:

"Good afternoon, madam. We are making a survey of re-frigerators. Would you please check to see if your refrigerator is running?"

[Long pause] "Yes, it is."

"Well, you'd better run after it before it runs out the door!"

Or he may act the part of an official of the telephone company:

"We are working on your line. Please do not answer your phone for the next thirty minutes. If you do, you may cause our repairman to be electrocuted."

Pretty soon the prankster calls back—several times if necessary—and when the phone is finally answered, he screams as if he were being fried on the line.

There are many variations of the repairman prank. A child may ask his victim to stand thirty feet away from the phone and whistle in order to determine whether the phone is working properly:

"Congratulations, you have just won a pound of bird-seed."

Or the "repairman" may be from the water company:

"Would you please check your kitchen faucet to see if water comes out. It does? Well, what did you expect—milk?"

A child may pretend to be a disc jockey or an official of a company which is sponsoring a contest:

"Can you name three cars that start with *P*?"

"Plymouth, . . . Pontiac, . . . uh . . ."

"Stupid, cars start with gas, not pee!"

"This is Radio station KMBC. If you can tell us the name of Roy Rogers' horse, you will win a prize."

"Trigger."

"Congratulations. You've just won a truckload of horse manure."

Obviously, it takes some skill on the child's part to bring this off. He must make his voice serious and grown-up; above all, he must not laugh. Children preparing to play telephone jokes conduct elaborate tryouts to see who can manage the best performance. Sometimes a handkerchief is placed over the mouthpiece to disguise a childish voice. We suspect that more often than not, the joke ends prematurely in a burst of giggles, or the caller is recognized for what he is. However, there is always the possibility of being taken seriously, and this spurs children on. To be accepted as an official adult with the ability to command or to dispense prizes is to be endowed with exhilarating power. You can make grownups do things, sometimes silly things. You can make them check their refrigerators or their water faucets, answer questions or even whistle. No mean trick.

Children may also pretend to be ordinary, nonofficial grownups. For even ordinary grownups, with money to spend, have powers that children envy. Being taken for an adult enables a youngster to set in motion the wheels of commerce. Children order carry-out dinners, pizzas, and taxis; they make restaurant and theater reservations. Usually the phony orders are placed in the name of a neighbor so that the delivery can be observed. Often the purpose of these jokes is not to harass the business establishment (grade-school children do not always realize what an inconvenience or loss their joke causes) or even to harass the neighbor. The real thrill comes from having made something happen.

Along the same line, but more harmless, are the calls to merchants asking for information. If the child is successful, the clerk politely answers a seemingly innocent question. The meat market and the tobacco store are frequent targets:

> "Do you have pigs' feet [or "... chicken legs?"]
> "Yes, we do."
> "Well, wear long pants and they won't show."

"Do you have Prince Albert in a can?"
"Yes, we do."
"Let him out before he suffocates!"

It's hard to keep from giggling during exchanges like these, but even harder during the following risqué routine. A child calls a sporting-goods store:

"Do you sell bowling equipment?"
"Yes, we do."
"What's the heaviest ball you've got?"
"Eighteen pounds."
"Oh, dear. Why don't you wear baggy pants? Maybe no one will notice."

The youngster who is able to see that through with a straight face is a real hero.

These pranks not only give chilren an opportunity to achieve prestige and status among their peers, but also increase their awareness of the ambiguity of language. That words can mean more than one thing at the same time is a phenomenon to be explored and tested. Some telephone pranks involve punning on the name of the party being called. Children search through the phone book for possibilities.

"Is this Mr. Roach?"
"Yes, it is."
"Well, this is Raid. Pssssst!"

"Is this the Lords' house?"
"Yes, it is."
"May I speak to Jesus, please?"

Under the mask of anonymity that the telephone provides, children may call members of the opposite sex whom they like but are too shy to talk to directly. A youngster may pretend to be someone else and carry on a long conversation, or may just hang up, having heard the loved one's voice. Unlike the pranks previously described, this particular kind of telephone call may be made by a child alone or in the company of one good friend. It is a means of exploring one's own feelings and reactions—feelings that may be too unfamiliar and private for just anyone to share.

Finally, there are those weird one-liners that children sometimes use in answering the phone. Children claim they say them just to be funny, but they are really tricks. A person making a phone call expects a conventional response. Instead, he sometimes hears:

"Morgan's Morgue—you stab 'em, we slab 'em,"

or

"Carson's Bakery—name your crumb."

Teen-age brothers and sisters regard such antics as *déclassé*, and parents don't usually appreciate them either. However, in spite of overwhelming disapproval, children continue to answer the telephone with such *bons mots* as:

"Joe's Pool Hall—Little Eight Ball speaking."

Riddles

The act of guessing a riddle has ominous undertones. Think of all those Greeks who were killed when they couldn't solve the riddle of the Sphinx: "What goes on four legs in the morning, two at noon, and three in the evening?" Finally Oedipus came along and answered, "A man. He crawls, then walks, and then, in his old age, uses a cane." Defeated, the Sphinx committed suicide.

Solving traditional riddles is a matter of life and death only in myths and fairy tales, but even the silliest modern riddle has something imperative about it. We want to give the right answer. We resist saying, "I don't know," even when it's hopeless.

And it often is, especially when we are riddling with a first-grader, who believes a riddle has only one right answer. Either you know it or you don't. A first-grader's riddles are not questions; they are challenges, or demands for a password—signs and countersigns.

Riddling is an ideal game for young children and adults because they can compete as equals; a child who wins can feel that his victory has been earned, not indulgently presented to him. Grownups may know some of the old stand-bys:

Why did the chicken cross the road?
To get to the other side.

What did one candle say to the other candle?
We're going out tonight.

Why does the rain fall in sheets?
To cover the river bed.

What did the big chimney say to the little chimney?
You're too young to smoke.

Why do they keep the cemetery gates shut?
People are dying to get in.

What did the pig say when the man grabbed him by the tail?
This is the end of me.

But adults are not likely to know all of a child's favorites:

What would happen if a girl ate bullets?
She would grow bangs.

What did the boy octopus say to the girl octopus?
I want to hold your hand, hand, hand, hand, . . .

What's long and green and lives in a trunk?
Elephant snot.

What do you call a friendly, helpful monster?
A failure.

What did the mother bullet say to the father bullet?
We're going to have a bee-bee.

What color is rain when it falls on a tin roof?
Pink, pink, pink.

What were Tarzan's last words?
Who greased the grapevi-i-ine?

What are they called when Batman and Robin get run over?
Flatman and Ribbon.

A child confronted with relatives he doesn't know very well but can't ignore has no reserve of small talk to draw on. But he does have riddles. And if, miracle of miracles, Aunt Sue or Uncle George knows some too, the child not only has fun with his relatives but learns some new riddles that he can use in the unending scrimmage of wit on the playground.

Not all of a child's riddles are suitable for Aunt Sue or Uncle George. Six-year-olds know:

What's S.T.P.?
Sticky toilet paper.

Nine-year-olds giggle over:

What made Miss Tomato turn red?
She saw Mr. Green pea.

And by sixth grade, many children know:

What goes in hard and dry and comes out wet and soft?
Bubble gum.

What's six inches long and has two nuts?
An almond bar.

Jack be nimble, Jack be quick,
Jack jumped over the candlestick.
Why was Jack nimble, why was he quick?

Great balls afire!

A ring-dang-do, oh what is that?
It's soft and round like a pussycat;

It's soft and round and split in two.
Oh, what is called a ring-dang-do?
    A girl's pee-pee.

What's green, and hops from bed to bed?
    A prostitoad.

What's white, and lies on the bottom of the ocean?
    Moby's dick.

Riddles like these rarely circulate in print, but the less shocking ones do. Many library books are entirely devoted to riddles. Children's magazines include them; readers are asked to send in their favorites. They even appear on bubble gum wrappers. They appeal to children, partly at least, as parodies of the threatening "riddles" that parents and teachers are always asking: "What have you been up to?" or "How much is six apples less three apples?" Answering these riddles is perilous, but after all is said and done a child can restore his soul by asking "catches" like:

If you have seven candles on a boy's birthday cake and eight on a girl's, which will burn the longest?
    Candles burn shorter.

A bus picks up four girls; then at the next stop, five boys. At another stop, it drops three girls and picks up two boys. At the next, it drops six boys. How many stops did the bus make?

Some catches that are in circulation have been around for a long time. For instance, a little girl in New York City challenges parents and friends with:

There once was a man going to St. Ives Place. He had seven wives; each wife had seven sacks; each sack had seven cats; each cat had seven kits. How many altogether were going to St. Ives Street?
    One.

This may have been old when it was written down in 1730. It

is essentially the same riddle today as it was then, although the narration has been shifted from first to third person, and St. Ives has become either an apartment house or a street in New York City.

Riddles are usually printed with one answer—*the* answer, a first-grader would say. But older children often think of a spoken riddle as a true question and try to figure it out even if they know they haven't heard it before. Sometimes they surprise the riddler by coming up with an answer he hasn't thought of.

What goes up and down but never really moves?
A staircase. A ladder. A road over a hill.

Lots of them go to the river but never drink?
Footsteps. Paths. Reflections.

But like parents and teachers, the riddlers always have the last word. A child asked us, "How do you know if a bear has been in the refrigerator?" We knew: "Footprints in the butter." The child was disappointed—that was his answer—but he invented a new answer on the spot: "No, in the pizza." Another tricky riddler lured us into a trap: "What moos?" "A cow." "No, an airplane going backward."

Comedians have long used two-answer "trap" riddles in their routines.

What has four legs and flies?
A dead horse.
Wrong! Two pairs of pants.

Had the Sphinx played at riddles this way, she would be in business yet. But the Sphinx played fair—and lost.

The most popular riddle in the United States right now seems to be: "What's black and white and red all over?" It is also the riddle that has attracted the most answers: "a newspaper," "a blushing zebra," "a skunk with diaper rash," "a bleeding penguin" or "a bleeding nun," "an Afro-American Santa Claus." There are several obscene answers and a few racist ones—"an integration march," for instance. This abundance may reflect a general belief that there are no right answers to anything in the twentieth century, just more and more ingenious interpretations. What has happened to the "newspaper" riddle may be part of the trend toward a "vastly increased dimension of exaggeration or of 'far-outness'" in the riddles and jokes of children which was found by Alta Jablow and Carl Withers, who studied these riddles and jokes first from 1940 to 1946 and again from 1962 to 1965.

Older, traditional riddles are tricky without being farfetched. The solution fits in an obvious way once it is revealed:

How deep is the ocean?
A stone's throw.

Often an older riddle contained several clues:

In marble walls as white as milk,
Lined with skin as soft as silk,
Within a crystal fountain clear,
A golden apple doth appear.
No doors there are to this stronghold,
Yet thieves break in to steal the gold.
An egg.

What is snow but snow it ain't,
Green as grass but grass it ain't,
Red as blood but blood it ain't,
Black as ink but ink it ain't. What is it?
A blackberry.

Contemporary versions of these riddles are much abridged:

No doors there are to this stronghold,
But thieves break in and take the gold.

A box without hinges, key, or lid,
Yet golden treasure inside is hid.

When is a blackberry green?
When it's red.

In fact, the most popular contemporary children's riddles are one-liners—joke riddles—in which "the most heterogeneous ideas are yoked by violence together; nature and art are ransacked for . . . comparisons. . . ."

> What's purple and plugs in?
> An electric prune.

In this case the solution is satirical; at least we assume that "an electric prune" is a satirical comment on a society that has produced the electric carving knife and the automatic pencil eraser. In other instances, the solution is simply farfetched, but almost always it involves an imaginary thing or event.

> What's green, faster than a bullet, and can stop a speeding train?
> Super pickle.

> What do you call a werewolf in a Dacron suit?
> A wash and werewolf.

> What's the famous dill-pickle game?
> Let's Make a Dill.

> What do you do if you're swallowed by an elephant?
> Run around until you're pooped out.

> What's red and white outside and gray and white inside?
> Campbell's cream-of-elephant soup.

> What's green and flies from planet to planet?
> An interplanetary cucumber.

> What do you get when you cross a rhino with an elephant?
> The 'ellif ino.

> What's green, wears a mask, and rides a horse?
> The Lone Pickle.

> What's the first building a vampire goes to in New York?
> The Vampire State Building.

> What's black and yellow and red?
> Burnt toast with ketchup and mustard.

The strain of violence in modern riddles shows a similar "far-out" quality.

What's black and white and black and white and black and white?
A nun or a penguin falling downstairs.

What's green and lies in the gutter?
A drunk Girl Scout.

What's yellow and lies on its side?
A dead school bus.

What's black and blue and bloody and rolls on the ground?
The next guy to tell me a riddle.

Why did the boy bury his mother under the step?
To get a stepmother.

And the more violent the riddles get, the less rational they seem to be.

What's the difference between unloading dead babies and unloading bowling balls?
You can't use a pitchfork to unload bowling balls.

What's blue and sits in a corner?
A baby in a baggie.

What's white and red all over and sits in a corner and cries?
A baby eating razor blades.

Perhaps the far-out character of some current riddles means that Americans, both children and adults, are simply exploiting every kind of ambiguity and implication in order to satisfy their sophisticated taste for complex and startling relationships.

But this aesthetic explanation may go hand in hand with Jablow and Withers' suggestion that our children see the world as "at best comically irrational, at worst violent and dangerous, and even meaningless." Our children may be connoisseurs of chaos.

ONE POTATO, TWO POTATO...

PERFORMANCES

Jump-rope

While America was a rural nation, jump-rope was mainly a boys' game. The boys did trick jumps—"cross hands," "double-rope," "pepper"—but used few rhymes. The girls liked jump-rope too, though. We can be sure of that, because in the 1850's the author of a children's book warned the girls that they should jump "with moderation," a sign that some were jumping with immoderate enthusiasm.

Then, sometime during the great migration of Americans from their farms to the towns and cities, the girls took over the old pastime of jump-rope. They had more time to play than their mothers had back on the farm, and more friends to play with. On smooth city streets they put together the dozens of games and hundreds of rhymes that make up modern jump-rope lore.

There are jump-rope rhymes about school, movie stars, politicians, history, bumblebees—you name it. But most fall into one of three overlapping groups; they are about domestic life, about boy friends, or about the game itself.

The largest group consists of the rhymes about domestic life; it includes those describing familiar tasks:

> Mable, Mable, set the table,
> Don't forget the salt, vinegar, mustard,
> *Pepper!* [the signal to turn the rope as fast as possible].

> Mix a pancake, stir a pancake,
> Pop it in the pan.
> Fry the pancake, toss the pancake,
> Catch me if you can.

> Grace, Grace, dressed in lace,
> Went upstairs to powder her face.
> How many boxes did it take?
> One, two, three, four . . .

112

Also in this group are rhymes portraying some pretty fierce sibling rivalries:

> Johnny over the ocean,
> [Or "Down by the ocean,"]
> Johnny over the sea,
> ["Down by the sea,"]
> Johnny broke a bottle and blamed it on me.
> I told Ma, Ma told Pa,
> Johnny got a whippin', ha-ha-ha!

> I had a little brother; his name was Tiny Tim.
> [Or "I had a little sister; her name was Bobby Sue."]
> I put him in the bathtub to teach him how to swim.
> ["I put her in the bathtub to see what she would do."]
> He ["She"] drank up all the water, he ["she"] ate up all
>   the soap,
> He ["She"] tried to eat the bathtub but it wouldn't go
>   down his ["her"] throat.
> My mother called the doctor, the doctor called his nurse,
> The nurse called the lady with the alligator purse.
> "Mumps," said the doctor. "Mumps," said the nurse.
> "Mumps," said the lady with the alligator purse.
> Out went the doctor, out went the nurse,
> Out went the lady with the baby in her purse.

> Fudge, fudge, call the judge, Mama has a newborn baby,
> Wrap it up in tissue paper, throw it down the elevator.
> First floor, stop; second floor, miss;
> Third floor, turn around; fourth floor, touch the ground;
> Fifth floor, close your eyes and count to ten.
> If you miss, you take an end.

And there are descriptions of illnesses and accidents:

> Mama, Mama, I am sick,
> Call the doctor, quick, quick, quick.
> How many pills must I take?

> Doctor, Doctor, can you tell
> What will make poor *Patsy* well?

She is sick and about to die,
That will make poor *Jerry* cry.
When he comes all dressed in blue,
That's a sign he'll marry you.

The most famous accident in jump-rope lore takes place in that most perilous of all the rooms in the house, the bathroom:

Alice, where are you going?
"Upstairs to take a bath."
Alice with legs like toothpicks
And a neck like a giraffe.
Alice in the bathtub,
Alice pulled the plug;
Oh my goodness, oh my soul,
There goes Alice down the hole.

Alice has had a long run. In 1939, children in Indiana were chanting:

Alice tall and slender,
Just like a giraffe,
Went one day to take her bath;
Billy Sunday, save her soul,
'Cause Alice is slipping down the hole.

Other domestic rhymes refer to food, relatives, clothing, money, drink, disobedience, and lies.

Jump-rope rhymes make use of both exact observation ("Mix a pancake, stir a pancake, . . .") and theatrical exaggeration ("Mama has a newborn baby,/Wrap it up in tissue paper, throw it down the elevator. . . ."). The latter is a form of tall talk used here to legitimize by its unreal exaggeration the expression of socially forbidden feelings. However, the girl who recites this rhyme does not necessarily hate her baby brother. She may not even have a baby brother. Jump-rope rhymes should be understood mainly as recitations of traditional "texts"—not as self-revelations.

Rope jumpers are naturally curious about the name of an

admirer, and some rhymes help them discover who he is. The
jumper may chant:

Ice-cream soda, Delaware punch,
Tell me the name of my honey bunch.
A, B, C, D, . . .

The initial on which she misses is regarded as that of her boy
friend.

Other rhymes describe problems that women may face—
being tied to an undesirable mate, being rejected—and these
verses are in startling contrast to the lyrics of popular commercial songs. The unhappy or rejected girl in popular songs is
usually forlorn and passive. The girls in the jump-rope rhymes
are a pretty resilient lot.

My mother gave me a nickel,
My father gave me a dime,
My sister gave me a lover boy
That kissed me all the time.
My mother took my nickel,
My father took my dime,
My sister took my lover boy
And gave me Frankenstein.
He made me wash the dishes,
He made me scrub the floor,
But I didn't like that a single bit,
So I kicked him out the door.

And consider the tough little Dutch girl; she gives you the facts
unmixed with moral platitudes:

I'm a pretty little Dutch girl,
As pretty as can be,
And all the boys on the baseball team
Are crazy over me.
They gave me all their apples,
They gave me all their pears,
They gave me fifty cents
And kicked me down the stairs.

ONE POTATO, TWO POTATO...

Girls also use rhymes in this group to tease one another:

> Down in the valley where the green grass grows,
> There sat *Nancy* as sweet as a rose,
> She sang and she sang and she sang so sweet,
> Along came *Ricky* and kissed her on the cheek.
> How many kisses did she get?

or

> My boy [or "girl"] friend's name is *Randy* ["*Anne*"],
> He ["she"] is so silly-silly,
> He ["she"] has forty-nine toes
> And a big, red nose,
> And that's the way my story goes.

Perhaps the most popular rhyme in the group about boy friends is this simple brag:

> I love coffee, I love tea,
> I love the boys and the boys love me.

Rhymes describing the action of the game may direct the enders, the girls who turn the rope:

> Blue bells, cockle shells
> [They wave the rope, getting the rhythm],
> Eevy, ivey, over
> [On "over" they begin to turn and start another rhyme].

But the most interesting rhymes governing the activity are those which announce virtuoso jumping exhibitions. For beginners, there is

> Bubble gum, bubble gum, chew and blow
> [The jumper blows a bubble];
> Bubble gum, bubble gum, scrape your toe
> [She drags one toe];
> Bubble gum, bubble gum, tastes so sweet,
> Get that bubble gum off your feet
> [She slaps the bottoms of her shoes].

Jump-rope is one of the few sports where the athlete does her own play-by-play commentary. Real pros chant longer rhymes:

> Teddy bear, teddy bear, turn around.
> Teddy bear, teddy bear, touch the ground.
> Teddy bear, teddy bear, tie your shoes.
> Teddy bear, teddy bear, read the news.
> Teddy bear, teddy bear, go upstairs.
> Teddy bear, teddy bear, say your prayers.
> Teddy bear, teddy bear, turn out the lights.
> Teddy bear, teddy bear, say good night.
> G-o-o-d-n-i-g-h-t.

> Ladies and gentlemen, children too,
> This young lady's going to boogie for you.
> She's going to turn around,
> She's going to touch the ground,
> She's going to shimmy shimmy shimmy till her drawers
>   fall down.
> She never went to college,
> She never went to school,
> But when she came back, she was a nasty fool.

> Policeman, policeman, do your duty.
> Along comes *Kathy*, the American beauty;
> She can hobble, she can wobble,
> She can do the twist, but I'll bet she can't do this:
> Jump on one foot, one foot,
> Jump on two feet, two feet,
> Jump on three feet, three feet,
> Jump on four feet, four feet.

> Spanish dancer, do the splits.
> Spanish dancer, do a high kick.
> Spanish dancer, turn around.
> Spanish dancer, touch the ground.
> Spanish dancer, skit, skat, skidoo!

A short rhyme that calls for unusual contortions is:

M, i, crooked letter, crooked letter, i,
Crooked letter, crooked letter, i,
Humpback, humpback, i.

The jumper must approximate the shape of the letters with
her feet as she spells "Mississippi." She lands pigeon-toed to
form an *M*, dots the *i*'s with her toe, and raises a knee to form
a *p*. Since *p* is the "humpback" letter, she also hunches over.

Besides doing these individual stunts, girls can team up and
jump face to face while one of them turns. Or, while enders
turn the rope, one girl can jump a circle around another, who
is jumping in place. Sometimes, to make jumping more difficult, girls shut their eyes.

Blondie and Dagwood went to town.
Blondie bought an evening gown.
Dagwood bought a pair of shoes.
Cookie stayed home to watch the news,
And this is what it said:
"Close your eyes and count to ten;
If you miss, you take an end."

Champion jumpers also display their skill by jumping "double-
Dutch"—that is, inside an eggbeater made of two ropes being
turned in opposite directions at the same time. Some girls
scorn fancy footwork, choosing instead to show their consis-
tency and endurance by jumping over a hundred times without missing. Occasionally, endurance jumps are involuntary;
girls announce:

Don't leave the rope empty,
If you do you'll suffer plenty!

In this game, someone must always be jumping, and the others
may choose not to relieve a disliked girl.

One group of fanatical jumpers that we know even combined jump-rope and hopscotch, swinging the rope over the
hopscotch diagram.

For a change of pace, there is Chinese jump-rope—"Indian
jumping" in parts of Philadelphia. The rope isn't turned. In-

stead, girls tie it together in a loop and stretch it around the ankles of the enders, or around the legs of two convenient heavy chairs. Actually, elastic is preferred, but a rope will do.

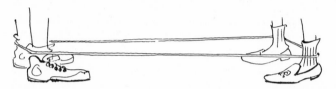

The jumper hops in and out on one foot several times. She hooks the near rope with the top of her foot, carries it across the other rope, and hops back.

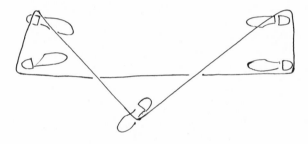

Next, the jumper hops inside the loop with both feet, hops out by straddling both sides, hops back in. This movement is repeated a number of times. Then the rope is raised to just below the enders' knees. All these jumps, except the one involving hooking the rope with one's foot, are repeated. The rope may also be arranged so that one side is higher than the other. The jumper jumps over the low side into the loop, then jumps out over the high side. Next she jumps backward over the high side back into the loop, then over the low side and out again.

Girls participate in rope jumping because it's fun, but the activity also has a variety of social functions. It's good exercise. It contributes to the girls' health. Perhaps more important, though, is the way it teaches them to combine competition and cooperation. It's sometimes said that jump-rope isn't competitive, but that isn't so. Everyone knows who the best jumpers are, and most girls would like to be counted among them. If jump-rope were purely competitive, however, jumpers could not also function as turners, for in that role they could easily make a rival miss; the turners would have to be impartial outsiders. But actually, one challenge in jump-rope is to achieve an ever tighter, ever giddier degree of cooperation, as in "red hots" (also known as "peppers" or "hot peppers"), in which the rope is turned faster and faster until the jumper misses. Her achievement is partly dependent upon her turners, who are at once partners and competitors. The game is no fun if the turners won't cooperate skillfully. On the other hand, it's perfectly all right for the turners as well as the other girls who are waiting to jump to shout:

> Miss, miss, little miss, miss;
> When she misses, she misses like this.

A jumper in Texas defiantly replies, "H-e-l-p!" She spells slowly because each letter means something: with *h*, she demands "high waters" or "hot peppers"; with *e*, she announces she'll jump with her eyes shut; *l* means she'll jump on one leg; and *p*, that she wants "peppers."

Jump-rope also gives each jumper a chance to play a socially powerful role. She can dispense a favor:

> Pom, pom, pompadour,
> [Or "Pop, pop, pop, gas-o-lin-a,"]
> *Sandy*'s calling *Sally* to the door,
> *Sally*'s the one who's going to have fun,
> So we don't need *Sandy* any more!

Or she can challenge a friend:

> Standing on the corner, chewing a piece of gum,
> Along came *Martha* and asked for some.

Martha, jumping in, says, "Give me some!" The jumper runs out, with Martha in hot pursuit. They run around one of the turners, through the rope, around the other turner, and back through the rope, forming a figure eight. If the jumper is finally tagged, or if she misses as she runs through the rope, she loses her place to Martha, who in turn offers the challenge to another girl.

Sometimes a spirit of camaraderie prevails and the object of the game is to see how many girls can jump together. The first jumper invites the second with:

> I love coffee, I love tea,
> I love *June* to jump in with me.

June jumps in and repeats the rhyme, picking another girl to join them, and so on.

Younger girls no doubt benefit from repeating rhymes that list the alphabet or the months:

> A, b, c, d, e, f, g,
> H, i, j, k, l, m, n, o, p,
> Q, r, s, t, u are out!

and

> I spy Peter
> Sitting on a heater;
> Ding dong! the fire bell!
> Up the ladder:
> January, February, March, . . .
> (Delaware, 1966)

The jumper names all the months of the year, then starts with "January" again and jumps out when she reaches the month she was born in.

And possibly some good nutritional information is dinned into the heads of the girls from Kansas and New York City who chant:

> Tomatoes, lettuce, carrots, peas,
> Mother said you got to eat a lot of these.

121

Jump-rope also provides a meeting ground where a new-comer can make friends. When many girls are waiting to jump, they say short phrases: "California oranges, tap me on the back!" or "Down by the river where the boats go—push!" On the word "back" or "push," a new jumper runs in and the old one runs out. No one jumps for long, but everyone gets a turn.

Some verses poke fun at propriety or authority. The performances of Sally Rand, the exotic dancer who was born in 1913, are still echoed on the playground:

> Sally Rand
> Lost her fan—
> Run, run, run,
> As fast as you can.

And the Jackson Five, on their trip to France, are dramatically impertinent:

> The Jackson Five went to France
> To teach the children how to dance,
> A heel and a toe and round you go,
> A heel and a toe and around I go,
> Salute to the Captain, bow to the King,
> Turn your back on the ugly old Queen.

In another rhyme, it is the king who is made fun of. The big daddy is reduced to an infant:

> King of France wet his pants
> Right in the middle of a wedding dance.
> How many puddles did he make?

Grade-school songbooks offer the children platitudes about abstract concepts like liberty and harmony. Jump-rope rhymes offer them the satisfactions of exactness and the joy of seeing domestic virtue triumph.

> Not last night but the night before,
> Twenty-four robbers came knocking at my door.

As I ran out, they ran in;
I hit them over the head with a rolling pin.

The violence here is as swift and matter-of-fact as it is in the
Border ballads of England and Scotland. The folk don't mess
around.

Jump-rope rhymes and folk ballads share another characteristic. They are composed partly of commonplaces—phrases that
are easily transferred from ballad to ballad or from one jump-
rope rhyme to another. Lines, even whole stanzas, are combined in new ways as the ballad singer puts on a performance.
The same thing happens when girls chant jump-rope rhymes.
We have already cited the story of the pretty little Dutch girl
who received apples, pears, and fifty-cent pieces. Here are
three other verses that use some of the same elements:

> My mother wanted peaches; my brother wanted pears;
> My father wanted fifty cents to fix the broken stairs.
> My boy friend gave me peaches; my boy friend gave me
>   pears;
> My boy friend gave me fifty cents to fix the broken stairs.
> My mother ate the peaches; my brother ate the pears;
> My father ate the fifty cents and fell right down the stairs.

> I am a little Dutch girl,
> As pretty as can be, be, be,
> And all the boys around my block
> Are crazy over me, me, me,
> My mother gave me peaches,
> My father gave me pears,
> My boy friend kissed me on the cheek,
> And fell right down the stairs.
> As I was walking down the street,
> I heard my boy friend say,
> To a little Dutch girl in strawberry curls:
> I l-o-v-e love you [or "h-a-t-e hate you"],
> I k-i-s-s kiss you ["s-l-a-p slap you," "k-i-c-k kick you"]
> On your c-h-e-e-k, cheek, cheek ["b-u-t-t butt, butt, butt"].

ONE POTATO, TWO POTATO...

Nine o'clock is striking; Mother, may I go out?
All the boys are waiting, for to take me out.
Some will give me apples, some will give me pears,
Some will give me fifty cents and kiss me on the stairs.
I don't want the apples, I don't want the pears,
I don't want the fifty cents to kiss me on the stairs.
I'd rather do the dishes, I'd rather scrub the floor,
I'd rather kiss the iceman behind the kitchen door.

(Missouri, 1943)

A verse that combines several different rhymes is used by children of West Indian descent living in the Canal Zone and Panama:

Blue bell, cracker shell,
Eeny, meeny, miney, moe,
Over!
Papa's in the garden digging potatoes;
Mama's in the kitchen baking cake.
Don't forget the vinegar, salt,
[Or "One, two, three, up the ladder,"]
And pepper, pepper, pepper!
["Children obey your parents, one-two-three."]

However, some jump-rope rhymes are more like contemporary literary poems than folk ballads. The logic of "Buster Brown," for instance, is surreal, proceeding on the basis of arbitrary rhymes instead of the logic of events:

Buster Brown went to town
With his pants on upside down.
He lost a nickel,
He bought a pickle.
The pickle was sour,
He bought some flour ["flower"?].
The flour was yellow,
He bought him a fellow.
The fellow was mean,
He bought a bean.

The bean was hard,
He bought a card.
And on the card
It said, *"Red hot pepper!"*

One of the popular "Cinderella" rhymes contains an apparently sophisticated instance of literary symbolism. Cinderella is one of the great characters of jump-rope literature, along with the ominous lady with the alligator purse, Tiny Tim, the Spanish dancer, and good old Johnny. Most of her adventures are described straightforwardly:

Cinderella, dressed in green,
Went upstairs to eat ice cream.
How many spoonfuls did she eat?
One, two, three, . . .

Cinderella, dressed in black,
Went upstairs and sat on a tack.
How many stitches did it take?
One, two, three, . . .

Cinderella, dressed in yellow,
Went downtown to buy some mustard.
On the way her girdle busted.
How many people were disgusted?
One, two, three, . . .

But consider one of her most popular adventures:

Cinderella, dressed in yellow,
Went upstairs to kiss her fellow,
Made a mistake and kissed a snake,
Came downstairs with a bellyache.
How many doctors did it take?
One, two, three, . . .

Freud has taught us to see sexual symbolism everywhere, especially in the speech of young children, who do not have the vocabulary or experience to express themselves directly.

Folklore, too, is regarded as a good place to find symbols, for isn't it the "unconscious" expression of the "folk"? Children's folklore, then, must be doubly blessed. And if the frog in the fairy tale who turns into a prince when he's taken to bed by the princess represents male genitals, certainly the meaning of Cinderella's snake is obvious—at least to literary-minded adults.

But the interpretation of a written text is one thing; that of a traditional performance, quite another. No jump-rope rhyme is meant to carry a burden of significance; its purpose is to help order a game. Also, the fact that "made a mistake" and "How many ——— did it take?" are commonplaces makes the linking of "mistake" and "take" to "snake" and "ache" look less significant and more accidental than it would be if the whole text were original. Furthermore, a bellyache seems reasonable to some little girls as the literal consequence of kissing a literal snake.

It is impossible, however, to dismiss the sexual implications of Cinderella's snake. Tradition limits a girl's choice of rhymes but does not dictate which of those available to her she actually selects. The subject matter of many of the rhymes obviously reflects the concerns of girls, one of which is sex. A version of the Cinderella rhyme that lacks the symbolic snake is fairly explicit:

> Cinderella dressed in yellow,
> Went upstairs to kiss her fellow,
> How many kisses did it take?
> One, two, three, . . .

But the fact that these are traditional verses used in traditional ways confuses any attempt to specify their meaning. A girl uses these verses as passwords to assert and maintain her membership in a group. To be sure, it must be assumed that to some degree she shares the interests of that group —interests which are expressed in the subject matter of the

group's verses. However, those verses also have a ritual significance that may override the meaning of the words they con-
tain; whatever is traditional has its own excuse for being.

Over six hundred jump-rope rhymes have been collected by
folklorists, but some are recited far more often than others.
Our nominations for the All-American Jump-rope Golds, the
Top Fifteen Hits on the Bricks, are: "Ice-cream Soda, Dela-
ware Punch"; "I Love Coffee, I Love Tea"; "Not Last Night
but the Night Before" (which is usually completed by some
version of "Teddy Bear" or "Spanish Dancer," both also top
hits in their own right); "I'm a Pretty Little Dutch Girl";
"Johnny Over the Ocean"; "Mable, Mable, Set the Table";
"Mama, Mama, I Am Sick"; "Fudge, Fudge, Call the Judge";
"I Had a Little Brother"; "Down by the River"; "Cinderella,
Dressed in Yellow"; "Grace, Grace, Dressed in Lace"; and "Blue
Bells, Cockle Shells."

Clapping Games

Nothing else two children do together is as intimate as a
clapping drill. While clapping, they are challenging each other
to ever swifter exhibitions of virtuosity, but they are also
helping each other. Their faces have a relaxed, yet blankly
rapt expression, broken now and again by brief grins as the
clap goes on without a miss. There can be few games that
offer the pleasures of pattern and closure more emphatically.

One function of the clapping session is to advertise a friendship. It's always a friendship between girls, though boys do
frequently take part in a game that might easily be mistaken for a clapping game—Categories. The players sit in a
circle; they clap their hands on their thighs, twice; clap their
hands together, twice; then snap their fingers, first those of
one hand, then those of the other. Between the first finger-
snap and the second, the person who begins names a cate-

gory—usually cars, trees, or animals. The next player says the name of a member of the category beginning with the letter *a*. The next names one beginning with *b*, and so on, always between finger-snaps. Boys who play Categories do clap, all right, but they don't touch other people. Also, in this game there is a competition between each player and everyone else. It is impersonal. Clapping is very personal.

Claps take place anywhere—even in class, if the teacher's not looking. There, the girls mouth the rhymes silently, and their hands don't quite touch. Usually only two girls do a clap, but sometimes eight or nine join in. They stand in a circle, and a girl either turns to face the girl beside her—first on one side, then on the other—or claps one hand with the girl on her right and one hand with the girl on her left. Girls have many ways of clapping: they clap hands high and low, or off to one side; they turn their palms in different directions, clap their own hands together, hit their own shoulders or thighs, cross their arms, snap fingers, bump hips, toss their arms in gestures like saluting or playing the violin, and suddenly freeze before beginning again.

In the clap "Head and Shoulders," each girl says "Head and shoulders" as she touches her head and then her shoulders; next, saying, "Baby one, baby two," which serves as a refrain, the two girls clap hands. This sequence is repeated. On the third repetition, the clappers say "Head and shoulders" twice, and after the refrain, go on to "Wrist and elbow," which is followed by:

> Davy Jones [they make singing motions],
> Jack Benny [they mime playing the violin],
> Ringo Starr [they mime playing the drums],
> Around the corner [they make a half a turn],
> Around the world [they turn around].

Then there is the family clap that begins:

> My mother works in a bakery,
>   Yum, yum [the clappers rub their stomachs].

My father works on a garbage truck,
  P.U.! Yum yum [they hold their noses and rub their
  stomachs].
My sister works for the phone company,
  Blah, blah, P.U.! Yum, yum [they hold "phones" to
  their ears, hold their noses, and rub their stomachs].

Many clapping rhymes also serve as jump-rope rhymes, but
some are used mainly for clapping. For instance:

Columbus went to sea, sea, sea,
To see what he could see, see, see,
But all that he could see, see, see,
Was the bottom of the deep blue sea, sea, sea.

Have you ever, ever, ever
In your long-legged life
Seen a long-legged sailor ["spider"] with a long-legged
  wife?
["Short-legged," "bow-legged," "pigeon-toed,"
  "bald-headed," or "pot-bellied" may be substituted
  throughout for "long-legged."]
No, I never, never, never
In my long-legged life,
Saw a long-legged sailor ["spider"] with a long-legged
  wife.

My boy friend's name is Fatty,
He comes from Cincinnati.
With a pickle for a nose,
And a great big mouth,
And that's the way my story goes.
[There are more stanzas to this verse.]

My mommy told me, if I was goody,
That she would buy me a rubber dolly.
But someone told her I kissed a soldier,
Now she won't buy me a rubber dolly.

When Pinocchio was one, he learned to suck his thumb,
Poor P-i-n-o-c-c-h-i-o, cross down.

When Pinocchio was two, he learned to tie his shoe,
Poor P-i-n-o-c-c-h-i-o, cross down.
When Pinocchio was three,
  he learned to climb a tree, . . .
When Pinocchio was four,
  he learned to shut the door, . . .
When Pinocchio was five,
  he learned to find a hive, . . .

This rhyme takes Pinocchio to age ten, rhyming "six" with "pick up sticks," "seven" with "go to heaven," "eight" with "roller skate," "nine" with "looked like Frankenstein," and "ten" with "pluck a hen." In some parts of the country, Pinocchio is replaced by Tiny Tim, and the refrain after the first line goes, "Thumbdiana, Thumbdiana, half past one": after the second line it becomes, ". . . half past two," and so on.

Zazo Witch was a wicked old witch.
Six lessons from Madam Old Zombie:
She taught me lesson one [*clap, clap*]
She taught me lesson two . . .
Six lessons from Madam Old Zombie.
(Massachusetts, 1968)

In the land of Oz ["Mars" in another dialect area],
Where the ladies smoke cigars,
Every puff they take
Is enough to kill a snake.
When the snake is dead,
They put roses in her head;
When the roses die,
They put diamonds in her eye;
When the diamonds break,
That's the end of sixty-eight.

We asked the girls who recited this rhyme about "sixty-eight." "That's just how it ends," they said.

Some clapping rhymes are taken from songs:

> Under the bamboo, under the tree,
> Big enough for you, my darling,
> Big enough for me.
> After we're married, happy we'll be,
> Under the bamboo, under the bamboo tree.
> If you'll be m-i-n-e, mine, I'll be t-h-i-n-e, thine,
> And I'll l-o-v-e, love you, all the t-i-m-e, time.
> You are the b-e-s-t, best, of all the r-e-s-t, rest,
> And I'll l-o-v-e, love you, all the t-i-m-e, time.
> Rock 'em up, sock 'em up, any old time,
> Match in the gas tank, boom-boom!

> Say, say, my playmate,
> Come on and play with me,
> And bring your dollies three,
> Climb up my apple tree.
> Slide down my rainbow,
> Go through my cellar door,
> And we'll be jolly friends
> Forevermore.
> So sorry, playmate,
> I cannot play with you.
> My dolly has the flu,
> Boo-hoo, boo-hoo, boo-hoo.
> Ain't got no rainbow,
> Ain't got no cellar door,
> But we'll be jolly friends
> Forevermore.

Parodies of "Playmate" are also popular:

Oh, little enemy,	Oh, little cockroach,
Come out and fight with me,	Come out and play with me,
....	I hate to step on you,
Climb up my poison tree.	Boo-hoo, boo-hoo, boo-hoo.
Slide down my rainbow,	Crawl down my rain barrel
Into my dungeon door,	And out my cellar door.
And we'll be jolly enemies	We won't ever be friends
Forevermore, one, two, three . . .	Forevermore.

ONE POTATO, TWO POTATO...

The following clapping rhyme takes the form of a dialogue with comment from a chorus:

ALL: Who stole the cookie from the cookie jar?
LEADER: *Nancy* stole the cookie from the cookie jar.
Nancy: Who, me?
ALL: Yes, you.
Nancy: Couldn't be!
ALL: Then who?
Nancy: *Elaine* stole the cookie from the cookie jar.
Elaine: Who, me?
ALL: Yes, you.
Elaine: Couldn't be! . . .

Some clapping rhymes are notable because they are funny:

My dog, Lima, loves to roam.
One day he came wandering home
Covered with burrs and quite unclean,
Where in the hell has lima been?

Others are thought to be a little improper:

The cutest boy I ever saw
Was sipping cider through a straw.
I asked him if he'd teach me how
To sip some cider through a straw.
He said of course he'd teach me how
To sip some cider through a straw.
So cheek to cheek and jaw to jaw,
We sipped some cider through a straw.
That's how I got my mother-in-law
And forty-nine kids that call me Ma.

Forty-nine kids! The girls called that "grossed out!"
Other claps include marvelous magic words:

Eeny, meeny, pasadini,
Alla, balla, boomerini,
Archie, parchie, liverarchie,
And your brother George.

Peach, plum, have a stick
Of chewing gum,
If you want the other half,
This is what you say:
Aman, aman, amandiego,
Sandiego, hocus pocus dominocus,
Sis, sis, siscumbah,
Rah, rah, rah.
(Virginia, 1966)

Kathaleena, macaleena,
Uppa sala wala vala
Oca poca noca was her name.
She had two teeth in the front of her mouth,
One pointed east, the other pointed south.
Kathaleena, macaleena, . . .
She had a neck like a ten-foot pole;
Right in the middle was a big fat mole.
Kathaleena, macaleena, . . .
She had two eyes in the front of her head;
One was green and the other was dead.
Kathaleena, macaleena, . . .
(Minnesota, 1968)

Children may clap on either the downbeat or the off beat.
Some clapping rhymes, like "Under the Bamboo Tree," seem
to lend themselves to off-beat clapping.

"Pat-a-Cake" has been drafted from the nursery for use as a
clapping rhyme; and Mr. Knick Knack (or Knickaback, or
Knickerbocker) has been created by children who have freely
associated elements from the first line of "This Old Man,"
a song commonly taught in school. ("This old man, he played
one, / He played knick knack on my thumb.")

Mr. Knick Knack, Knick Knack, number one,
He sure got drunk on a bottle of rum,
Now let's get the rhythm of the hands, clap, clap.
Now you've got the rhythm of the hands,
Now let's get the rhythm of the feet, stomp, stomp.

133

ONE POTATO, TWO POTATO...

Now you've got the rhythm of the feet,
Now let's get the rhythm of the eyes.
Now you've got the rhythm of the eyes,
Now let's get the rhythm of the hips, woo, woo.
Now you've got the rhythm of the hips, woo, woo,
Now let's get the rhythm of the number *five!*

Like all rhymes in oral tradition, clapping rhymes go through many transformations.

The space is true love forever,
Twilight lights in heaven,
Singing my song to you.
What is the me-ea-eaning
About the flow-ow-ower?
This is my sto-o-ory,
My story of love
From me to you.
My heart goes bum-pe-ty bump
bump,
Bum-pe-ty bump bump,
Bum-pe-ty bump bump bump.
[Repeat lines 3 through 8.]
My eyes go twink-ke-ty twink
twink,
Twink-ke-ty twink twink,
Twink-ke-ty twink twink twink.
[Repeat lines 3 through 8.]
My heart goes cha-cha-cha cha
cha,
Cha-cha-cha cha cha,
Cha-cha-cha cha cha cha.
(Canal Zone, 1974)

The spades are true love
together,
Twilight's in heaven,
Bring back my love to me.
The flowers purple and
green,
They're made of sausage and
cream.
Somewhere there's
Cha-cha-cha boom-e-ay,
Cha-cha-cha boom-e-ay,
Cha-cha-cha boom-e-ay,
One, two, three,
One, two, three,
One, two, three,
And a boom, boom, boom.
(Indiana, 1972)

The spades go tulip together,
Twilight together,
Bring back my love to me.
What am I thinking of?
I do not know,

The spades go tulips
together,
Tie them together,
Bring back my love to me.
What is the meaning

134

For love is the story,
The story of
Eeny, beeny,
Cha-cha cheenie,
Ooh, ah, bubbleeney,
Cha-cha-cha.
There goes Liberace.
(Canal Zone, 1974)

Of all these flowers?
This is my story,
My story of-a love-a to-a
   you-a
Cha-cha-cha.
My heart goes pump
   pa-ri-ump pump
Pump pa-ri-ump over the
   sight of you.
[Repeat from line 3.]
Cha-cha-cha!
(Massachusetts, 1968)

The Spanish two hearts in heaven,
Working together,
Bring back my love to me.
What is the meaning
Of all the flowers?
These flowers that tell the
Story of l-o-v-e
Love! Love! Love!
(Wisconsin, 1975)

The space goes two lips together,
Twilight's forever,
Bring back my love to me.
I saw a ship sail away,
It sailed a year and a day, a day.
It took my true love away, true love away,
To the city of Love,
From me to you.
What is the meaning, meaning,
Of all these flowers, flowers,
They tell the story, story,
The story of death from me to you.
(St. Thomas, Virgin Islands, 1972)

In Spain there're two lips together,
Twilight forever,

135

ONE POTATO, TWO POTATO...

Bring back my love to me.
What is the meaning of this,
Of all these flowers,
They tell my story,
My story of love to you.
We will get married,
Where shall we live,
In Sunny Spain or Gay Paree?
We will have children of course,
And then we'll get a divorce,
And then we'll marry again.
This is the end.
(Canal Zone, 1970)

There are many more clapping rhymes. We can't cite them all, but we don't want to leave out Old Miss Mary Mack. She's been around for so long—the *grande dame* of the claps.

Miss Mary Mack, Mack, Mack,
All dressed in black, black, black,
With silver buttons, buttons, buttons,
All down her back, back, back.

Children add different endings to this verse. In New York City, Miss Mack becomes a comic character in a silent film:

She went upstairs to make her bed,
She made a mistake and bumped her head;
She went downstairs to wash the dishes,
She made a mistake and washed her wishes;
She went outside to hang her clothes,
She made a mistake and hung her nose.

Her behavior is sometimes exceedingly improper:

She could not read, read, read,
She could not write, write, write,
But she could smoke, smoke, smoke,
Her father's pipe, pipe, pipe.
She asked her mommy, mommy, mommy,
For fifteen cents, cents, cents,

136

To see the boys, boys, boys,
Pull down their pants, pants, pants.

In the following version, her accident-prone nature proves to be her undoing:
She went upstairs to make her bed,
She hit her head and now she's dead.

The most common ending may be:

She asked her mother for fifty cents, cents, cents,
To see the elephant, elephant, elephant,
Jump over the fence, fence, fence.
They jumped so high, high, high,
They reached the sky, sky, sky,
And never came back, back, back,
Till the Fourth of July, ly, ly.

Miss Mary Mack wasn't always a clapping rhyme. She seems to have started out as a riddle. The answer was "coffin."

Sex Roles in Performance Games

Games that encourage outstanding performances by individuals, rather than by teams or partners, easily become pastimes. When there is no one around to play with, a child can spend an afternoon sharpening his or her skills all alone, starring in front of an imaginary crowd. The nature of the skills that are sharpened, however, depends on whether the child is a girl or a boy.

What are conventionally thought of as girls' games require a player to master a set of patterned motions, as in clapping, for instance, and in jump-rope. The game of jacks, too, calls for a set of patterned responses, though they vary slightly according to the position of the jacks. A jacks player has to sweep the jacks into a cave made by an arched hand resting on the floor ("pigs in a pen"), put each jack into her cupped palm ("picking cherries"), circle the ball with her hand before catching it ("around the world"), or make a series of gestures in the process of retrieving the jack ("sweep the floor, move the chair, pick it up, and put it there").

A girl playing hopscotch does her ancient dance back and forth over one of a variety of patterns, pausing only to retrieve her marker.

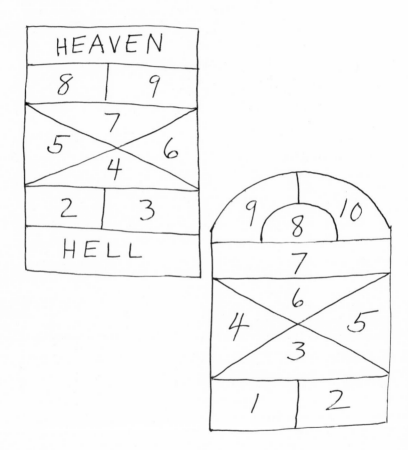

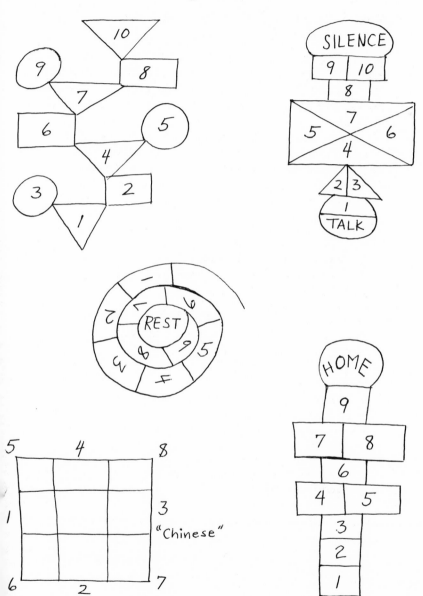

"Chinese"

ONE POTATO, TWO POTATO...

Normally hopscotch is a game of skill, not strategy, but some girls let a player call for an advantage. A call of "Alligators!" "Octopus!" or "Pippi Longstockings!" entitles a player to lie full length upon the diagram before throwing her marker, and a call of "Red, white, and blue!" entitles her to tiptoe along the outside line in order to reach a good position.

Virtuoso ball-bouncing, like clapping and jump-rope, enhances a girl's rhythmic sense, a matter of some consequence, since rhythms play an important though still mysterious part in language facility and in our general well-being. A few ball-bounce rhymes challenge a girl to co-ordinate unchanging patterns of ball-bouncing, recitation, and mime.

> Mickey Mouse he had a house
> [The player bounces the ball against a wall],
> Clapped his hands,
> Stamped his foot,
> Wiggled his tail,
> Sat in a pail
> [The player imitates sitting],
> Jumped out of the house
> [She jumps over the ball].

A more popular rhyme challenges a girl to think ahead to the next stanza while she is reciting and bouncing her ball. In the first stanza all the names must start with *A:*

> My name is *Alice*; my husband's name is *Al*;
> We live in *Alabama*; and we sell *apples.*

In the next stanza all the names must begin with *B*; in the third, with *C*, and so on. Girls soon memorize sets of names for each letter, but a lapse of memory or an unwise attempt at originality may cause a ball-bouncer to experience that giddy and pleasurable (when it occurs in the context of a game) panic that ensues when time is running out and one can't think of what to say.

Often girls use a simpler rhyme like:

> One, two, three, a nation,
> I received my confirmation
> On this day of declaration,
> One, two, three, a nation.

We can talk more confidently about girls' games than about boys' games. Girls' games are likely to be played by girls only. Boys show little interest in them. Girls, on the other hand, will join whatever game the boys are playing these days. Nevertheless, we think of baseball, stoopball, Johnny on a Pony, tops, marbles, Skelly, and the like as boys' games. Certainly they are different from those games traditionally associated with girls.

They don't, for example, require that a boy master extended, repetitious patterns. Instead, the players of these games must learn to calculate and to respond to a developing situation. Take stoopball, or curb-ball. The "hitter," who may be a member of a team or may be "standing" all the rest of the players, throws a ball at a curb or step, or at the place where a wall and sidewalk meet. If an opposing player catches the rebounding ball before it hits the ground, that's an out. Sometimes a hitter actually runs to bases; sometimes each bounce counts as a base. The definition of a homer and a foul varies according to the architecture of the neighborhood. While the hitter winds up, the other players wait, alert but relaxed; they will respond when—literally—they see which way the ball bounces.

Skelly, or Skillzies, is a popular game in New York City. With a flick of his fingers a player skids a bottle cap or poker chip from number to number on a square "board" that is chalked on the sidewalk or street. One version is played on a "board" that looks like this:

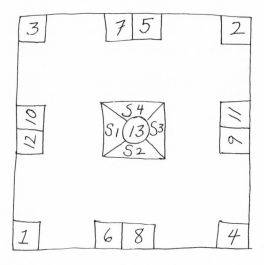

A player tries to move his bottle cap from 1 to 13 and back to 1. If his cap lands on the number he was aiming for, he gets another turn. The player whose cap hits an opponent's cap has the right to flick that cap as far away as he can. If a player's cap lands on one of the "skells," or "skellies," that surround the number 13, that player loses his turn until one of his friends hits his cap out of the "skell." The other players are willing to help out someone who is stuck in a "skell" because whoever hits out the cap is entitled to advance his own cap one, two, three, or four squares, depending on which "skell" is involved. After coming back from 13 to 1, a player "goes to skelly"—moves his cap through the four "skells." Then he shoots it back to 1, and at that point, his cap becomes a "killer." A player with a "killer" aims not at the squares but at the other players' caps. A cap that has been hit five times by a "killer" is removed from the game.

What this game teaches its players is judgment. Each boy must calculate his shots in relation to the other players' caps and foresee the relationship of his cap to theirs if he misses.

There is no rhythm, no pattern; a player surveys the board, takes his shot, and evaluates the consequences.

Tops, too, is a boys' game in which the responses require judgment rather than repetition of a pattern. Once, boys everywhere in the United States played tops, but the game's popularity has steadily declined since its heyday in the 1890's. However, it's still widely enjoyed in Latin America, and the influence of Latin immigrants is one of the things that keeps tops spinning in the United States.

Tops is often a scapegoat game. The least popular boy has to spin down his top first, as a target. The other boys stand almost placidly, winding their tops and eying the terrain. Then, calculating distance, speed, direction, and the exact moment, they take their steps and whip loose their tops. Each hopes his top will collide with the target top and crack it or at least pop off a piece of it.

Folk games have long reflected the sex roles approved of by society. And in the past, boys' games, besides being less patterned and requiring more calculation than girl's games, were also often rougher. Girls were discouraged from playing Johnny on a Pony because it was considered indecorous for a girl to spread her legs in public; they were also discouraged from wrestling with boys in Ring-a-levio and from squatting behind the plate or sliding home in baseball.

But for some time now, society has been growing increasingly tolerant of rough play by girls. The recent court cases involving the girls' right to participate in Little League baseball don't indicate a new militancy among grade-school girls. They were playing Johnny on a Pony and Ring-a-levio long before they demanded a Little League uniform. But while girls have taken to playing boys' games, they have not given up playing their traditional girls' games. Boys, on the other hand, have shown less interest in expanding their repertoire. In fact, for at least fifteen years after World War II, the number of games they enjoyed seemed to be growing smaller and smaller. In 1961, the psychologists B. G. Rosenberg and Brian Sutton-Smith found implications that it was "much more deviant behavior for a modern boy to play at, say Dolls, Hopscotch, Jacks, Houses, Schools, Cooking, Jump rope, Musical chairs, Simon says, and Singing games than it was for a boy to play at these things in earlier historical periods. . . ."

Possibly a generation of boys brought up by feminists, opposed to sexual stereotyping, will reverse this trend. At present, it's too early to tell. We know some boys who have shown interest in girls' games, to the chagrin of their fathers, and we have watched grade-school boys take part in hopscotch, jacks, and jump-rope. But clapping is still emphatically a girls' game. Grade-school boys seem to define their role more by what they won't do than by what they do.

Singing Games

For a long time, singing games provided young adults with an acceptable excuse for flirting, dancing, and kissing. About 1800, even New England Puritans approved of a game called Marriage. A couple took the floor, and the girl sang:

> Come, my dearest partner, and join both heart and hand;
> You want you a wife, and I want me a man.
> So married we will be, if we can agree,
> We'll march down together, so happy are we.

Her partner replied, fitting his actions to his words:

> Now I must part, and leave you alone,
> So fare you well, my true love, till I return.

The girl circled the room, singing:

> I mourn, I mourn, for that is the cry,
> I'm left all alone, and I'm sure I shall die.

Coming together again, they addressed first each other and then their friends, who were lined up two by two:

Oh, here comes my love, and how do you do?
And how have you been since I parted with you?
There is a scene secure from all harm,
Please give us joy by the raising of the arm.

Their friends made an arch with their arms. The first couple paraded under the arch, then paused:

Now we are married, and never more to part,
Please to give a kiss from the bottom of the heart.

The next couple then took a turn.

The popularity of games like this among young adults was long reflected on the playground, where younger children played Knights of Spain, once said to be "a universal favorite." In this game, three boys advanced toward three seated girls, one of whom was the "mother." The boys sang first; the mother replied.

"Here come three lords out of Spain,
A-courting of your daughter Jane."

"My daughter Jane is yet too young,
To be ruled by your flattering tongue."

"Be she young, or be she old,
'Tis for the price she may be sold.

So fare you well, my lady gay,
We must turn another way."

"Turn back, turn back, you Spanish knight,
And scour your boots and spurs so bright."

"My boots and spurs they cost you nought,
For in this land they were not bought.

Nor in this land will they be sold,
Either for silver or gold.

So fare you well, my lady gay,
We must turn another way."

> "Turn back, turn back, you Spanish knight,
> And choose the fairest in your sight."

> "I'll not take one nor two nor three,
> But pray, Miss *Lucy,* walk with me."

A knight promenaded with the girl he had chosen. Returning to the mother, he said:

> "Here comes your daughter safe and sound,
> In her pocket a thousand pound,

> On her finger a gay gold ring,
> I bring your daughter home again."

Versions of this and similar songs continued to be sung in the United States as part of a marriage game during the first half of the twentieth century, but they are not widely known today.

One can still see courtly singing games played, however, in societies that have not yet grown self-consciously "natural." In the interior of Panama, we observed a large group of children spontaneously play singing games during recess. In one game requiring partners, a twelve-year-old boy bowed to a tiny six-year-old girl, indicating that he had picked her. The children giggled and she blushed, but she conquered her shyness, raised her chin, and enacted her role as *La Señorita* with grave aplomb. She knew how a lady traditionally should behave. In the United States, adult models are much less well defined.

The singing games our children like best are those which permit a certain amount of individual assertiveness or physical release. These elements may always have had more appeal to children than the more formal aspects of singing games. Father Damian Webb, a British folklorist, has remarked that in the only spontaneous game of Oranges and Lemons he ever saw, most of the song's verses had been cut out so the children could get down to the serious business, which went more or less like this: "Here comes a chopper to cut off your great fat bleeding block of a head." The most popular ring game in our collection is a version of Drop the Handkerchief that has dispensed with singing altogether in order to focus on the action of the chase. In Duck, Duck, Goose, the children sit cross-legged while one player walks behind them, saying "Duck" each time he taps a child on the head. When he says "Goose," the one he taps must jump up and try to catch him before he can race around the circle and take the "goose's" place.

The following game gives children a chance for complete physical abandonment. The children move in a ring, suiting their pace to the words, as they sing:

> Motorboat, motorboat, go so slow,
> Motorboat, motorboat, get up and go,
> Motorboat, motorboat, go so fast,
> Motorboat, motorboat, step on the gas!

Usually the circle ends in a heap.

Self-assertion and self-expression also seem to be the main goals of those who play Mary Died, I Went to Old Kentucky, and Billy, Billy. Once, these games may have been played only by blacks. We first saw Mary Died played by an integrated group after a Girl Scout meeting in 1970, but the black girls took the leading roles in that game, and had taught the others. Since then, we have seen it played by all-white groups.

In Mary Died, the children form a circle around a leader, who begins:

> "Mary died."
> "How'd she die?"
> "She died like this."

The leader makes a face and takes a comic position.

> "She died like this."

Everyone imitates the leader, who then continues:

> "Mary died."
> "Where'd she die?"

"We-ell, she lived in a place called Tennessee
Wore a short skirt above her knee,
Gonna shake that finger,
Hands up! Tootsy, tootsy, tootsy toes,
    Wherever she goes."

With "Hands up," everyone joins in and imitates the leader's actions.

"Hands down! Tootsy, . . ."
"Touch the ground, . . ."
"Do the twist, . . ."
"Like this, . . ."

Finally, the leader spins around with her eyes shut, singing:

"Mary never went to college,
Mary never went to school,
I just found out she's an educated fool!"

and points to a new leader.

It's interesting to compare Mary Died with popular nine-teenth-century singing games that refer to death. The game Jenny Jones was perfectly serious throughout:

"We've come to see Miss Jenny Jones, Miss Jenny Jones,
    Miss Jenny Jones,
We've come to see Miss Jenny Jones,
And how is she today?"
"She's upstairs washing, washing, washing, . . .
You cannot see her today."
"We've come to see Miss Jenny Jones, . . ."
"She's upstairs ironing, . . ."

This went on until the answer was, "She's dead." Then the question was, "What shall we dress her in?" Various colors were suggested, but the final decision was usually white, which turned Jenny into a ghost who chased the other players. Southern children's reason for rejecting the color blue was, "Blue is for Yankees and that won't do."

Another nineteenth-century favorite portrayed a mixture of sentimentality and callousness about death:

> Water, water, wine flowers, growing up so high;
> We are all young ladies, and we are sure to die,
> Except Mistress *Alice*, she's the finest one.

The verse goes on to tell about the young lady's beau, and ends with her about to marry; however,

> *Alice* is sick and ready to die,
> That will make poor *Joseph* cry,
> *Joseph, Joseph,* don't you cry,
> You'll get married by and by.

In neither of these songs is there anything as macabre as "She died like this," followed by a comic pose.

Many contemporary songs, however, are accompanied by an exhibitionistic comic dance, for example:

> I went to old Kentucky, the old Kentucky fair;
> I met a senorita with buckles in her hair;
> Oh shake 'em, shake 'em, shake 'em if you can.
> If you don't know how, do the best you can.
> Round and round and round she goes,
> Where she stops, nobody knows.
> Point to the east, point to the west,
> Point to the one you love the best.

After the last line, the circle breaks up as everyone does her own thing, imitating clowns, dancers, singers, or parents.

Sometimes (as in Chicago, 1963) girls choose partners and line up in two lines. They sing:

> This is the way you Billy, Billy, Billy,
> This is the way you Billy, Billy.

Then one of the girls steps out and dances down between the lines as everyone sings:

All night long,
Oh, shake 'em, Miss Sally, Sally, Sally,
Oh, shake 'em, Miss Sally,
All night long.

The dancer takes her place at the other end of the line, and the figure is repeated until everyone has had a turn.

When they play Teensy, Teensy, Tiny O, girls form a circle around a leader, who teases one of the players by singing:

"*Ellen* has a boy friend."

The others respond:

"Teensy, Teensy, Tiny O. [All do a dance step,
   crossing their legs back and forth.]
How do you know so?
Teensy, Teensy, Tiny O." [All do the dance step.]

The dialogue continues, as the leader replies:

" 'Cause you told me so."
"Teensy, Teensy, Tiny O. [All do a dance step,
"Can you monkey it?"
"Teensy, Teensy, Tiny O." [All stoop like a monkey.]
"Can you twirl it?"
"Teensy, Teensy, Tiny O." [All twirl one finger.]
"Can you twist it?"
"Teensy, Teensy, Tiny O." [All wiggle their hips.]
"S-t-o-p—stop!" [With eyes closed, the leader turns
   around, one arm extended, and picks a new leader.]

Contemporary children play both traditional and modern versions of Rise, Sally, Rise. The traditional version is a quiet game. One girl kneels and hides her eyes. The others move around her in a circle as they chant:

Little Sally Waters, sittin' in a saucer,
Crying her eyes out for someone to come,
Rise, Sally, rise, and dry out your eyes,
Point to the east, point to the west,
Point to the one you like the best.

150

One modern version of Sally Waters goes:

> Little Sally Walker, sittin' in her saucer,
> Rise, Sally, rise, go wipe your weepin' eyes,
> Go fly to the east, go fly to the west,
> Go fly to the one you love the best.
> Put your hands on your hips and let your backbone slip.
> Ah, shake it to the east, ah, shake it to the west,
> Ah, shake it to the one you love the best.

Although many of the older games are still collected—A Tisket, a Tasket, A Paper of Pins, Nuts in May, Did You Ever See a Lassie?, Cat and Mouse, Rig-a-Jig-Jig, The Needle's Eye, Looby Loo, In and Out the Window, and Skip to My Lou—we suspect that they are kept alive largely by teachers who find them in school songbooks. However, two of the most ancient singing games are still going strong on their own: London Bridge and Ring Around the Rosie. Some children particularly like to play them in swimming pools, where a tug of war or "All fall down" is a special delight.

Autographs

Autograph books are as popular as they ever were, though fashions in autographs have changed since the 1880's. Children then had at their command more sober sentiments than children do today. Consider these two from Laura Ingalls Wilder's *Little Town on the Prairie*:

> The rose of the valley may wither,
> The pleasures of youth pass away,
> But friendship will blossom forever
> While all other flowers decay.

> In memory's golden casket,
> Drop one pearl for me.
>   Your loving friend, . . .

Or this, from a late-nineteenth-century textbook from Pennsylvania:

ONE POTATO, TWO POTATO...

Now the time has come to part.
Sad the Echo to my heart.
But let these after lives be chaste and pure,
that we may meet again to part nomore [sic].

But not all nineteenth-century verse was so sober:

May you sail down
the river of time like
a bob tailed chicken
on a sweet potato vine.

Though most contemporary verses have a comic twist, a few are almost as serious as anything in great grandmother's autograph book.

Roses are red,
Violets are blue,
I was so glad
To have a friend like you.

Red as roses,
White as snow,
I am your friend
From head to toe.

I met you as a stranger,
I took you as a friend,
I hope we meet in heaven
Where friendship never ends.

Moralistic rhymes urging one ever upward are fairly common:

Study hard,
Don't be a flop,
Sooner or later,
You'll reach the top.

Don't worry if your jobs are small
And your rewards are few.
Remember that the mighty oak
Was once a nut like you.

One ironic rhyme suggests that success has a price:

As you slide down the banister of life,
May the splinter of success stick in your butt.

Words of caution are not unknown:

When you're a teen-ager
And think you're sweet,
Take off your shoes
And smell your feet.

When you fall in the river
There is a boat,
When you fall in the well
There is a rope,
When you fall in love
There is no hope.

Love many, trust few,
Always paddle your own canoe.

Not all advice is in rhyme. An Indiana girl urged a friend, "Carry a big stick and drink plenty of water." Later we heard an adult use the same line; he assured us that he was quoting Theodore Roosevelt!

Often traditional rhymes simply plead:

Remember *m*; remember *e*;
Put them together—remember me.

Remember Grant,
Remember Lee,
To hell with them,
Remember me.

Curiously, just as one of the major themes of modern poetry is the process of writing a poem, so an important theme of modern autograph verse is the autograph itself.

It makes me giggle,
It makes me laugh,
To see me writing
My own autograph.

ONE POTATO, TWO POTATO...

Whenever you look through this book,
Upon this page you'll frown
And curse the one who spoilt this book
By writing upside down.

Well you asked me to scribble,
And scribble I will,
Just remember your friend
That writes downhill.

I auto cry,
I auto laugh,
I auto sign
My autograph.

I'm a pilot without a plane
Who just dropped down to sign my name.

Other verses express sentiments that are insulting, in a friendly way, or irrelevant:

Roses are red,
Flowers are blue,
Your mother is pretty,
What happened to you?
[Or "What you need
Is a good shampoo."]

I saw you in the ocean,
I saw you in the sea,
I saw you in the bathtub—
Oops, pardon me.

I'd cross the hottest desert,
I'd swim the deepest sea,
I'd cross the highest mountain,
But I can't come over tonight because it's raining.

By the sewer I lived,
By the sewer I died,
They called it a murder,
But it was sewer-cide.

Girls like to comment on sex:

> If all the boys
> Lived over the sea,
> What a wonderful swimmer
> *Janet* would be.

> Some kiss under a lily,
> Some kiss under a rose,
> But the best place to kiss a boy
> Is right under his nose.

Everyone likes puzzle messages:

> UR 2 sweet 2 B 4 gotten.

> URAQT and INVU.

> 2 y's u r,
> 2 y's u b
> I c u r
> 2 y's 4 me.

> 2 young
> 2 go
> 4 boys
> 4 ever
> ──────
> 8 I nice

> Don't B 2 ♯
> Don't B 2 ♭
> Just B ♮

Children understand the impersonal nature of these traditional rhymes and so may shift to prose to convey genuine feelings. The trouble is, most of them aren't very adept at original, sincere expression:

> To a nice friend, good luck.

> It's been lots of fun sitting behind you this year.

> You're one of Sandy's nicest friends. Stay that way.

155

A rare child will try his hand at original verse. To a girl who was leaving the country, a budding poet wrote:

> It's hot in Panama,
> I hope you know,
> But I'm sorry to say
> Up here there's snow.

Another partly original rhyme is this bit of blarney from a young miss in Tennessee:

> Hooby dooby dee,
> You are one I might never see.
> As the Irish might say,
> May the sunshine brighten your spirits,
> And the light winds soften your heart.

But when children grow tired of trying to be original—and they have a good many autograph books to sign—or if they are dissatisfied with the quality of their attempts at sincere expression, they can always fall back on tradition. A few of the old standbys are in prose: "I hope our friendship lasts until Ivory soap sinks," or "Yours till America drinks Canada Dry," but most are in rhyme. And some of these have been in use since before the Flood. For instance:

> When you are old
> And out of shape,
> Remember girdles
> Are 2.98.

A more recent version:

> When you get old
> And out of date,
> Remember face transplants
> Are only 100,000.98.

Saying good-by isn't easy; it's especially difficult for children leaving the sixth grade. They are leaving a certain phase of their lives, and they all know that even if they attend the same junior high (which they may not) all their relationships in that much larger school are going to be different. Autograph rhymes provide them with an appropriate rhetoric of good-by.

NOTES

JEERS

Common Insults and Comebacks

Jeering among the Tonga of Zambia and American Indian tribes is described by Max Gluckman in *Politics, Law and Ritual in Tribal Society* (Chicago: Aldine, 1965), pp. 97–104, 194–95, 304–12. In *Law and Warfare,* edited by Paul Bohannan (Garden City, N.Y.: Natural History Press, 1967), K. O. L. Burridge describes "Disputing in Tangu," pp. 205–32, and E. Adamson Hoebel discusses "Song Duels Among the Eskimo," pp. 255–62. Johan Huizinga relates play to law in *Homo Ludens* (Boston: Beacon Press, 1955), Ch. IV, with particular reference to Greek and Roman legal orations, p. 87. David J. Winslow discusses "Children's Derogatory Epithets" in *Journal of American Folklore,* 82 (1969), 255–63. "Don't say it,/Your mother'll faint . . ." is from David J. Winslow, "An Annotated Collection of Children's Lore . . . ," *Keystone Folklore Quarterly,* 11 (1966), 164. The background of "Puddentaine" is related in Iona and Peter Opie, *The Lore and Language of Schoolchildren* (Oxford: Clarendon Press, 1959), p. 157. The quotation from Bruno Bettelheim is in "The New Illiteracy," *Encounter,* 43 (Nov. 1974), 15. Janet and Mark appear in *The First Preprimer* of the Harper & Row Basic Reading Program (New York, 1966). "Hot squat" is recorded in Anna K. Stimson, "Cries of Defiance and Derision, and Rhythmic Chants of West Side New York City, 1893–1903," *Journal of American Folklore,* 58 (1945), 125. Stephen Spender's comment is in "Meditations on America," *Columbia Forum,* 3 (Spring 1974), 4. We have not included anything about Playing the Dozens, a kind of verbal dueling popular among some urban blacks (and now taken up by some whites), because it seems to us more characteristic of junior-high and high-school students than of grade-school children.

ONE POTATO, TWO POTATO...

Ambushes, Scapegoats, and Punishments

Jinks and Cooties are discussed in Mary and Herbert Knapp, "Tradition and Change in American Playground Language," *Journal of American Folklore*, 86 (1973), 135–41. Club Fist is described in *The Boone County Headlight* (Harrison, Arkansas), Oct. 30, 1975, p. 2; and in Peggy Bradley Boaz, "Take It Off; Knock It Off; Or Let the Crows Pick It Off," *Tennessee Folklore Society Bulletin*, 29 (1973), 77–78. Swatter Go Find is recommended by Margaret E. Mulac, *Games and Stunts for Schools, Camps, and Playgrounds* (New York: Harper & Row, 1964), p. 115.

The Battle of the Sexes

Laura Ingalls Wilder's anecdote about a "greeny" is from *Little Town on the Prairie* (New York: Harper & Row, 1953), p. 192. The Yiddish saying is from Lillian Mermim Feinsilver, *The Taste of Yiddish* (New York: Yoseloff, 1970).

JOKES

Tricks and Wit

Edshu's remark is from Leo Frobenius, *Und Afrika sprach . . .* (Berlin: Vita, Deutsches Verlagshaus, 1912), pp. 243–45, as quoted in Joseph Campbell, *The Hero With A Thousand Faces* (New York: Pantheon, 1949), p. 45. The translations of the names Odysseus and Antikleia are by G. E. Dimock, Jr., "The Name of Odysseus," *Hudson Review*, 9 (1956), 52–70. We are also indebted to Roger D. Abrahams, "Trickster, the Outrageous Hero," in *Our Living Traditions*, edited by Tristram P. Coffin (New York: Basic Books, 1968), pp. 170–79.

Telephone Jokes

The best article on telephone jokes is Norine Dresser, "Telephone Pranks," *New York Folklore Quarterly*, 29 (1973), 121–30.

Riddles

William Hugh Jansen discusses the functions of riddling in America in "Riddles: Do-It-Yourself Oracles," in *Our Living Traditions*, pp. 204–14. Mac E. Barrick discusses multiple-answer riddles in "The Newspaper Riddle Joke," *Journal of American Folklore*, 87 (1974), 253–57. Alta Jablow and Carl Withers discuss their studies of children's jokes and riddles, first in the forties and then in the sixties, in "Social Sense and Verbal Nonsense in Urban

Children's Folklore," *New York Folklore Quarterly*, 21 (1965), 243–57.

Jump-rope

Roger D. Abrahams lists most of the rhymes and the important articles on jump-rope published before 1969 in his *Jump-Rope Rhymes: A Dictionary* (Austin: University of Texas Press, 1969). The warning to girls to jump in moderation is quoted in Peter L. Skolnik, *Jump Rope!* (New York: Workman, 1974), p. 23. The 1939 rhyme about Alice is from the archives of the Folklore Institute of Indiana University. Indian jumping is mentioned by Skolnik in *Jump Rope!*, p. 67. "I Spy Peter" was collected by Ruth Hawthorne, "Classifying Jump-Rope Games," *Keystone Folklore Quarterly*, 11 (1966), 117.

Clapping Games

For a discussion of clapping games and examples of rhymes from several states, see Maureen Kenney, *Circle Round the Zero* (St. Louis, Mo.: Magnamusic-Baton, 1974).

Sex Roles in Performance Games

Skelly is described in John and Carol Langstaff, *Shimmy Shimmy Coke-Ca-Pop!* (Garden City, N.Y.: Doubleday, 1973), pp. 30–31; in James Wagenvoord, *Hangin' Out: City Kids, City Games* (Philadelphia: Lippincott, 1974), pp. 29–37; and in Fred Ferretti, *The Great American Book of Sidewalk, Stoop, Dirt, Curb, and Alley Games* (New York: Workman, 1975), pp. 230–33. Playing tops is discussed in *Hangin' Out: City Kids, City Games*, pp. 48–51; and its decline in popularity is traced in the surveys in Brian Sutton-Smith and B. G. Rosenberg, "Sixty Years of Historical Change in the Game Preferences of American Children" in *Child's Play*, edited by R. E. Herron and Brian Sutton-Smith (New York: John Wiley & Sons, 1971), pp. 18–50. The quotation from Sutton-Smith and Rosenberg is on p. 48.

Singing Games

Marriage is recorded in William Wells Newell, *Games and Songs of American Children* (second ed., 1903; reprint ed., New York: Dover Publications, 1963), p. 59; Knights of Spain is described on pp. 39–40. The relative popularity of singing games at different times is suggested by Leah Rachel Clara Yoffie, "Three Generations of Children's Singing Games in St. Louis," *Journal of American Folklore*, 60 (1947), 1–51; and by Jean Olive Heck, "Folk Poetry and Folk Criticism," *Journal of American Folklore*, 40 (1927), 1–77. Father Damian Webb's observation is from "Singing Games," *The Listener*, 81 (May 9, 1969), 639. Jenny Jones is from Newell, *Games and Songs of American Children*, p. 243. Yoffie also discusses this game, as well as Water, Water, Wine Flowers, in "Three Generations of Children's Singing Games in St. Louis," pp. 12–13.

Autographs

The nineteenth-century autograph rhymes come from Laura Ingalls Wilder, *Little Town on the Prairie*, pp. 188–89; and from Mac E. Barrick, "Some Nineteenth Century Autograph Verses," *Keystone Folklore Quarterly*, 8 (1963), p. 113.

4 | Coping with the Here and Now

RESISTANCE

Folklore helps people to cope with the here and now in three ways. It helps them to escape from the unsatisfactory present into fantasy, consoles them by reminding them that their troubles aren't unique, and by virtue of its formal, traditional nature, provides a safe, accepted means of expressing social hostility. Thus folklore helps relieve individual frustration without destroying the *status quo*.

In some cultures, this sort of coping is formalized. In Ghana, for instance, during the breaks of a formal storytelling session, the Ashantis ridicule and mimic their leaders, their gods, even the sick. At that time a person can mock things that it is unacceptable to criticize anywhere else. In the United States, parodic songs provide a similar, though informal safety valve for the resentments of American school children.

Parodies

Parodies are more than high-spirited entertainment. They are a way of asserting one's perceptiveness and independence. We adults parody proverbs to show that we aren't taken in

161

—by traditional wisdom in general, and by romantics, snobs, bureaucrats, and the like, in particular.

> Absence makes the heart go wander.
> Better *nouveau* than never.
> Do not enumerate your fowl until the end product of the incubation process has been finalized.

We parody our favorite authors to get back at them for sweeping us off our feet. We want to show that we see through their tricks, but this doesn't always mean that we have stopped loving them—only that the enchanted honeymoon is over.

Commercials in Parody. Children, too, use parodies to demonstrate that they aren't taken in, but when they parody commercials, it's not immediately clear just what they aren't taken in by. A person hearing a child chant the following might reasonably assume that he was disenchanted with specific products:

> Winstons taste bad, like the last one I had.
> No filter, no flavor, just plain toilet paper!

> Sani-Flush, Sani-Flush,
> Cleans your teeth without a brush.

> Comet, it makes your teeth turn green,
> Comet, it tastes like gasoline [or "Listerine," "Vaseline"],
> Comet, it makes you vomit,
> So buy some Comet and vomit today!

> Everything tastes better
> With Blue Vomit [i.e., Blue Bonnet margarine] on it!

Research paid for by the advertising industry itself seems to confirm this supposition. Second-graders are said to have a "concrete distrust" of some commercials; by sixth grade the youngsters' distrust is "global"—they are suspicious of them all.

But though children may distrust commercials, their parodies provide only ambiguous evidence of that attitude. After all, how many grade-schoolers smoke Winstons? How can they be disenchanted with a product they don't use? No commercial has ever claimed that Sani-Flush or Comet is good for cleaning teeth, so what exactly is being criticized? The Blue Vomit verse seems to say that Blue Bonnet margarine tastes terrible, but mothers tell us that kids love having it in the house, so they can recite the parody while spreading the dreaded vomit on their toast.

The appeal of these parodies—of any parody—is largely based on style. One thing children dislike about commercials is the intrusive, we-know-best tone, which they also hear in many of the sales pitches of parents and teachers. In response, kids gleefully distort the advice they are given. They recommend Sani-Flush for toothpaste and warn that Pepsi-Cola makes you sick.

> Pepsi-Cola hits the spot,
> Ties your belly in a knot,
> Tastes like vinegar, looks like ink,
> Pepsi-Cola is a stinky drink.

> Pepsi-Cola is a drink,
> Pour it down the kitchen sink,
> Tastes like vinegar, looks like ink,
> Pepsi-Cola is a stinky drink.

> McDonald's is your kind of place;
> They serve you rattlesnakes,
> Hot dogs up your nose,
> French fries between your toes,
> And don't forget those chocolate shakes,
> They're from polluted eggs.
> McDonald's is your kind of place;
> The last time that I was there,
> They stole my underwear,
> I really didn't care,
> They were a dirty pair.
> The next time that you go there,
> They'll serve my underwear.

ONE POTATO, TWO POTATO...

McDonald's is your kind of place.
Scooo-oobie.

Oh! I wish I wasn't an Oscar Mayer wiener,
That is what I wouldn't want to be
Because if I was an Oscar Mayer wiener,
There would soon be nothin' left of me.

You'll wonder where your teeth went
When you brush your teeth with Pepsodent.

The insistent, repetitious, intrusive theme songs of certain programs have the same effect as commercials and have inspired their share of parodies. The parodied theme of the Daniel Boone show became part of children's racist lore; that of "The Addams Family" became part of fartlore; that of "It's About Time," a science-fiction serial, became a jeer or trick. A child recites, "It's about TIME! It's about SPACE! It's about *Henry*'s ugly face!" or ". . . It's about time I slapped your face!" and follows up with a slap.

While many of these parodies drop out of children's lore after the commercial or show is withdrawn from the air, others live on and on.

Parodied versions of the theme song of the Popeye cartoons, which were first shown in the movies and later televised, have become an enduring part of the repertoire of children's songs. The spinach-eating hero changes his diet:

I'm Popeye the sailorman,
I live in a garbage pan,
I eat all the worms
And spit out the germs,
I'm Popeye the sailorman, toot, toot.

Children like parodies of advertised products so much that they will even collect commercially prepared parodies such as those chewing gum cards now discontinued but which once "advertised" Cheapios, Duzn't, Liptorn Soup, Crust Toothpaste, Ajerx, 6-Urp ("the gassy one"), Squabble ("the nasty

164

game"), and Heartburn ("the unnatural cereal"). Some adults believe that by collecting these cards, children are learning to fight back at the advertisers who would teach them to say "Gimme." But children don't tell their mothers not to buy these products. Rather, through the parodies they defend themselves against becoming mere bundles of reflexes that are dominated by the ads. They reserve for themselves the possibility of disagreeing, but they don't necessarily dislike the products. What they especially like is seeing the officious official world turned upside down.

And inside out. They may resent being the targets of commercials, but they love to deliver them. Reciting "Comet, it makes your teeth turn green," children can have it both ways. They can mock the advice they've been given, while enjoying the texture and patterns of popular culture. And they have ample opportunity to observe the style of commercials. According to a study by Action for Children's Television, children's programs offer a commerical on the average of once every 2.9 minutes. Brand names become verbal toys:

> Pepsi-Cola went to town,
> Coca-Cola shot him down,
> Dr Pepper fixed him up,
> While drinking a bottle of Seven-up.

Though criticism of particular products is not the point of children's parodies of advertising, the youngsters are aware of the untruthfulness of ads in general. Seven- to ten-year-olds, who are more perceptive than younger children and more idealistic than older ones, are "angry" about what they regard as the immorality of commercials. Writing in the *Harvard Business Review*, researchers who have studied the effect of advertising on children express concern that seven- to ten-year-olds are unable to cope with "socially accepted hypocrisy" without becoming cynical about morality and business. We can't say how much hypocrisy should be socially acceptable or how much cynicism is bad, but we do know that children are not entirely dependent upon adults for guidance in these matters. To some extent, they cope with the hypocrisy of commercials on their own, by mocking them.

And they mock not only commercials but also the basic principle of an acquisitive society—that any problem can be solved if only we buy the right brand:

> Black and white were up tight
> Until they tried Ultra Brite!

Nursery Rhymes in Parody. Parodies of nursery rhymes are slightly different from other parodies that children know. By the time a child is ready to parody nursery rhymes, the originals no longer play much of a role in his life. Thus nursery-rhyme parodies serve as epitaphs on the propaganda of the nursery, and also allow a child to boast of his new, more realistic vision of life.

> Hickory, dockory, dock,
> Three mice ran up the clock;
> The clock struck one,
> And the other two escaped with minor injuries.

> Little Miss Muffet
> Sat on a tuffet,
> Eating her curds and whey.
> Along came a spider
> And sat down beside her,
> And said, "What's in the bowl, bitch?"

> Twinkle, twinkle little star,
> How I wonder what you are.
> If I may, if I might—
> Oh, shucks! it's a satellite.

> Jack be nimble, Jack be quick,
> Jack stand still; you're making me sick.

> Mary, Mary, quite contrary,
> Don't eat the raspberry—*puut!*

166

Peter, Peter, pumpkin eater,
Had a wife and couldn't keep her,
So he put her in a pumpkin shell
And threw her out the window, the window,
The second-story window.
He put her in a pumpkin shell
And threw her out the window!

Mary had a little lamb.
The doctor was surprised.
But when MacDonald had a farm,
The doctor nearly died!

Christmas Carols, Patriotic Songs, and Religious Verses in Parody. Around Christmas time, carols and popular Christmas songs are dinned at us from every side. Schools and churches train choirs to sing them; merchants broadcast them in stores —hoping they will trigger a buying frenzy. Adults wearily try to close their ears, passively accepting their fate. Children, inspired by some imp of the perverse, assert themselves by singing parodies. However, since the parodies are themselves traditional, a child is likely to learn some of them before he learns the originals; the result is that the originals may seem to him like washed-out versions of the parodies, at least until he can get the priorities straight.

Joy to the world, the school burned down,
And all the teachers died.
If you're looking for the principal,
You'll find him on the flagpole
With a rope around his neck, . . .

We three kings of Orientar,
Tried to smoke a rubber cigar;
It was loaded and exploded,
And that's how we traveled so far.

We three kings of Orient are,
Tried to smoke a rubber cigar;
It was loaded and exploded. Boom!

ONE POTATO, TWO POTATO...

Jingle bells, Santa smells,
From thirty miles away,
Blows his nose in Cheerios
And eats them every day.

Jingle bells, Batman smells,
Robin laid an egg;
Batmobile lost a wheel,
And Joker broke his leg.

Jingle bells, Santa smells,
Teacher's on the way;
Oh, what fun it is to ride
In a six-seat Chevrolet.

Jingle bells, shotgun shells,
BB's all the way;
Oh, what fun it is to ride
In Grandma's Chevrolet.

Jingle bells, jingle bells,
Santa Claus is dead;
Someone took a BB gun
And shot him through the head.

The following parodic version of "Jingle Bells" comes from
Brazil:

Dingo bell, dingo bell,
Acabou o papel.
Nat faz mal, nat faz mal,
Limpa com o jornal.

Roughy translated, it means:

Ding bat, ding bat,
We've run out of paper.
That's all right, that's all right,
Wipe with a newspaper.

In a widely known folk version of "Rudolph, the Red-
Nosed Reindeer"—the song about the humble outcast who
wins acceptance because his deformity turns out to be the very

thing needed to save the community—this little deer becomes
a cowboy gunman who murders in order to gain the social approval of the hoods he wants to be his bunkhouse buddies.
It's a brilliant commentary on the sanctimonious moral of
the original song:

> Rudolph, the red-nosed cowboy,
> Had a very shiny gun,
> And if you ever saw it,
> You would turn around and run.
>
> All of the other cowboys
> Used to laugh and call him names;
> They never let poor Rudolph
> Join in any poker games.
>
> Then one foggy Christmas Eve,
> Sheriff came to say,
> "Rudolph with your gun so bright,
> Won't you shoot my wife tonight?"
>
> Then all the cowboys loved him
> As they shouted out with glee,
> "Rudolph, the red-nosed cowboy,
> You'll go down in history."

Parodies of patriotic songs serve much the same purpose
as parodies of Christmas songs.

> [The Star-Spangled Banner]
> Oh-oh say can you see
> Any bedbugs on me?
> If you do, take a few
> 'Cause I got them from you.
>
> [America]
> My country 'tis of thee,
> I'm going to Germany
> To see the king.
> His name is Donald Duck,
> He drives a garbage truck,

169

ONE POTATO, TWO POTATO...

He lives in home and house
With a city mouse.

Another version is:

My country's tired of me,
I'm going to Germany
To serve the king.
I'll eat their sauerkraut
Until my eyes pop out,
And then I'll probably shout,
"*Hotsy totsy;* I'm a Nazi!"
(Indiana, 1967)

[God Bless America]
God bless my underwear,
My only pair,
Stand beside it and guide it
Through the hole and the wear and the tear.

[Yankee Doodle]
Yankee Doodle went to town,
Riding on a turtle,
Turned the corner just in time
To see a lady's girdle.

By singing these parodies a child is showing that the originals
are important to him. However, he's also fending off the depersonalization that accompanies the insistent celebration of
patriotism in some schools—the pledge of allegiance every
morning, flag ceremonies at assemblies, and patriotic songs in
music class.

Parodies of religious verse have been used in the past to
shock the sanctimonious. However, we collected only one
verse of this type:

My eyes have seen the glory of the coming of the Lord,
He is driving down the valley in a green and yellow
Ford,
One hand on the throttle and the other on a bottle
Of———beer.

Most modern religious parodies seem to be rather affectionate. As a child parodies bedtime prayers, the funeral service, hymns, and biblical verses, he strikes up a good-natured teasing partnership (one-sided, of course) with sanctity.

Catholic children know:

> Hail, Mary, full of grace,
> Bless my boy friend's happy face,
> Make [*sic*] his hands that are so strong,
> Make them stay where they belong.
> (Massachusetts, 1968)

However, many of the parodies of "Hail, Mary"—such as "Hail, Mary, full of grace,/Four balls, take your base," or ". . . Give me a horse in the second race"—seem to be more popular among adults. Some Protestant children know, "Stand up, stand up for Je-sus! Oh, for Christ's sake, sit down." And children of almost all denominations share unofficial versions of the Office of the Dead, a popular target for parodists since the Middle Ages. Among the many variant lines that may follow "Ashes to ashes, dust to dust," are:

> Two twin beds, only one of them mussed.
> You'd look better with a knife in your bust.
> If the Lord don't get me, the devil must.
> If it weren't for your ass, your belly would bust.

Children also share numerous versions of "Now I Lay Me."

> Now I lay me down to sleep,
> A bag of apples at my feet.
> If I die before I wake,
> You'll know it was a stomach ache.
> (Rhode Island, 1964)

> Now I lay me down to sleep;
> My car is parked across the street.
> If it should roll before I wake,
> I pray the Lord put on the brake.

171

ONE POTATO, TWO POTATO...

George Monteiro, who collected many scriptural parodies in Rhode Island, remarks that a ten-year-old boy recited the following with "wicked relish":

> Now I lay her on the bed,
> I pray to God I'll use my head.

Many of these religious parodies are passed from child to child, but adults seem to contribute toward keeping some of them, especially parodic graces, in circulation. On a camping trip a joking father will say:

> Good bread, good meat,
> Good God, let's eat.

Or at Thanksgiving, a lubricated uncle may announce that dinner's ready with:

> In the name of the Father, Son and Holy Ghost,
> The first to the table gets the most.

These marvels are, of course, subsequently repeated by children among themselves.

But today's snippets of religious parody make a poor showing compared to the variety and verve of the parodies originated by English monks between the eleventh and the fifteenth centuries. During this age of faith, parodic masses were devoted to Bacchus and Venus. Hymns to the Virgin became hymns to wine. The catechism and the paternoster, even the Latin grammar book, were parodied, and biblical phrasing was used to tell dirty stories. In comparison, the following is mere fluff:

> Praise God, save the Queen,
> Shoot straight, keep clean.
> Thank you, Lord, for what we've got;
> Pass the taters while they're hot.
>   (Canal Zone, 1974)

Antischool Songs. For most children today, the school is almost as omnipresent and demanding as the church was for

172

English monks in the late Middle Ages. The children's most popular parodic songs are devoted to reviling the school and its teachers. These parodies differ from those we have already discussed in that they aren't meant to mock the song they are based on. "Battle Hymn of the Republic," for instance, merely provides a convenient melodic and grammatical frame for the children's resentment:

> Mine eyes have seen the glory of the burning of the
> school.
> We have tortured all the teachers,
> We have broken every rule,
> We are marching down the hall
> To hang the principal,
> Our gang is marching on.
> Glory, glory hallelujah,
> Teacher hit me with a ruler;
> I hit her on the bean
> With a rotten tangerine
> And she ain't no teacher any more.

Like any popular folk song, this one has innumerable variants. We have collected over fifty. For example, children may sing:

> We have barbecued the principal,
> Destroyed the PTA,

or

> We have stood in every corner,
> We have spit on every wall.

The chorus sometimes runs:

> I shot her in the mouth
> With a loaded forty-four,
> And her teeth came marching out,

or

> I shot her in the seater
> With a forty-five repeater,

173

or

> I hit her in the rear
> With a bottle of————beer,

or

> I shot her in the butt,
> With a rotten coconut.

One may also sing:

> Teacher hit me with a ruler,
> The ruler turned red,
> And the teacher fell dead.

There are many other possibilities.

Children sing another parody of the "Battle Hymn" too, but it is much less popular. It is mainly a camp song:

> I wear my pink pajamas in the summer when it's hot.
> I wear my flannel nightie in the winter when it's not.
> And sometimes in the springtime, and sometimes in the
>   fall,
> I jump right in between the sheets with nothing on at
>   all.
> Glory, glory hallelujah,
> Glory, glory what's it to ya?
> Balmy breezes blowin' through ya
> With nothing on at all.

Every bit as popular as the antischool version of the "Battle Hymn" are the antischool versions of "On Top of Old Smoky," sometimes referred to as a mountain lonesome tune. The traditional verses that are sung by adults quaver mournfully of false-hearted lovers who "hug you and kiss you/And tell you more lies/Than the crossties on the railroad,/Or the stars in the skies." The antischool version is a good deal more cheerful. It is sung with bloodthirsty glee:

> On top of Old Smoky,
> All covered with blood [or "sand"],

I shot my poor teacher
With a forty-four gun ["a red rubber band," "a blue
    rubber band," "a forty-eight slug"].
I shot her with pleasure,
I shot her with pride,
I couldn't have missed her,
She's forty feet wide ["—and that's the truth!" may be
    added].
I went to her funeral,
I went to her grave,
Instead of throwing flowers,
I threw a grenade ["bomb"].

A variant is:

On top of old Smoky,
All covered with blood,
I shot my poor teacher
With a twenty-two gun.
I shot off her right hand,
I shot off her left,
I shot off both legs,
I shot off her head.

There is, incidentally, a second children's version of "On Top
of Old Smoky," which is a true parody of the "Old Smoky"
sung by adults and not just a convenient frame for comment
about teachers. Like the mountain lonesome version about false-
hearted lovers, this one is sung with a plaintive whine. Its sentimental tone, however, is undercut by the object of the
singer's concern—a poor meatball—and in many variants, by a
sternly moralistic close: one's actions have irreparable consequences; all the pity in the world won't save the meatball.

On top of spaghetti, all covered with cheese,
I lost my poor meatball 'cause I had to sneeze.
It rolled off the table and onto the floor,
And then my poor meatball went out of the door.
It went in the garden and under a bush,
And then my poor meatball was nothing but mush.

175

So if you have spaghetti, all covered with cheese,
Hold on to your meatball and try not to sneeze.

The children's antischool songbook also includes versions of
the dwarf's song from Walt Disney's *Snow White,* "The
Marines' Hymn," "Ta-Ra-Ra-Boom-De-Ay," "Row Row, Row
Your Boat," and "Chiquita Banana."

Heigh ho, heigh ho, I bit the teacher's toe,
She bit me back, the dirty rat,
Heigh ho, heigh ho, heigh ho, heigh ho, heigh ho,
It's off to school we go,
With hand grenades and razor blades,
Heigh ho, heigh ho.

From the halls of *P.S. 92* [or *"Ashdale* pri-i-son"]
To the shores of Bubble Gum Bay,
I will torture every teacher,
Spit mud and gum and clay;
I will fight for extra re-e-cess,
[or "First to get rid of arithmetic"]
I will keep my desk a mess.
From the halls of *P.S. 92* [*"Ashdale* prison"],
I'm the teacher's personal ["number one"] pest!

Tra-la-la-boom-de-ay,
We have no school today,
Our teacher passed away,
We shot her yesterday.
We put her in the bay,
She scared the sharks away,
And when we fished her out,
She smelled like sauerkraut [or "sour trout"].
Tra-la-la-boom-de-ay,
We have no school today.

Apparently a version of "Ta-Ra-Ra-Boom-De-Re" was part of
Mama Lou's act at Babe Connor's *maison de joie* in St. Louis
in 1888. Henry J. Sayers cleaned it up; Lottie Collins introduced it to respectable society in London in 1891, and children
have been singing their disrespectful versions ever since.

Row, row, row your boat,
Gently down the stream.
Throw your teacher overboard,
Listen to her scream. *HELP! Ahg.* Gulp.

The original advocates oriental detachment: "Life is but a dream." The parody advocates decisive action, as does the parody of "Chiquita Banana":

I'm Chiquita Banana, and I'm here to say,
If you want to get rid of your teacher today,
Just peel a banana, put it on the floor,
And watch your teacher slide out of the door.

Not all songs about school are so bitter or exultantly vengeful. Some strike a note of resigned passivity:

Over land, over sea,
Over *Mr. Johnson's* knee,
There's a paddle awaitin' for me.

I've been working on my homework,
All the livelong day.
I've been working on my homework,
Just to pass the time away.
Can't you hear the teacher saying,
"Spit out that bubble gum!"
Can't you hear your mother shouting,
"Get that homework done!"

These antischool songs wouldn't be so popular if they didn't reflect widespread genuine feelings, but the traditional character of these songs ritualizes and depersonalizes children's resentments—usually.

For instance, on one of our interview forms, the words of "Old Smoky" were written in a progressively more illegible fifth-grade hand. Suddenly, the penmanship became copperplate. "Yes," the teacher told us. "Tom asked me to help him finish." Both student and teacher recognized the formulaic, impersonal nature of the parody.

177

Not all of its versions are impersonal, however. We doubt that Tom would have asked for help in writing:

> On top of Old Smoky,
> All covered with blood,
> I found poor *Mrs. Richards*
> All stuck in the mud.
> A knife in her stomach,
> A sword in her head,
> I came to the conclusion
> *Mrs. Richards* was dead.

Even this variant, though directed at a particular person, is not militant. It's a fairy tale, not a revolutionary anthem. Compare by way of contrast the following. It is sung to the tune of "The Air Force Song":

> Off we go into the peace group yonder,
> Looking for yippies to chase,
> There goes one, tearing our flag asunder,
> At him boys, step on his face,
> . . . .
> Those filthy reds, we'll break their heads,
> Nothing can stop the hard hats today.

Unlike the other parodies, which turn up in different versions in school after school, this song was reported by just one student at one school. It doesn't boast of defying or destroying the authorities; it advocates punishing those who challenge them. Nowhere does it touch upon the traditional concerns of grade-school children. "Asunder" is literary diction, and the verse lacks the specific detail often present in children's songs. We find no rotten tangerines or red rubber bands or .44 guns, no surreal violence piled on violence—burning schools, knifed and tortured teachers, corpses blown apart by grenades —of the kind that distances children's traditional songs (and fairy tales) from reality. Everybody knows that no one will really hang the principal from the flagpole, so it's all right to sing about it. This adult parody of "The Air Force Song" on the other hand suggests the possibility of real violence.

Students distance themselves from the school through parody in other cultures as well as in our own. A young man from Taiwan told us that his school song began, "Oh, beautiful school with its trees, where our pen and brush exist next to each other," while the unofficial version went, "Oh, high arched bones, pigs' feet and soy sauce, cooked eggs, plus sausages to go with rice, how good it tastes." He told us he and his elementary school friends also parodied the couplet, "Lifting my head I see the moon;/Lowering my head I think of home." The boys said, "Lifting my head, I see the blackboard;/Lowering my head, I think of lunch."

Shockers

Children's traditional shocking rhymes and jokes have not been collected to any great extent in the United States, but there is good reason that they should be. We need to know something about their nature, distribution, and variety in order to distinguish the standard and traditional versions from the distorted or original creations of the psychologically troubled child.

Nevertheless, some readers may feel that the less said about shockers, the better. "What's the use of giving kids ideas?" asked one mother. We told her of another young mother who wanted to help us collect material. At our request, she asked her first-grader what songs he and his friends sang on the school bus. His eyes got big, and he refused to tell: "Oh, Mama, you'd be shocked." And she was—because all along, she'd assumed that *she* was protecting *him.*

Children enjoy a brief escape from social restraint—a ritualistic rebellion—when they recite shockers, and they gain a certain kind of prestige among their peers. Shockers also help educate them, not just about sex, but about language. And, paradoxically, shockers help reinforce existing social taboos.

ONE POTATO, TWO POTATO...

There is, of course, the question of what is and what isn't shocking. We can't answer this any better than the Supreme Court, but some sort of classification, however arbitrary, seems useful.

Kindergartners and sixth-graders don't recite the same shockers.

> Peek-a-boo,
> I see you,
> You look like a piece of doo!

and

> Nanny, nanny boo-boo,
> stick your head in doo-doo!

are popular with the younger set, but by sixth grade some girls are singing, to the tune of "Ta-Ra-Ra-Boom-De-Re":

> We are the tomboy girls,
> We wear our hair in curls.
> We never play with toys.
> [or "We sit with boys in cars."]
> We always flirt with boys.
> ["And smoke big, black cigars."]
> We wear our dungarees
> Above our dirty knees
> And keep our sweaters tight
> To keep the boys in sight.

Sixth-grade boys try to shock the girls—and to get used to their own sexuality—by reciting:

> Jack be nimble, Jack be quick,
> Jack jump over the candlestick.
> But Jack wasn't nimble, Jack wasn't quick,
> Now Jack's in the hospital with a French-fried dick,

or

> Roses are red, violets are blue.
> Hey, you with the knockers! Let's screw.

180

The shockers that children prefer vary not only with the age of the children but also with the age in which they live. William Allen White, that eminently respectable and admirable Kansas editor of the early years of this century, recalls that back in the 1870's he and his friends knew "ribald rhymes and Rabelaisian catches and catcalls" and were "dirty little devils, as most kids are when they are leaving the portals of babyhood and becoming boys." When White was eight, he and his gang would smear mud in indecent patterns on their naked bodies, then stand near the railroad bridge. As old Number Four chugged by, the future pillar of the Republican party in Kansas would dance about and make obscene gestures at the passengers.

Not all contemporary shockers, at least as we think of the term, are about sex or the excretory process. To the tune of "Frère Jacques," youngsters may proclaim:

Marijuana, marijuana,
L-S-D, L-S-D,
College kids are [or "Sister Mary's"] making it,
High-school kids ["all the nuns"] are taking it,
Why can't we? Why can't we?

"Clean" shockers are often learned at summer camps. By singing them, children assert a degree of control over their own squeamishness and immaturity.

Everybody's doing it, doing it, doing it,
Picking their nose and chewing it, chewing it, chewing
it.

Granny's in the cellar,
Oh Lordy can't you smell 'er,
Makin' biscuits on the dird-o-dirty stove.
In her eye there is a matter
That keeps drippin' in the batter,
And she whistles while the [here the singers sniff
audibly]

181

ONE POTATO, TWO POTATO...

Runs down her nose,
Down her nose, down her nose,
She whistles as the [*sniff*] runs down her nose.

We all like greasy grimy gopher guts,
Insulated monkey's feet [or "Mutilated monkey meat"],
Little birdies' dirty feet,
French-fried eyeballs, floatin' in a pool of blood,
Come on everybody! Let's eat!
I need a spoon!

Nobody likes you, everybody hates you,
I'm gonna get some worms,
Big, fat juicy ones,
Itty-bitty ones,
Fuzzy-wuzzy little worms.
First you'll bite the heads off,
Then you'll suck the guts out,
Oh, what juicy worms,
Big, fat juicy ones,
Little itty-bitty ones,
Little fuzzy-wuzzy worms.
Up goes the first one,
Down goes the second one,
Oh, how delicious worms,
Big, fat juicy ones.
First one's greasy, goes down easy,
Second one's little and squirmy,
Third one's rusty,
Fourth one's busty,
Fifth one sticks on your tongue.
No one knows how girls can stand them!
Three times a day and in between!

These rhymes shocked and delighted us when we sang them thirty-five years ago, and they make us squirm a bit today, but most people probably would reserve the label "shocking" for verses that use or flirt with taboo words.

She wore no pants
To the kootchy-kootchy dance;

She just wore grass
To cover up her—donkey.

Bars, bars, bars, bars,
Bars, bars, bars, bars,
Bars on the ceiling,
Bars on the floors,
Bars on the windows,
Bars on the doors.
Cedar School is a prison camp,
Room *10* is a cell,
Mrs. *Smith* [the principal] is the warden,
I wish she'd go to
Hello, Mrs. *Graham,*
Johnson broke the window,
Behind your desk is glass,
If you fall upon it, you cut your
Ask me no questions,
Tell me no more lies,
The boys are in the bathroom,
Zipping down their
Flies are in the corner,
I have to say good-by.

Verses that flirt with taboo words, as these do, serve to remind children that certain words are, indeed, forbidden. Other verses flirt with descriptions of taboo behavior.

I love you big, I love you mighty,
I wish your pajamas were next to my nightie.
Now don't get excited, now don't lose your head,
I mean on the clothesline instead of in bed.

Perhaps less obvious is the fact that a child who actually uses a taboo word in a song is thereby also affirming the rule against using it. To mention such words casually, without recognizing anything unusual about them, would weaken the power of the taboo, but to introduce them in the formal context of a song that is meant to be shocking affirms that the taboo still exists—and is worth violating. Moreover, children need to

183

know what words are forbidden—reserved, that is, for moments of stress—in polite society, and the school is not allowed to impart this information.

By and large, children and adults agree on what words are taboo; "ass," however, is much more shocking to children than it is to adults. The children proclaim:

> Robin Hood, Robin Hood, running through the grass,
> Little John, Little John, shot him in the ass.
> Thought he was a deer,
> Hit him in the rear,
> Oh, Robin, poor Robin will never sit again.

Or, to the tune of "You're in the Army Now":

> In 1955, my mother learned to drive,
> She stepped on the gas and blew off her ass
> In 1955.

> He's Popeye, the sailorman,
> He lives in a frying pan,
> He turns on the gas to burn off his ass,
> He's Popeye, the sailorman.

> I was goin' 'round the corner doin' ninety
> When the chain on my motorcycle broke;
> I went sliding through the grass
> With the muffler up my ass
> And my titties playin' "Dixie" on the spokes.

Bathroom shockers are also popular:

> The night was dark, a scream was heard,
> A man got hit by a low-flying turd.

> Birdie, birdie in the sky,
> Why'd you do that to my eye?
> Gee, I'm glad that cows don't fly.

> How dry I am, how wet I'll be,
> If I don't find the bathroom key.
> I found the key, now where's the door—
> Oops, too late, it's on the floor.

> I see London, I see France,
> I see *Betsy's* underpants.
> They ain't green, they ain't blue,
> They're just filled with number two.

And, of course, many shockers are about sex. A common playground chant is:

> Tarzan swings, Tarzan falls,
> Tarzan lands right on his balls.

(A sixth-grade teacher told us about a boy who was playing with several ball bearings. He dropped them and they rolled to the front of the room. Exasperated, the teacher demanded, "Okay, who's got the steel balls?" From the back of the room, someone squeaked, "*Sup-er-maan!*")

There are many versions of "A Place in France" in circulation.

> There's a place in France
> Where the ladies wear no pants,
> And the men all wear bikinis,
> And the children suck their wienies [or "drink martinis"].

Almost everyone recognizes that the sort of traditional sex education children "pick up in the street" is inadequate and misleading. As a result, we have sex-education programs in many schools. But these programs do not make all of our children's traditional sex lore obsolete. Knowing what sex is all about is one thing; integrating that knowledge into one's personality is something else. Words always help tame new ideas —and traditional words help more than original ones:

> My Bonnie lies over the ocean,
> My Bonnie lies over the sea,
> My daddy lies over my mommy,
> And that's how they got little me.

Traditional jokes also serve this purpose. An example is the following joke, which has been around in one form or another for at least thirty-five years:

ONE POTATO, TWO POTATO...

A child sees his mother in the shower and asks, "What's
   that?"
"That's my pocketbook."
Later, the child sees his father in the shower and asks,
   "What's that?"
"That's my roll of money."
The child then asks, "Why don't you put your roll of
   money in Mama's pocketbook?"

In variants of this joke, the mother may speak of her bun,
gorilla, socket, garage, or fruit bowl; and the father—corre-
spondingly—of his hot dog, banana, plug, car, or banana.

> Down by the river where nobody goes,
> Along came *Susan* without any clothes,
> Along came *Christopher* swinging a chain,
> Down went the zipper and out it came,
> Six months' swelling, nine months later,
> Out it came, a bald-headed monster,
> Swinging a chain.

This is a folk warning. Young girls recite it blithely enough as
they jump rope, but teen-agers remember it as "really kind of
scary."

Another educative aspect of shockers, generally overlooked,
has to do with their impact on a child's grasp of the complexity
and richness of language. A man in Oregon laughed when he
heard about the kind of rhymes we were collecting, and told us
of a speech he learned in Pittsburgh in 1959, when he was
seven. He remembered how old he was because that summer
his conscious awareness of sex increased dramatically. A junior-
high-school boy, a newcomer to the neighborhood, made himself welcome by teaching shockers to the natives. The man said
that he and his friends didn't fully understand the following
speech, but knew it was dirty and recited it all the time:

> My name is ———. I was sitting in my office late
> one night when I heard this knock at the door, nearly

scared me out of my secretary. A woman stepped in. I found myself staring at two thirty-eights, then she pulled her gun. She said that she heard that I was the best private dick in town, but she wanted to see my credentials. I showed it to her and was hired. She said she would give me a ride and I hopped on, then we went down to her car. It had a flat tire. She pumped, I pumped, she pumped, I pumped, she pumped, I pumped, then we got the jack. We were driving along when a rock flew through the window and hit her where it hurts, broke my glasses, too. When we got to her door, I went in, then out, then in again, then she found the key. We went to the kitchen, where she had some cake. I had a piece, then another piece, then we cut the cake. She told me she had thirteen sisters. They were all very fine. I felt like a jack rabbit jumping from hole to hole. When I got to my office the next day, I realized how much I missed her. I had a lump in my throat and a lump in my pants. I called in my secretary.

We find this shocker impressive. The children who recited it learned a few things about sex, to be sure, but they also developed an ear for metaphor, innuendo, puns, tone, and—yes —aesthetic form: the references to the secretary frame the hero's adventures and provide closure. All this can be taught in class, of course, but somehow the effect is not the same. A traditional function of poetry has always been to talk about the unspeakable; that's one thing that makes it fun. And one reason children fail to learn how much fun artistic language can be is that we try to protect them from the electrifying interplay of language and sex. We either pretend sex doesn't exist or explain it in defused language.

Many adults take it for granted that shockers are circulated only by "bad" kids. Even parents who agree that their children are familiar with some shockers tend to assume that they have learned only the milder ones. But many "shocking shockers" are widely known. The school bus is a particularly good place for children to share them. Not all songs and rhymes repeated on the bus are shockers. "A Hundred Bottles of Beer on the Wall" and other old stand-bys are popular, but so are:

> Old MacDonald sittin' on a fence,
> Hittin' his knee with a monkey wrench,
> Missed his knee and cracked his balls,
> Pissed all over his overalls.

> Little bird with yellow bill,
> Sittin' on the window sill,
> Lured him near with crumbs of bread,
> Then I crushed his fuckin' head!

> I'm Popeye the garbage man,
> I live in a garbage can,
> I love to go swimmin' with bare-naked [or "bow-legged"] women,
> I'm Popeye the sailorman!

Teasing shockers are also popular:

> Tra-la-la-boom-de-ay,
> We'll take your pants away,
> And while you're standing there,
> We'll take your underwear!

> I don't go out with girls any more,
> I don't intend to marry,
> I just go out with boys I adore,
> Oops! I'm a fairy.

To illustrate the strength of the shocker tradition, we offer the following:

> I went to the store to get a poun' a butter,
> Seen a girl a-sittin' in a gutter,
> Picked up a rock and hit her in the cock,
> Chased me half around the block.

We collected this rhyme from a white, ten-year-old boy in a depressed, semirural area of Indiana in 1970. The first two lines echo,

> Far are ye gaein'?
> Across the gutter.
> Fat for?
> A pund o' butter,

which is part of a perfectly innocent rhyme current in Britain about 1910. We supposed the last two lines were a local, back-woods invention, or possibly a not generally known shocker that we would collect from boys with reputations for "talk-ing dirty." But the next variant of this verse that we came across was volunteered in 1973 by a white, ten-year-old, mid-dle-class girl in the Canal Zone. Her family had come to the Zone from a small town in the Southwest.

> I went downtown to buy a stick of butter,
> Saw an old lady peeing in the gutter,
> Picked up some glass and hit her in the ass,
> Never saw an old lady run so fast.

A twenty-year-old white girl then told us that she and her friends used to sing the following song when they were in grade school in the Zone in the early sixties. Lines 3 through 6 are yet another variant of the verse we first collected in Indiana:

> I was walkin' through the jungle with my dick in my
>   hand,
> I'm the coolest mother-fucker in the Congo land,
> I look up a tree and what did I see?
> A goddamn monkey tryin' to pee on me!
> Picked up a rock and hit him in the cock,
> Goddamn monkey chased me forty-five blocks.
> Turned the corner and what did I see?
> A hundred naked ladies just a-waitin' for me.
> I fucked ninety-eight of 'em till my balls turned blue,
> Took a shot of whiskey and fucked the other two.

ONE POTATO, TWO POTATO...

This is a "toast," a type of oral narrative usually collected from urban, black males. Later, in the Folklore Archives at Indiana University, we found parts of this toast reported by an eleven-year-old white boy who attended an integrated school in Indianapolis in 1970.

> Old Casey Jones was a son-of-a-bitch,
> Drove his train in a hell of a ditch,
> Ran off the start with his dick in his hand
> . . . .
> And lined fifty women up against the wall,
> And bet fifty dollars he could fuck 'em all.
> Fucked forty-eight till his balls turned blue,
> Backed off, jacked off, and fucked the other two.

Our experience with these verses has taught us never to underestimate the geographic distribution of folk rhymes or to assume that acquaintance with a certain verse or kind of verse is restricted to members of one sex, class, or race.

REFLECTIONS

Prejudice: Blacks

None of the rhymes that refer to sex or scatology, however, are as truly shocking as this counting-out rhyme, collected in New York in the 1880's:

> Penny, come Penny, come down to your dinner,
> And taste the leg of the roasted nigger,
> For all you good people, look over the steeple,
> To see the cat play with the dog.

We know that the attitude of most whites toward blacks at that time was aggressively racist, and it shouldn't surprise us that the man who collected this rhyme doesn't seem to have been shocked by it. But it does. He took pleasure in announcing that in all his oral and written communication with children the nearest thing to an oath used by a child was "Gracious Peter!" But he let pass without comment the line about feeding the leg of a roasted man to a pet. That's the kind of thing that brings a historical period uncomfortably to life.

Of the three main groups abused in children's rhymes—blacks, Jews, and orientals—blacks have always received the most attention. Children's verses have thus reflected both the general attitude of the majority toward blacks and the importance of blacks in American society. However, an individual child's attitude toward blacks cannot automatically be deduced from the rhymes he uses.

Between the 1880's (when American children's lore was first collected) and the 1930's, aggressive racist lore was present in abundance. For instance, among the rhymes employed by children to choose the It for a game of Hide and Seek were:

> Butter, eggs, cheese, bread,
> Hit the nigger on the head,
> If he hollers, hit him dead,
> Eggs, butter, cheese, bread.
> (Massachusetts, New York)

> Nigger, nigger,
> Pull the trigger,
> Up and down the Ohio River,
> Rigger, jigger,
> Nary snigger,
> In a row we stand and shiver.
> (Indiana)

> Nigger, nigger, never die,
> Black face and shiny eye,
> Crooked toes and broken nose,
> And that's the way the nigger grows.
> (Philadelphia)

> I know something I won't tell,
> Three little niggers in a peanut shell,

191

ONE POTATO, TWO POTATO...

> One was black, one was blacker,
> One was the color of chawin' tobacker.
> (North Carolina, Michigan)

During this period, white boys treasured homemade sling-shots called "nigger-shooters"; they found "nigger-toes" (Brazil nuts or licorice) in their Christmas stockings; and on the Fourth of July, they lit small fireworks called "nigger-chasers." In New York about 1891, when two white boys met a Negro each of the boys tried—for luck—to be the first to cross his fingers, draw them down his friend's coat sleeve, and say "Grease!" In Missouri boys posed riddles like:

> There was a little green house, and in the little green house there was a little white house, and in the little white house there was a little red house, and in the little red house was a whole bunch of niggers. What is it?
> A watermelon.

And white children jeered both blacks and fellow whites with rhymes such as:

> Run, nigger, run; de patterol'll ketch you;
> Run, nigger, run; it's almost day.
> The nigger run, the nigger flew,
> The nigger tore his shirt in two.
> (New York, North Carolina)

> Nigger, nigger, black as tar,
> Tried to ride a 'lectric car,
> Car broke down and broke his back,
> Poor little nigger wanted his money back.
> (Tennessee)

> Did you ever, ever, ever in your life, life, life,
> See a nigger, nigger, nigger, kiss his wife, wife, wife?
> (North Carolina)

> Nigger, nigger, never die
> Big flat nose and shiny eye,
> Mouth as big as a steamboat slip,

192

India rubber nose and lip, lip.
Nigger eat scrap iron, yes he do;
Nigger he chews glue.

      (North Carolina, New York, Michigan)

Teacher, teacher [or "Policeman, policeman"], don't
 whip me!
Whip that nigger behind the tree!
He stole the honey and I stole the money.
Teacher, teacher, wasn't that funny?

      (Kansas, North Carolina, South Carolina)

In the twenties, "nigger" was so completely acceptable to many
Americans that it appeared in school cheers, like the following
from a grade school and a high school in Utah:

Nigger, nigger, pull the trigger;
Sis-boom, bully nigger.

Nigger, nigger, hoe potato,
Half past alligator,
Slick-ra-dah,
——— High School, ——— High School, rah, rah, rah!

Sometime between 1930 and 1960, some of the most vicious
racist lore declined in popularity; however, it didn't disap-
pear. In the forties in Georgia, a child would hold his hands
apart as if to measure, while he chanted:

Takes this much to kill a nigger,
Takes this much to kill a Jew,
Takes this much to kill you!

After each line the child moved his hands farther apart, and on
the last word, he doubled up his fist and smashed his friend
on the shoulder. In many schools the thing for a child to shout
if he was outnumbered in a quarrel was, "Two against one's
nigger's fun!" And almost everyone knew:

Arty, smarty, had a party,
Nobody came but a big fat darky.

ONE POTATO, TWO POTATO...

A possible source for the American rhyme is this British version:

> Mrs. Harty gave a party.
> Nobody came.
> Then her brother gave another.
> Just the same.

In Kansas, from about 1910 to 1918, there was a formulaic response to "Arty, Smarty." After the last line—"Nobody came but a big fat darky"—the child to whom the jeer was directed could reply, *"And that was you!"* As Kenneth Porter points out, "To *be* a Negro (even if only in fantasy) was considerably worse even than to have a Negro for a guest (also in fantasy)."

Racist lore has wide circulation among grade-school children even today, but during the sixties and seventies the general temper of this lore has changed. A child will still sometimes say, "Last one there's a nigger baby," or call a playmate "a dirty nigger." But today his own companions may tell him that they disapprove of the word "nigger." That's something new. Of course, a few of the old racist taunts are still around. Once a rhyme becomes established in the children's tradition, it dies hard. Somewhere, some child continues to know it, even though it is no longer in general circulation. That is the case with this counting-out rhyme:

> Had a little nigger,
> Would not grow any bigger,
> Put him in a Wabash show.
> Fell out the winder,
> Broke his little finger,
> One, two, three, four, five.
>
> (Indiana, 1971; Canal Zone, 1973)

And girls still sometimes sing the following song when they "stay over" with each other:

> Three little niggers laying in bed,
> One rolled over and the other one said,

194

"Boom, boom, boom, I see your hiney,
Boom, boom, boom, so black and shiny,
Boom, boom, boom, you'd better hide it,
Boom, boom, boom, before I bite it."
(Indiana, 1971; Canal Zone, 1974)

The last four lines of this song, minus the "Boom, boom, boom," are used as a popular taunt: the boy shouts the part beginning "I see your hiney" when a girl shows her underwear. A boy who knew only this portion of the song was puzzled when we asked him what "black and shiny" meant. He thought a moment and told us he guessed it referred to a girl's panties. No, he'd never seen shiny, black panties on a girl, but he'd heard about them.

By the sixties, blacks were acquiring new roles in childlore as well as in society at large, as is illustrated by this jump-rope rhyme:

Three little Negroes dressed in white,
Wanted to go to Harvard on the tail of a kite,
The kite string broke and down they fell.
They didn't go to Harvard, they went to . . .
Now don't get excited, don't turn pale,
They didn't go to Harvard, they went to Yale.
(Michigan, 1961)

Still condescending, but a world different from "Penny, come Penny."

And by 1971, the black folk ritual of "giving skins" (slapping palms)—which Clarence Major in his *Dictionary of Afro-American Slang* considered "distinctively black" and manly —had spread to some white grade schools. There has always been an exchange of folk beliefs, rhymes, and customs between blacks and whites, but the whites' adoption of skins differs from Huck's learning black lore from Jim. Skins is a public ritual, not a private belief. And everyone knows it was originally a black ritual. White children told us that they usually gave skins during a happy moment in a game, but that they also gave skins outside of game situations. One boy said he and his dad exchanged hand slaps every morning after breakfast. No longer distinctively black, the practice still seems to be considered manly. A girl told us, "Boys do it. I don't."

During the sixties, a growing number of grade-school children came to recognize "nigger" as a taboo word, but that gave it a new kind of status with them. For instance, the theme song of the Daniel Boone television show gave rise to a parody that went:

> Daniel Boone
> Was a ma-a-an,
> Yes, a bi-ig man,
> But the bear was bigger,
> And he ran like a nigger [or "chigger"]
> Up a tree.

This has a racist message, obviously, but the rhyme's popularity also had something to do with the newly acquired status of "nigger" as a taboo word. By using it—or its cousin "chigger" —out loud a child could enjoy some of the *frisson* he used to get from reciting one of the traditional shocking rhymes with the forbidden "bad" words, words that had lost much of their magic by the late sixties. It would be an error to cite the parody of the Daniel Boone theme as no more than an example of the persistence of racist attitudes. To be sure, it was that. But its popularity also reflected a growing awareness on the part of children of certain aspects of racism. Children who use "nigger" as a thrill word are acknowledging its impropriety.

Some of the continuing popularity of "A fight, a fight,/A nigger [or "black"] and a white," may also be explained by the partial success of the civil-rights movement. First reported in use about 1910, this rhyme may at a somewhat earlier time have served to rally the white community when an actual fight between a black and a white took place. By 1910, however, it was employed to describe fights between white boys, giving their encounters some of the drama of a race war. In the in-

tegrated schools of the seventies this rhyme is once again sometimes a literal description, but more often than not it advertises
a fight in an all-white school between two white boys. It
glamorizes the incident—makes it seem as significant as something on the six o'clock news.

No doubt the best-known racist rhyme in the United States,
both in the past and today, is "Eeny, Meeny." Versions of this
counting-out rhyme go back to revolutionary times, but it was
not until the passage of the Fugitive Slave Law in 1850 that
the second line was changed to "Catch a nigger. . . ." One version advised, "Catch a nigger by the thumb/If he hollers, send
him hum"—i.e., home, back down South. Others proposed making the fugitive ransom himself: "Make him pay you fifty dollars," or, even more demanding: ". . . make him pay,/Twenty
dollars every day." The most popular version, however, said
simply that he should be let go when he hollered. Curiously,
too, most versions speak of catching the fugitive "by his toe"—
an unusual means of detaining a man. Charles Francis Potter
suggests that "by his toe" may be a child's folk translation of a
French-Canadian version of "Eeny, Meeny" that goes:

> Meeny, meeny, miney, mo,
> *Cache ton poing derrière ton dos*
> [Hide your fist behind your back].

As early as the 1880's, genteel mothers were encouraging
their children to substitute some other word for "nigger" in
"Eeny, Meeny." At first they had very limited success, but
slowly replacements like "lion," "tiger," "monkey," "rabbit,"
and "dummy" began to be accepted. During moments of national crisis, "Hitler," "Tojo," "Castro," and "the Viet Cong"
have appeared in the rhyme. Today "nigger" is still used, but
less often than numerous other words. White children we
talked to were well aware of the racist connotations of the word
and told us that they said "catch a tiger" or "catch a rabbit"
when they recited "Eeny, Meeny" in the presence of black
playmates. Some of them, however, when playing with an all-

white group sometimes use the traditional form of the verse. This does not necessarily indicate latent racism. Even today, when racial sensitivity is high, the formulaic quality of "Eeny, Meeny" sets it apart from ordinary language.

But the effort of mothers to purge their children's vocabularies should be given its due. Considering the poisonous racial attitudes that prevailed at the turn of the century, the gentility that made racist epithets taboo in many white, middle-class homes and that gradually made "nigger" taboo in the rhymes of many middle-class children was probably marginally beneficial. It did not prepare children actively to resist the attitudes of race hatred which they found in society at large, but it encouraged them to regard overt expressions of racism as vulgar and contemptible, and that was a step toward perceiving racism as wrong. The homage gentility pays to virtue may be hypocritical, but we have a scary way of sometimes becoming the persons we pretend to be.

Rhymes about Orientals

Rhymes and jokes about orientals are less common and less aggressive than those about blacks. The most popular ones make fun of the presumed stupidity, the smell, or the eating habits of the Chinese.

> Ching chong Chinaman
> Sittin' on a fence,
> Tryin' t' make a dollar out of fifteen cents.

> Ching chong Chinamen
> Eat dead rats.

> Ching chong Chinaman,
> Chop, chop, chop,
> Eatin' all the candy in the candy shop.

> Chink, Chink, you stink!

A guy goes into this Chinese restaurant and orders a Coke. He drinks it and says, "Hey, this Coke tastes funny."

And the waiter says, "Me Chinese, me play joke, me put pee-pee in your Coke."

There are fewer slurs about the Japanese. The only really popular one is:

"Do you like cheese?"
"Yes."
"You're a dirty Japanese."

Clearly the child is attracted by the sound, not the sense, of this exchange.

The sound "ese" rather than any racial antagonism is also behind the oriental references in this sex joke collected from a first-grader. The jokester pulls the corners of his eyes up and says, "Chinese." He pulls them down and says, "Japanese." He puts his hands on his knees and says, "American-knees." Then he pulls out his shirt at the chest and asks, "What are these?"

A primitive appreciation of inherited traits motivates the jokester in the following performance. He first slants his eyes upward as he says, "A Japanese"—now he slants his eyes down—"married a Chinese, and the baby they had looked like this." Now he slants one eye upward and the other down.

In a similar vein, Chinese children on Taiwan shout verses about the appearance and eating habits of Americans. Our rhymed version of one of their verses is based on a literal translation by David K. Jordan:

The American's nose is supersized.
It sticks out between two pale-blue eyes.
He likes to eat bread because it's white.
It follows that he likes to bite
Light-yellow corn, and since corn is round,

ONE POTATO, TWO POTATO...

> He likes to eat a great big mound
> Of wheatflower balls that are so slick—
> Of course, he loves a young boy's dick.

A variant ends with the American eating dog shit.

We don't know if Chinese children taunt each other with such rhymes or save them to shout at Americans. Certainly, if American children saved their anti-Chinese rhymes to shout at Chinese, the rhymes would soon be forgotten. What keeps them alive is that American children use them against one another.

Jewish Rhymes

Among the anti-Jewish rhymes from the first half of this century collected by Nathan Hurvitz are:

> Red, white, and blue,
> Your mother is a Jew,
> Your father is a Chinaman
> And so are you.

> In 1492,
> Your father was a Jew.
> He walked on the grass
> And fell on his ass,
> In 1492.

> One, two, you're a Jew.
> Three, four, your mother's a whore.

> The girls in France
> Wear tissue paper pants,
> And the things they do
> Is enough to kill a Jew.

However, not all references to Jews in playground rhymes during the first part of the century were hostile. In Cincinnati in 1927, children played a variant of the popular singing game sometimes known as Three Dukes or Three Kings in which they substituted Jews for the nobility. The players sang a song that announced a Jew had come "A-riding, riding, rid-

200

ing." He was asked why he had come and replied, "To get married." The girls offered themselves as brides but were rejected: "You're all too dirty and greasy." With democratic aplomb, they asserted, "We're just as good as you are," whereupon the Jew picked a bride and they marched off. The song was repeated until all had been chosen.

Dukes, ducks, kings, knights, and Jews all appeared in variants of this singing game. Their common denominator seems to be an attractive exoticness.

Rhymes tying Jews to labor strife and to President Franklin Delano Roosevelt were popular, but we suspect that they were repeated mainly by teen-agers and adults. They resemble children's rhymes but are unusually sophisticated in their subject matter—the labor movement and Roosevelt's political maneuvering. And they seem to us to have an aggrieved, almost whiny tone that isn't characteristic of children's rhymes.

> Heigh ho, heigh ho, we'll join the C.I.O.
> We'll pay our dues to the goddamn Jews
> Heigh ho, heigh ho.

> Franklin said to Eleanor,
> "Eleanor, how are you?"
> Eleanor said to Franklin,
> "I got some advice for you.
> Roses are red, violets are blue,
> You kiss the niggers,
> I'll kiss the Jews,
> And we'll stay in the White House
> As long as we choose."

We don't doubt that some sixth-graders recited these rhymes, but we imagine they were more at home with the straightforward aggressiveness of:

> Sheeny, sheeny, alley-picker,
> Your father was a Jew,
> And your mother was a nigger.

Aleph, beis, gimel, dollar,
Hit a nigger [or "Jew"], make him holler.

Jews sometimes responded with jeers of their own, for example, "Hocus, pocus, kiss my *tokus!*" a mixture of bogus Latin, English, and Yiddish. Also:

Shakespeare, a kick in the rear,
Merry *kratz-mine-tokus*
And a happy new year.

Another Jewish response was to add a different ending to "The girls in France/Wear tissue-paper pants." A Jewish boy would complete the rhyme by shouting:

And the things they do, *oy, oy,*
Is enough to kill a *goy.*

Jewish children also recited many other rhymes that were part of the Jewish branch of American childlore. Shockers and parodies were popular; "Ain't Gonna Rain No More" became:

A rabbi sat on the railroad tracks
[He was] saying his *brokus,*
Along came a choo-choo train
And knocked him in the *tokus.*

They might proclaim:

Holy Moses, King of the Jews
Wiped his ass on the *Daily News.*
The paper was thin
And what a fine mess the king was in.

Yankee Doodle went to town
A-riding on a *ferdl,*
Er fohrt arein in barber shop,
Un shert zich op dos berdl.

Jewish children jumped rope to versions of "Red, White, and Blue," for example:

Red, white, and blue,
Your mother is a Jew,
Your father is a curly head
And so are you.

The variant of "Red, White, and Blue" that includes "Your father is a Chinaman" was also used by Jewish children, as was:

Red, white, and blue,
The color of a Jew.

Hurvitz suggests that this may represent an effort of Jewish children to identify themselves as true Americans.

Today, anti-Jewish playground verses are far less popular than they once were, but the traditional stereotype has not disappeared. On many playgrounds, if you won't "give bites" of your candy bar, you are a "dirty Jew" or a "stingy Jew"; if you bargain, you are "jewing down" someone. Since all minorities "stink," we weren't surprised to collect, "P.U., you smell like a Jew." The old "Red, White, and Blue" may well still be in use in the United States, but the only version we collected is a counting-out rhyme popular among West Indian children living in the Canal Zone.

In 1970, the following was collected in Indiana:

There was an old lady lived in a shoe.
The dirty old Jew
Didn't know what to do.
Finally one day a man came to screw
And taught that old Jew what to do.

This rhyme is not popular or widespread, however. A very different, more light-hearted tone is found in the more generally known autograph rhyme:

Roses are red,
Violets are bluish,
It it weren't for Christmas,
We'd all be Jewish.

Polish Jokes

How does a Polack spell "farm"?
E-i-e-i-o.

Poles, Jews, and blacks are the most common victims in joke-lore, but jokes about Poles differ from those about Jews and blacks in two ways. First, while the stereotypes of the Jew and the black are relatively complex, the stereotype of the Pole is simple. Jews are supposed to be stingy, rich, sexually exotic, timid, pushy, overprotective of their children, loud, intelligent, unclean, and much more. Blacks are supposed to be stupid, dirty, flashy dressers, sexually aggressive, natural thieves, happy-go-lucky, rhythmically talented, easily frightened, fierce bogeymen, lazy, and so on. The Poles of jokelore are just poor, dirty, and stupid.

How do you get eight Polacks into a VW?
Throw in a penny.
How do you get them out?
Throw in a bar of soap.

How do you sink a Polack ship?
Put it in water.

How do you tell it's a Polack house?
The toilet paper is out to dry.

The second difference is that the act of telling a so-called "Polack" joke seems not to serve the same function as that of telling a joke about Jews or blacks. When non-Jewish, white grade-school children tell a joke about Jews or blacks, they are trying to assert the otherness and inferiority of these groups. But whom exactly is the speaker differentiating himself from when he tells what is known as a Polack joke? He is not, as a rule, thinking of actual Poles, although a similarity does exist between American Polack jokes and German jokes about Poles, and the latter are certainly directed at Poles as a nationality. For although in some parts of the United States, Poles form an identifiable group, in most of the country, they do not. Often, an American who tells a so-called Polack joke will substitute the name of some other nationality which seems to him to be lower class. In Texas, one may substitute the name of a group of college students who are obviously not lower class but whom it is traditional to tease for being "hicks." A fifth-grade Texan told us this one:

> How do you confuse an Aggie?
> Put him in a roundhouse and tell him to point to the corner.

Some students of jokelore believe that the ethnic joke reflects the joke-teller's aggressive attitude toward a nationality that he perceives as rising on the social scale. Others, however, assert that no American associates the Polack in Polack jokes with real people.

Certainly the children we talked to did not seem to associate Polacks with Poles. Though wary about telling us jokes about blacks or Jews, they eagerly volunteered Polack jokes. Possibly they took it for granted that we shared with them a prejudice against Poles; it is more likely, however, that school children believe no one will disapprove of jokes about an unreal person who is poor, dirty, and stupid—even his dogs are stupid.

> Why do Polack dogs have flat noses?
> From chasing parked cars.

There is, however, another dimension to some of the jokes of this type. Those jokes that focus on stupidity may be told as "little moron" jokes; indeed, some of them may have originated as jokes of this kind. The little moron is not lower class. He doesn't fit into any social scheme. His stupidity is a kind of craziness. He ignores the laws of nature:

> How does the little moron tie his shoe?
> [The joke-teller puts his left foot on a chair, then bends over to tie his right shoe.]

D'j'hear about the little morons who were building a house? One went to his boss and asked if they should build from the bottom up or the top down. The boss said, "The bottom up, dummy," and the little moron yelled to his friends, "Tear her down, boys; we got to start over."

Nor does he recognize the conventions of language:

Why'd the little moron cut a hole in the rug?
He wanted to see the floorshow.

He is a noodle, a numbskull, and is related to the trickster-fool discussed in the section on "Tricks and Wit" in Chapter 3. The trickster-fool is oblivious to all social convention or restraint:

Why did the little moron kill his mother and father?
He wanted to go to the orphans' picnic.

Even when a joke specifies Polacks or Aggies, the teller may have in the back of his mind the mythical fool whose failure to recognize the laws of nature, language, or society makes us feel superior because we do recognize them.

Political Rhymes

Political jeers are different from racial, ethnic, and religious jeers, but the difference is often overlooked.

Racial, ethnic, and religious jeers threaten the fabric of society by asserting the unworthiness of certain groups to participate fully in that society. Jeers of this kind are not about a conflict that can be settled by a vote or by compromise after an election.

Political jeers are popular only for a short period of time before and after an election. To some extent they cut across class, ethnic, racial, and religious lines. They represent institutionalized, limited conflict. And they are reassuring. Where there is no public political conflict, there is no politics.

Nevertheless, many educators view all conflict as bad. They are devoted to the "melting pot" theory of public education, which leads them to minimize or ignore differences between groups, to devitalize history, and to encourage a blind faith in the benevolence of authority from the President right down to the classroom teacher. Their goal is to create one nation, indivisible.

A child may indeed want to see authority figures as benevolent, since he is weak and they are strong. And certainly the public school should function as a "melting pot," uniting a nation that is "neither a land nor a race." But this sort of education can lead the child to grow up with the feeling that "most people" are just like he is. And this feeling, though comfortable, makes the world a harder place to understand.

The child's discovery during an election year that good friends know rhymes belittling the candidates his parents have praised is a revelation. He finds himself living in a much larger, less familiar world. He realizes that old friends have parents quite unlike his own and that inside the houses he walks by on his way home from school live people with outlandish beliefs who worship strange gods.

Political jeers can bring about educational experiences that are difficult to match in an orderly classroom. The lesson they teach varies from child to child, and there is no way to test an individual on what he's learned. Fundamentally, however, the lesson has to do with the discovery that other people really are "other," not just reflections of the child himself. Awareness of that fact encourages a healthy alienation, a distancing that reveals some of the multiple, overlapping allegiances that both divide us and bind us together.

City, county, even congressional elections fail to rouse excitement on the playground. It takes a presidential election campaign to do that. Ed Cray, who collected many of these campaign rhymes, refers to them as "quadrennial perennials."

Back in 1888, Republicans taunted Cleveland's supporters with, "Ma, Ma, where's my Pa?" alluding to Cleveland's illegitimate child. Defiant Democrats repeated the line but added, "Gone to the White House, ha, ha, ha."

ONE POTATO, TWO POTATO...

Cleveland really did have an illegitimate child, but whether a candidate did or not, it was popular to taunt him with:

> Shame, shame, oh what a shame!
> ———'s got a baby without any name.

Other late-nineteenth-century rhymes include:

> McKinley rides a white horse,
> Bryan rides a mule,
> McKinley is a gentleman,
> Bryan is a fool.

> McKinley's in the White House
> Kissing all the ladies,
> Bryan's in the backhouse
> Washing nigger babies.

From Franklin Delano Roosevelt's administration to the present, folklorists have kept closer track of what is said on the playground during an election year.

> Roosevelt's at the front door
> Talking to a lady,
> Landon's in the high chair
> Crying like a baby.

> Roosevelt's a Jew,
> Wallace is a thief,
> Put them in the White House,
> Then go on relief.

> Sixty needles and sixty pins,
> Sixty dirty Republikins.

> Sixty rats and sixty cats,
> Sixty dirty Democrats.

That rhyme echoes this much earlier one:

> Coffee and gingerbread hot from the pans,
> We'll serve to good Republicans,

Fried rats and pickled cats
Are good enough for Democrats.

Other Roosevelt rhymes were:

Roosevelt's in the White House
Waiting to be elected,
Dewey's in the garbage can,
Waiting to be collected.

Roosevelt, Roosevelt,
Sittin' on a fence,
Tryin' to teach Dewey
Plain ol' common sense.

Subsequent election years inspired:

I've always been a Democrat,
A Democrat I'll always be,
But I wish I was a dog
And Truman was a tree.

Whistle while you work,
Stevenson's a jerk.
Eisenhower has more power,
Whistle while you work.

Updated versions of "Roosevelt's in the White House" and
"Roosevelt, Roosevelt, Sittin' on a Fence" were shouted during
the Kennedy–Nixon campaign, as was this jump-rope rhyme:

Down in the valley where the green grass grows,
There sits Kennedy, sweet as a rose.
Along came Nixon and kissed him on the cheek,
How many kisses did he receive?
One, two, three, . . .

And in 1960, Nancy Leventhal collected

Two, four, six, eight,
Who do we appreciate?
Kennedy, Kennedy.

Why? Why?
He's going to die!
When? When?
Two P.M.
Where? Where?
In the electric chair!

More recently we have heard:

Goldwater, Goldwater, he's our man
He belongs in a garbage can.

Nixon yea! Wallace boo!
Humphrey is a dirty foo [Jew?].

Nixon, Nixon, he's our man
The hero of the nation
The only thing that's wrong with him
Is mental retardation!

The preceding quatrain was collected in 1974, not an election year, but one of unusual political excitement.

No one knows what happens to campaign rhymes between election years or how exactly they are resurrected. At least one—sung to the tune of "Tramp! Tramp! Tramp! The Boys Are Marching"—proved so popular that it didn't go away when the election was over. It eventually lost its political meaning, becoming a popular jump-rope rhyme that is recited by children who have no knowledge of its political antecedents:

Vote, vote, vote for *Billy Martin*
Chuck old *Earnie* out the door,
If it wasn't for the law,
I would punch him in the jaw,
And we won't have *Earnie* any more.
                    (London, 1916)

Intermediate stages are recorded in several places, including Abrahams' dictionary of jump-rope rhymes:

Vote for *Jane,*
Here comes *Betty* at the door,

> *Betty* is a lady and knows how to vote,
> So we won't need *Jane* any more.

Today, in many localities, it's simply:

> Pom, pom, pompadour,
> *Sally's* calling *Elly* to the door,
> *Elly* is the one who's going to have fun,
> So we don't need *Sally* any more!

ACCOMMODATION

Fartlore

This small category of jeers has been neglected by scholars. But there is every reason to believe that rhymes and sayings related to flatulence go back a good many years. The fart has been with us for some time, and it seems unlikely that children would let it pass without comment. In this respect they differ from folklorists, even those who have specialized in children's lore.

Sometimes, though, folklorists have recorded fartlore inadvertently. In 1889, the Reverend Walter Gregor presented a collection of counting-out rhymes from northeast Scotland to the Buchan Field Club. Included in his collection is:

> I think, I think,
> I fin a stink,
> It's comin' from y-o-u!

The child upon whom the "u" fell was beaten with bonnets until he cried "Peas!" This rhyme may have been used to count out, but its primary purpose was to identify and condemn the farter.

Though we can't cite much fartlore from the past, we know that children today have a repertoire of codified expressions related to farting. They sing traditional "consciousness-raising" songs on the subject. A first-grader wrote out the following song for his teacher as part of an assignment. Needless to say, she was expecting something else.

> Wayr is the groom
> hes in the dresen room
> wy is he thar
> he ript his unar wayir
> how did he do it
> he maed a fart and blue it.

The tune, of course, is the wedding march from *Lohengrin*. Another verse goes:

> Here comes the bride,
> All dressed in pink.
> Open the windows
> To let out the stink.

"Stink," by the way, doesn't always refer to a smell. "You stink" can mean "I don't like you," or "I disagree." When the following verse, which is clearly an example of fartlore, is used as a counting-out rhyme, "stink" means merely "you are out."

> Inka blinka, bottle of ink,
> Cork fell out, and you stink.

"Excuse me, *but!*" is said by a child who is butting into a line—or by one who has just farted. Other announcements are less ambiguous.

> Going down the highway
> A hundred and fifty-four.
> I cut a super gas
> That blew me out the door.
> The wheels couldn't take it,
> The engine fell apart,
> All because of my
> Supersonic fart!

"The Caisson Song" surfaces as:

> G.I. Joe, G.I. Joe,
> Accidentally let one go
> And he blew all
> The Germans away!

Then there are:

> Ten, twenty, thirty, forty, fifty, or more,
> Snoopy let a fart in the grocery store,
> And Lucy tried to hold her breath.
> Snoopy let another one
> And killed all the rest.

> Fat and Skinny went to bed.
> Fat let a fart and Skinny fell dead.
> Fat called the doc; the doc said,
> "Any more of this and we'll all be dead."

At Christmas time, among the parodic versions of carols that are heard on the playground is:

> God rest you merry gentlemen,
> And rest ye merry heart,
> Feen-a-mints are just the thing
> They'll surely make you fart.
>   (Rhode Island, 1964)

The child who sings this rhyme is daring and bold. He has said the word "fart" and thus defied a mild verbal taboo. But in defying the verbal taboo he has reminded himself of the more important taboo against actually farting. A verse that is more widely known is

> The Addams family started
> When Uncle Fester [or "Henry"] farted.
> I think they're all retarded,
> ["They all came out retarded,"]
> The Addams fam-il-y. [Two farting noises follow.]

213

ONE POTATO, TWO POTATO...

This is sung to the tune of the theme of "The Addams Family," a popular children's television show. Sometimes it is followed by a second stanza:

> The mother is a German,
> The father is a spy,
> And I'm the little stinker
> That called the F.B.I.
> That's the Addams fam-il-y. [Two farting noises follow.]

When a child "cuts one" or "lets one," his friends may chant:

> *Suzie* is a nut,
> She has a rubber butt,
> And every time she turns around
> She goes putt-putt.

> *Linda* is a dope,
> She ate a bar of soap,
> Bubbles here, bubbles there,
> Bubbles in her underwear.

> You look like a pig,
> You smell like one, too.
> My mommy told me not to play
> With someone like you.

Or the farter's friends may shout one-liners: "Pink, pink, you stink!" "Dead birds!" "Tweetie on wood!" "You may think you're a big cheese, but you only smell like one!" Some children, reflecting the current problems of the adult world, send up the alarm "Air pollution!"

The farter may apologize by making his offense into a joke. Raising his hands as if gripping high handle bars, he turns his wrists and stamps on the ground with one foot. "What are you doing?"

"Just starting my motorcycle."

Only the uninitiated fail to flee at once. From a safe distance, his friends can jeer, "Smell it, tell it, go downtown and sell it!"

On the other hand, some verses brazenly celebrate the occasion:

> Beans, beans are good for your heart.
> The more you eat, the more you fart.
> The more you fart, the better you feel,
> So eat beans for every meal.

This has variants:

> Beans, beans are a musical fruit.
> The more you eat, the more you toot.
> The more you toot, the better you feel,
> So eat beans for every meal.

Fartlore also includes superstitions and folk wisdom. Some children call out, "Light a match, quick!" when they smell a fart, believing that the flame will purify the air. Others shout, "Knock on wood!" The last one to do so is said to eat the fart. When a person in a group announces, "Somebody let one," and looks around accusingly, the guilty party may respond with the old saying, "The one who smelt it, dealt it," and be believed because everyone knows that the best way to keep from being accused of farting is to accuse someone else first.

In the late nineteenth and early twentieth centuries, children shouted the following rhyme, whose meaning is not entirely clear to us:

> Jane, Jane, had a machine [pronounced "machane"],
> Jo, Jo, made it go.
> Frank, Frank, turned the crank,
> His mother came out and gave him a spank,
> And sent him over the garden bank.

This rhyme as a whole is apparently forgotten today, but we did pick up two variants in the seventies:

215

Jean, Jean, had a machine,
Jo, Jo, made it go.
Art, Art, let a fart,
And blew the whole thing apart.

Mark, Mark, let a fart,
And his butt fell apart.

These sayings, rhymes, and jokes illustrate the way children's folklore meets needs that are not officially recognized by the school or by adult society. In our culture, farting is a social *faux pas* of the highest order—so serious that when it occurs we have nothing appropriate to say. For polite adults, it is beyond language. But what adults endure in silence, children forcefully condemn.

Roses are red,
Violets are blue.
If skunks had a college,
They'd name it for you. P.U.

The child who farts is almost always the butt of a jeer; thus he is reminded of a cultural prohibition. At the same time, the formulaic nature of these jeers testifies to the frequency and the ordinariness of the situation, and thereby reduces embarrassment to manageable proportions. Moreover, the existence of songs like "Beans, Beans," which are often sung by several children in unison, acknowledges that the problem is sometimes uncontrollable. Indeed, occasional mass flatulence among sixth-graders is one of the unheralded occupational hazards that their teachers must face.

Kissing Games

"Kiss" is a powerful word on the playground. Plenty of jeers attest to the mixture of fascination and horror the idea of kissing has for children: "Missed me, missed me, now you got to kiss me!" "Georgie Porgie puddin' and pie, kissed the girls and made them cry!" "Yellow, yellow—go kiss a fellow!"

"*Lucy* and *Eddy,* sitting in a tree, k-i-s-s-i-n-g!" Those who shout these jeers are not, of course, thinking of the kisses they exchange with Mommy or Daddy. They have in mind another kind of kissing altogether—the kind that marks a significant step in the child's gradual declaration of independence from his family.

Some children are natural-born friendly kissers. Such children soon realize that kissing will impress and intimidate their less kissy peers. Sometimes a pair of friendly kissers puts on a show for the peasants. We knew two third graders who used to walk home for lunch together. When they came to the parting of the ways, they would kiss—right out there in front of God and everybody. They were going to be married, they said. It gave them terrific prestige. But in fourth grade, though they still often walked home with each other, they called off the show. Kissing had become a more complicated matter.

When children begin to toy with the idea of erotic kissing, they rely on childlore to provide them with laboratory conditions, so to speak, where they can perform some safe, traditional experiments before going out to do field work.

Kissing games are most popular in junior high, where almost everyone plays them. In grade school, children know fewer of these games and are less likely to have played them. But the number of sixth-graders who have participated in kissing games is not insignificant. Usually, the majority of the class have done so.

Grade-school kissing games include Truth or Dare, Tag Kiss, Post Office, Choo-choo, and Spin the Bottle.

TRUTH OR DARE: The leader requests a player to choose between the alternatives, and goes on to ask the question or set the dare, which may be something like, "Kiss *Esther* on the ear."

TAG KISS: The boys chase the girls; then the girls chase the boys. In the version we have seen, a boy catches a girl and kisses her. The two of them are supposed to wait on the sidelines until all the other girls have been caught. But usually, when most of the girls have been caught, the roles are suddenly reversed without any specific signal, and the girls chase the boys.

POST OFFICE: The rules vary. Often there is a postmaster, who starts by telling a girl that there is a letter for her with a specified number of stamps—i.e., kisses—on it in the next room (where a boy is waiting). Soon the boy comes out, while the girl stays in the room. The postmaster consults with the girl, then tells a second boy that he has mail waiting for him, and so on.

CHOO-CHOO or PONY EXPRESS: The game is started by a girl and a boy imitating a train. The first person is the engine; the second puts his or her hands on the engine's hips. They choo-choo off to another part of the house. When they stop, the leader kisses the second person. On the next trip, the train picks up another "car." Soon the train includes everyone. Kisses—sometimes slaps, too—are passed back each time it stops. The order in which the "cars" are attached is not prescribed by the game but neither is it entirely voluntary. It is not good form to be choosy. Often the person nearest the train when it stops is expected to join it.

SPIN THE BOTTLE: The players sit in a circle. A player in the center spins a bottle or a flashlight and must kiss the person it points to when it stops spinning. The person who is kissed then moves to the center of the circle.

Grade-schoolers also report Rum and Coke, Slap-Kiss-Hug, and Pass or Fail, but these seem to be mainly junior-high games. Sixth-graders who go to seventh- or eighth-grade parties play them and carry marvelous stories about them to their friends.

Rum and Coke is a dance game. Everybody dances until a leader calls out "Rum!" Then partners must kiss each other, until he says "Coke!" Then everybody switches partners. In Slap-Kiss-Hug, a player is blindfolded. The leader asks, "Who would you like to do this to?" while holding two fingers on

218

his cheek (the sign for a slap) or over his lips (the sign for a kiss) or on his shoulder (the sign for a hug). When an answer has been given, he asks the question twice more, using the other two signs. The blindfold is then removed, and the victim must slap, kiss, and hug the people he specified. In Pass or Fail, there is less game and more kissing. The boys line up, and one by one, the girls go down the line, kissing the boys. A boy says "Pass" or "Fail" after each kiss. "If they like you, they tell you you've failed," a girl remarked.

Traditional kissing games protect a child in several ways. Some—such as Spin the Bottle, Choo-choo, and the versions of Post Office that require the player to choose a number instead of a name when he is consulted by the postmaster—excuse a child from selecting a partner (a most onerous task for younger children) and eliminate the possibility of being deliberately left out. The psychologist Brian Sutton-Smith observes that as played today Post Office is often a game of chance, differing in this respect from older versions that required a specific choice. This change may indicate that younger children, who want some protection from the perils of choosing, are now playing kissing games.

Also, the public or semipublic nature of these games excuses players from kissing "like they do in the movies." And the game atmosphere masks the occasional rejection of a partner. In Post Office, for example, a tricky girl may "stamp" a boy on his toes instead of on his lips, thus turning a kissing game into an ambush game.

Like games, local customs sometimes legitimize kissing. In the Canal Zone, and perhaps also elsewhere, if a boy takes a girl to a movie and the numbers of their tickets total twenty-one, he gets to kiss her. Grade-school boys know about this practice but don't look forward to it. They tell us that the boy "will *have* to kiss her," as if it were a penalty.

Among older children, customs like kissing if the numbers on the movie tickets add up to twenty-one, or every time the performers in the movie kiss, or every time a car with one light goes by, lead to increasingly informal kissing and to personal commitments, which is as it should be. Traditional kissing games aren't meant to keep a person out of deep water forever—only to provide a shallow end where children can get their feet wet.

Special Days

Children have little or nothing to say about how most of the well-known holidays are celebrated. They are in complete charge, however, of certain special days invented by themselves and generally unknown to adults.

Christmas and Easter are full of folk customs—hanging stockings, decorating the tree, buying new clothes, hunting eggs—but adults decide which of these customs will be observed. Adults are also in charge of Thanksgiving. The celebration may involve traditional family recipes, but will include little that can be called children's lore. Wishing on the wishbone, maybe. In like manner, a family may associate private traditions with Mother's Day or Father's Day, but these holidays have no traditional links with childlore.

Similar observations can be made about most of the other holidays marked on the calendar. Children do have the tradition of setting off fireworks on the Fourth of July, but this custom has been curtailed in recent years, and rightly so. May Day has become Law Day or Loyalty Day. Thus do we counter the Communists, who parade on May 1 and claim it as their special day. Little is left of the old pagan celebration of the returning spring. No budding boys and girls get up at dawn to go and bring in the May. Our last report of real May baskets being left on a little girl's front porch was from Lansing, Kansas, in 1940. Valentines' Day, with the assistance of the greeting-card industry, has survived a little better. In many grade schools exchanging valentines is still an important event. Compassionate teachers arrange things so that every child will get a few, for children covet them shamelessly and compare the sizes of their stacks.

Halloween is still celebrated after a fashion, helped along by costume manufacturers and pumpkin farmers, but it's not the holiday it once was. In some neighborhoods, adults have tried to transform it into an occasion for children to collect money for UNICEF. But Halloween was changing long before the UNICEF people got hold of it.

Earlier in this century, Halloweeners were mainly boys who disguised themselves to conceal their identities while they played tricks on adults, removing from a house, for instance, the front-porch steps, a length of guttering, or the screen or storm doors—all in near silence. Gregory P. Stone has pointed out that tricks like these required foresight, skill, and diligence. The destructive tricks played by contemporary Halloweeners—slashing tires, egging houses, breaking windows, burning leaves—are accomplished as easily as they are conceived.

But most contemporary Halloweeners are not interested in tricks of any kind. They want loot. They show up at the houses of strangers dressed as traditional goblins and witches but also as Bugs Bunny or Carol Burnett. Their costumes are meant not to disguise them but to be admired.

They come to beg—well, actually to collect, since they believe they have a right to what the householder gives them. In pagan times, people offered food to the dead on Halloween. Later, people doled out soulcakes to anyone who came by, but mainly to the poor. Today, we give candy to the well fed, who arrive with shopping bags. These bagmen are accompanied by their parents, who protect them from marauders who might make off with the loot. The adults also inspect the goodies. Tales of razor blades in apples and of drugs in soft candy have become part of the folklore of every neighborhood.

The old-time Halloween trickster lived in a small town or in a well-defined neighborhood and had a certain intimacy with his victim. To some degree, this familiarity must have regulated the behavior of them both. In today's more anonymous neighborhoods there is good reason for adults to try to eliminate entirely the destructive aspects of Halloween. However, our substitute for the traditional tricks may not, at first glance, seem much of an improvement, being a celebration of gluttony.

But a begging holiday appears somehow appropriate for big cities. It gives children license to approach strangers and reminds people that they live in a neighborhood, even if they don't spend much time there. The modern Halloween has absorbed an earlier New York City custom of begging on Thanksgiving. The playwright William Gibson has recalled how in the early twenties boys and girls traded clothes, put them on backward, blackened their faces with burnt cork, and went out to sing to the neighbors on Thanksgiving. After each song, they called, "Anything for Thanksgiving, Mister?" and neighbors would give them fruit and candy; from apartment houses, people would throw down pennies wrapped in twists of newspaper.

A shadow of the old trickster's Halloween remains alive today in the ritual demand, "Trick or treat." But many children don't even understand what they are threatening. They think the phrase means, "Trick *for* treat," and that if asked they must do a jig or something else to pay for their candy. Usually, they aren't asked. They show off their costumes, collect their loot, and march off to the next house, occasionally punctuating the night with the Halloween rhyme:

> Trick for treat,
> Smell my feet,
> Give me something good to eat!

April Fools' Day is in a much lower key than Halloween. Both children and adults still celebrate it, but casually. The traditional tricks—salt in the sugar bowl, "Your shoelace is untied," and so on, each followed by a derisive "April Fool!" are still played. And in some schoolyards one may still hear:

> April Fool, go to school,
> Tell your teacher she's a fool.
> If she slaps you, don't you cry.
> Take your books and say, "Good-by!"

Adults and children also cooperate, somewhat less casually, to celebrate birthdays. Adults give the traditional spankings, preside over the blowing out of the candles, and lead the birthday song. But not all children repeat the official verses; instead, some of them sing:

> Happy birthday to you,
> You belong in a zoo!
> You look like a monkey,
> And you smell like one, too!

Most party games, like Pin the Tail on the Donkey or Musical Chairs, are imposed on children by adults, but some—Murder, or Killer, for example—are partly kept alive by the children themselves. In Murder, one player is secretly designated the murderer (perhaps by being the one to choose the queen of spades, or whatever card has been decided on, from a pile of cards). The players all sit in a circle, staring at one another. When the murderer winks at somebody, that person announces, "I'm dead." The "murders" continue, and the remaining members of the group try to identify the murderer before they too are wiped out. (There is also a kissing game called Murder. A girl is kissed. The detective enters and tries to deduce the perpetrator.)

Only a few special days are completely free of adult influence. Toesday is one of them. On any Tuesday, a child may shout, "It's Toesday!" and everyone, at once, is on guard. All day long, children try to stamp on each other's toes. At places of special danger, like bus stops, children who are celebrating Toesday protect themselves by walking around on their heels, with their toes in the air.

Weddingsday is another children's holiday. On such a

223

ONE POTATO, TWO POTATO...

Wednesday, if a boy touches a girl, it's a sign they will marry. A touch may lead to a mock wedding, usually at a bus stop. In some schools, if you wear white on Weddingsday, you are proof against the prophetic touch.

Queersday, on Thursday, is probably more widely celebrated than Toesday or Weddingsday. If you wear yellow to school on Queersday, you are "queer." In some schools, the incriminating color is green. Children know that to be queer is bad, but many of them understand the word only literally; months or even years may go by before they learn its connotations for adults.

Dress Up day isn't as popular at present as it was in the late sixties. It was not a day when the children dressed up; rather, it was a day when the boys pulled the girls' dresses up. In schools where it was a regular feature, girls were always prepared. They knew of the boys' plans and came to school wearing shorts under their dresses.

Monday and Friday apparently don't need any dressing up. On Monday, a child meets the friends he hasn't seen all weekend; on Friday, he is released from "prison."

The day the children are released for summer vacation is the greatest of all their special days. They cry:

> School's out! School's out!
> Teacher let the monkeys out!

and

> No more pencils, no more books!
> No more teacher's dirty looks!

And the shout of some daring child rises above the others:

> School's out! School's out!
> Teacher let the fools out!
> One went east, one went west,
> One went up the teacher's dress!

Underground Games and Traditional Toys

In 1975, the members of a Seattle play group were spending a good deal of time making, playing with, and trading toy hydroplanes. The boys took apart the two-piece, clip-type clothespins and glued together three of the pieces to form an abstract model of a hydroplane.

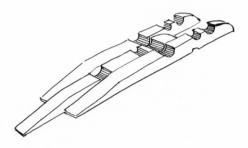

Some of their models were whittled a bit and painted—gussied up more realistically.

But this activity was unusual. As a rule, children don't much occupy themselves with homemade toys these days—except in the classroom, where playthings of any kind have always been forbidden, and if discovered, confiscated. The classroom is no place for expensive, store-bought toys, but it is just the place for readily abandoned, traditional ones.

One of the most popular classroom toys is a fat, triangular

225

football that the boys make by folding a piece of notebook paper. It looks like this—actual size:

They flick it with their fingers, back and forth across a desk or table—sometimes from one table to another. If it comes to rest hanging over the edge of the table, that's a touchdown. If a boy calls for a field-goal attempt, his opponent makes goal posts by placing the tips of his index fingers together and raising his thumbs.

You have to hold the folded football on end with one hand and "kick" it with the index finger of the other in order to get it aloft.

Knowing how to fold paper is important. Boys fold paper into footballs. Girls fold the pages of their autograph books. Boys fold paper into airplanes and into balloons that they can pop between their palms. Girls fold notes. Note-folding is an art in which form is far more important than content. Here are five popular patterns:

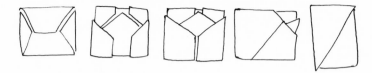

Girls also fold a thingamajig that foretells the future and a love charm. These are described in the section on "Cartomancy, . . ." in Chapter 5. And both boys and girls fold paper into something that can be considered a hat or a boat, whatever you want to call it, mostly for the fun of making it.

Other underground toys are soda-straw blowguns for spitballs, slingshots made from two fingers and a rubber band for paper wads and bobby pins, and rockets made from the silver paper that is wrapped around a stick of gum. To make a rocket, you place your finger tip so that it reaches halfway up the paper, wrap the paper around the finger tip, and twist the top into a point. Then you place the rocket on the hole formed by your fist. You blast off by smacking the palm of

your other hand against the bottom of your fist. The higher your missile goes when the teacher's back is turned, the higher your prestige in the community. A student who is not daring enough to send up rockets may draw eyes and eyebrows on his hand to make a puppet. Using his other hand, he can cause his puppet to stick out its tongue at someone.

ONE POTATO, TWO POTATO...

Not all underground amusements, however, involve special toys. In a typical class, while the teacher is explaining about the Erie Canal, all sorts of games are in progress. The whole class may be playing Cooties. Here two boys are having a formal pencil fight. One boy holds up his pencil; the other tries to break it with his pencil. He only gets one try. If he is unsuccessful, he has to hold up his pencil as the target. Two other boys are surreptitiously playing ticktacktoe. Over there, two girls are playing the more popular dot game. Each girl in turn draws a line between two dots. The one who

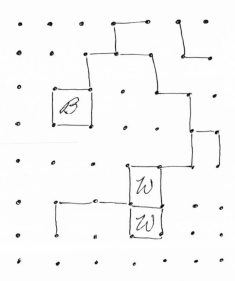

closes a square initials it and takes another turn. The person with the most initialed squares at the end of the game has won.

In the back row, students are showing each other visual riddles, like this one:

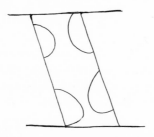

It's either a giraffe passing a window or a bear climbing a tree. At another desk a boy is playing string games in his lap, making a teacup or a Jacob's ladder. A girl staring intently at her open book is trying to figure out the old puzzle that looks like this:

Another version looks like this:

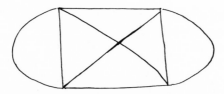

The idea is to try to draw a single line that crosses every line on the figure without crossing any line twice. Meanwhile, two boys have started a slow-motion race to the pencil sharpener, each trying to go fast enough to win but not fast enough to distract the teacher from her concern with the Erie Canal.

Soon, however, the students will be trying to distract her —playing the old game of making noises to drive the teacher crazy. A child will begin clicking his ball-point pen, but will not continue long enough to be identified. Another will twang a bobby pin against the bottom of a desk. A real folk artist will bring forth wonderful noises, using only his own body. He may crack his knuckles, make a popping sound with one finger in his mouth, belch at will, or whistle between two fingers. Children who have such skills are extravagantly admired.

Not all popular folk toys are used in the classroom. Girls still put together clover chains, and they split dandelion stems to make useless but appealing ornaments that look like this:

Boys still construct parachutes out of a handkerchief and a rock, though the prevalence of Kleenex has resulted in this toy's becoming almost obsolete. Tricksters make a kind of jack-in-the-box from a button, a bobby pin, and a rubber band. They seal the contraption in an envelope which they ask an unwary victim to open.

Coins are also popular toys. They are used, among other things, for table soccer, which can be played at home or in the lunchroom at school. You put three coins in a pyramid in the middle of the table—like racked billiard balls. Flick the top coin to start the game. Each time, you must flick one coin between the other two as you move toward your opponent's end of the table. If your coin fails to pass between the other two, you lose your turn. If it hits one of the other coins, you lose your turn. If your coin stops so that all three coins are lined up, you stand the center coin on edge and spin it. If at the end of the spin it has passed between the other two coins, you keep your turn. When you are in position to try for a goal, your opponent must create it by making the old horns sign with his fist (raising his index finger and his pinky) and placing his knuckles against the edge of the table.

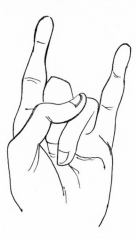

There is no way that toy manufacturers can produce a game that will outshine the folk version of table soccer. Nothing has to be lugged out of the closet; there are no pieces to lose; and you can always pick up the game and go buy an ice-cream cone if it gets boring.

NOTES

RESISTANCE

Parodies

William R. Bascom discusses "Four Functions of Folklore" in *The Study of Folklore,* edited by Alan Dundes (Englewood Cliffs,

ONE POTATO, TWO POTATO...

N.J.: Prentice-Hall, 1965), pp. 279–89, and quotes R. S. Rattray on Ashanti customs, p. 290. Daniel J. Dieterich discusses children's "global" distrust of commercials in "Public Doublespeak: Teaching About Language in the Marketplace," *College English*, 36 (1974), 478–79. The indignation of seven- to ten-year-olds about advertising is assessed by T. G. Bever, M. L. Smith, B. Bengen, and T. G. Johnson in "Young Viewers' Troubling Response to TV Ads," *Harvard Business Review*, 53 (Nov. 1975), 109–20. John R. Krueger cites "My Country's Tired of Me" in "Parodies in the Folklore of a Third-Grader," *Southern Folklore Quarterly*, 32 (1968), 66–68; and George Monteiro looks at "Parodies of Scripture, Prayer, and Hymn" in *Journal of American Folklore*, 77 (1964), 45–52. Comments on religious parody in the Middle Ages are in George Kitchin, *A Survey of Burlesque and Parody in English* (London: Oliver, 1931), pp. 2–3. For "Ta-Ra-Ra-Boom-De-Re" see David Ewen, *American Popular Songs* (New York: Random House, 1966), p. 386.

Shockers

William Allen White's reference to dirty-minded Kansas boys is from *The Autobiography* (New York: Macmillan, 1946), p. 45. The 1910 gutter/butter rhyme is in Iona and Peter Opie, *The Lore and Language of Schoolchildren* (Oxford: Clarendon Press, 1959), p. 10.

REFLECTIONS

Prejudice: Blacks

"Penny, Come Penny" is No. 817 in Henry Carrington Bolton, *The Counting-Out Rhymes of Children* (1888; reprint ed., Detroit: Singing Tree Press, 1969). His remark about "Gracious Peter!" is on p. 25. The next four rhymes are from Bolton (Nos. 696, 733, 741, 777); and from Emelyn E. Gardner, "Some Counting-Out Rhymes in Michigan," *Journal of American Folklore*, 31 (1918), 532. "Nigger-shooters" and other expressions are recorded in Kenneth Porter, "Racism in Children's Rhymes and Sayings, Central Kansas, 1910–1918," *Western Folklore*, 24 (1965), 191–96; and in William Allen White's *Autobiography*, p. 73. The "Grease!" superstition is from Frederick Starr, "A Page of Childlore," *Journal of American Folklore*, 4 (1891), 55–56. The watermelon riddle is in Ruth Ann Musick and Vance Randolph, "Children's Rhymes from Missouri," *Journal of American Folklore*, 63 (1950), 433. New York versions of "Run, Nigger" and "Nig-

ger, Nigger, Never Die" are in Anna K. Stimson, "Cries of
Defiance and Derision, and Rhythmic Chants of West Side New
York City, 1893–1903," *Journal of American Folklore*, 58 (1945),
124–29. The Tennessee rhyme is in James Agee, *A Death in the
Family* (New York: McDowell, Obolensky, 1957), p. 217. The
rhymes from North Carolina are in *The Frank C. Brown Collection of North Carolina Folklore*, 7 vols. (Durham: Duke University Press, 1952), Vol. I, pp. 179, 204. See also Gardner, p. 534.
Versions of "Teacher, Teacher" are in *Brown*, p. 195; Bolton (No.
735); and Porter, p. 194. School cheers using "nigger" are in
Ray B. Browne, "Children's Taunts, Teases, and Disrespectful
Sayings from Southern California," *Western Folklore*, 13 (1954),
197. In "Racism in Children's Rhymes and Sayings . . ." Porter
also discusses "Arty Smarty," p. 194, and cites an incident in which
one child criticized another for using "nigger," p. 191. The jump-
rope chant about Negroes going to Harvard is in Roger D.
Abrahams, *Jump-Rope Rhymes: A Dictionary* (Austin: University of Texas Press, 1969). Clarence Major defines "skins" in
Dictionary of Afro-American Slang (New York: International
Publishers, 1970). The origin of "A Fight, a Fight" is discussed
by Porter, p. 195. And the history of "Eeny, Meeny" is recounted
by Charles Francis Potter in *Funk & Wagnalls Standard Dictionary of Folklore, Mythology and Legend*, 2 vols. (New York: Funk
& Wagnalls, 1949), Vol. I.

Rhymes about Orientals

The Taiwanese verses are discussed by David K. Jordan, "Anti-
American Children's Verses from Taiwan," *Western Folklore*, 32
(1973), 205–209.

Jewish Rhymes

Nathan Hurvitz's article, "Jews and Jewishness in the Street
Rhymes of American Children," *Jewish Social Studies*, 16 (1954),
135–50, is the best source of Jewish rhymes in childlore. Inter-
esting variations are found in Emelyn E. Gardner, "Some Count-
ing-Out Rhymes in Michigan," pp. 534–35. The "Three Jews"
variant of Three Dukes is in Jean Olive Heck, "Folk Poetry and
Folk Criticism," *Journal of American Folklore*, 40 (1927), 8.
Hurvitz also includes some childlore in "Blacks and Jews in
American Folklore," *Western Folklore*, 33 (1974), 301–25.
"There Was an Old Lady" is from the archives of the Folklore
Institute of Indiana University.

233

Polish Jokes

Alan Dundes discusses the function of ethnic slurs in "A Study of Ethnic Slurs: The Jew and the Polack in the United States," *Journal of American Folklore*, 84 (1971), 186–203, as does Andrea Greenberg, "Form and Function of the Ethnic Joke," *Keystone Folklore Quarterly*, 17 (1972), 144–61.

Political Rhymes

". . . neither a land nor a race" is quoted from "American Letter," by Archibald MacLeish, *Collected Poems 1917–1952* (Boston: Houghton Mifflin, 1952), p. 65. "Shame, Shame" and "McKinley Rides a White Horse" are from B. A. Botkin, *A Treasury of New England Folklore* (New York: Crown, 1947), p. 911. "McKinley's in the White House" and "Roosevelt's a Jew" are from Ed Cray, "The Quadrennial Perennials," *Western Folklore*, 23 (1964), 199–201. The rhyme about pins and Republicans is in Carl Withers, *A Rocket in My Pocket* (New York: Holt, Rinehart and Winston, 1948), p. 192. "Coffee and Gingerbread" is in Botkin, p. 911. Versions of several of the remaining rhymes are in Cray's article and in the Opies' *The Lore and Language of Schoolchildren*, pp. 348–49. "Down in the Valley" was collected by Martin Light, "Politics in a Jump Rope Rhyme," *Journal of American Folklore*, 76 (1963), 133. "Two, Four, Six, Eight" is in Cray's article, p. 200. The Billy Martin rhyme is in Norman Douglas, *London Street Games* (1916; reprint ed., London: Johnson Reprint, 1969), p. 32.

ACCOMMODATION

Fartlore

A little fartlore is scattered through the journals, but the genre is largely unexplored. The rhyme collected by Walter Gregor is in *Counting-Out Rhymes of Children* (1891; reprint ed., Darby, Pa.: Norwood Editions, 1973), p. 32. The Feen-a-mint rhyme is in George Monteiro, "Parodies of Scripture, Prayer, and Hymn," p. 50. "Jane, Jane" is No. 792 in Bolton, *The Counting-Out Rhymes of Children*.

Kissing Games

Different kinds of kissing games are discussed in Brian Sutton-Smith, "The Kissing Games of Adolescents in Ohio," *The Folkgames of Children* (Austin: University of Texas Press, 1972), pp. 465–90.

Coping with the Here and Now

Special-Days

Earlier and more recent Halloweens are compared in Gregory P. Stone, "Halloween and the Mass Child," in *The American Culture,* edited by Hennig Cohen (Boston: Houghton Mifflin, 1968), pp. 257–65. A history of Halloween and interviews with contemporary Halloweeners are in Catherine Harris Ainsworth, "Halloween," *New York Folklore Quarterly,* 29 (1973), 163–93. William Gibson's recollection is in *A Mass for the Dead* (New York: Atheneum, 1968), p. 70.

5 | Coping with the Unknown

Superstitions

Superstitions function in confusing and complicated ways in the lives of both children and adults. A person may literally believe that a black cat brings bad luck, that a rabbit's foot or a particular shirt brings good luck, or that certain days are lucky for him. Certainly many children have such beliefs and sometimes this superstitious faith is dangerous. Kenneth Pease and Barbara Preston, at the University of Manchester, discovered that British children of ages five through eight were using a safety jingle taught them at school as a charm. The jingle warned them to look left and right before crossing a street. They were reciting it before crossing, as instructed, sometimes even turning their heads, but they weren't looking. They were depending on the rhyme to insure their safety.

On the other hand, many children regard superstitions with varying degrees of detachment and disbelief. A youngster who insists that breaking a mirror will bring seven years of bad luck will, a minute or two after breaking one, be playing happily, apparently unconcerned about the effects of his mishap. The idea that there are laws governing luck and the future is satisfying to children, but at the same time, all that

stuff about breaking mirrors is felt to be just superstition when
it comes down to a particular case.

Some children take a rather scientific view of superstitions.
As parents and teachers, we would like to make things easy
for our children, to give them all the answers to all the questions that life poses. But evidently there is something so en-
joyable about discovering things for one's self that a child
who really believes his parents' assertion that there is no such
thing as a ghost will repress his faith in their reliability in
order to see for himself if doing the goose step will bring
Hitler's ghost to haunt him, as all the kids say it will. His
refusal to accept the results of his parents' experience and
wisdom without checking for himself is unquestionably ineffi-
cient, perhaps ungrateful, but it is very scientific.

And both children and adults cling to superstitions for
reasons that have nothing at all to do with belief. The superstition that you should hold your breath while passing a cemetery is really more of a game than a belief, especially if there
are two children in the car. Each tries to outlast the other.
"Step on a crack, break your mother's back,/Step in a hole,
break your mother's sugar bowl" is also the basis of a game.
Girls play it as they walk home from school. They link arms,
and marching and swaying, try to avoid cracks and holes as
they recite the rhyme.

Superstitions serve as passwords, too. Nobody learns superstitions from the official curriculum, so if we share a superstition with someone, we know that we also share, to some
extent, an unofficial past.

And superstitions may serve as private rituals. We know of
one middle-aged man who when he sees the first star of evening never fails to recite a version of "Twinkle, Twinkle,
Little Star" that ends, "I wish I may, I wish I might,/I wish
this wish on you tonight." He is not superstitious, but the
rhyme comforts him, gives some continuity to his life. He
says that he repeats it because he's always done so.

Many of us use superstitions to mock our rationalistic pretensions. We knock on wood or cross our fingers while waiting for a computer print-out, not because we think such gestures will effectively influence the "outcome of our input," but to acknowledge to ourselves and others our own fallibility.

Often, the superstitions that are taken most seriously by children are not the traditional ones, but personal inventions. "I used to test myself all the time," one child told us. "If I could take my dad's coffee to the table without spilling any in the saucer, that meant something. If I could finish reading a page before the song on the radio was over, that meant something, too." A boy said, "I used to spit all the way home from school. If I hit a crack, that was good luck for the next day. That was my only *true* superstition." Another boy told us, "I used to be afraid to turn over in my bed in the morning. I thought the room was full of ghosts or something. But they couldn't get me as long as I didn't move. Finally, I'd jump out real fast, before they could close in. I always beat them, but sometimes I'd wait a long time to catch them off guard."

But traditional superstitions still play a sizable role in children's lives. The following list is the merest sample, and we have not included superstitions based on local plants or geographic features. Like Huck Finn, children today know cures and weather lore as well as signs of good and bad luck. Indeed, many of the neatly dressed children who were entering projects in "science fairs" proved to have a great deal more in common with Huck Finn than we had anticipated.

Good Luck

1. If you see a red truck, say, "Red truck, good luck."
2. A penny minted the year you were born is good luck.
3. For good luck, keep a penny in your shoe.
4. If you find a penny on the street, that's good luck.
5. If you find a praying mantis, that's good luck.

6. A four-leaf clover is good luck.
7. Seeing a rainbow is good luck.
8. Seven is a lucky number.
9. Put the front of your hair in two braids for luck.
10. When you take a test at school, bring along something pretty, like a gold ring, for good luck.
11. A ladybug is good luck. When you see one, say, "Ladybug, ladybug, fly away home; your house is afire and your children alone."
12. When you see a white horse, cross your fingers for luck. (Not too many years ago, it was popular to "stamp" a white horse. When a person saw one, he licked his thumb, wiped it in the palm of his other hand, and stamped the palm with the bottom of his fist. He held his thumb up, like the handle of a rubber stamp. This custom hasn't entirely disappeared. A boy in La Marque, Texas, reports that he stamps white horses, and a boy in Wisconsin Rapids, Wisconsin, reports that he stamps robins.)

Bad Luck

13. Thirteen and three are unlucky numbers.
14. Opening an umbrella in the house is unlucky.
15. Walking under a ladder will bring bad luck.
16. If a black cat crosses your path, watch out.
17. If a bird flies in the window, somebody will die.
18. Spilling salt brings bad luck. To stave off this effect, throw some over your left shoulder.
19. To avoid bad luck while riding in a car, hold your breath while passing cemeteries, lift your feet while crossing railroad tracks, and close your eyes while going under bridges.
20. If you step over someone's legs and do not go back over them, you will die. In some places, it is believed that the person who is stepped over is the one who will die.

21. If you put your underwear on inside out, changing it back will bring bad luck.

Wishing

22. If you see a postman or a red truck, cross your fingers and make a wish. Then, keep your fingers crossed until you see a dog, and your wish will come true; if you don't keep your fingers crossed, you will have bad luck.
23. If you see an eyelash on someone's cheek, tell the person to make a wish and guess which side the eyelash is on. If the guess is correct, the wish will come true.
24. After a girl ties five knots in a string, she ties it around a girl friend's wrist. The friend makes a wish for each knot and vows to tie threads on the wrists of from one to ten other girls. If a boy pulls the thread from her wrist, her wishes will come true.
25. Find a dandelion that has gone to seed, make a wish, and try to blow off all the seeds. If you do so, your wish will come true.
26. If you are riding in a car through a tunnel, ask the driver to honk, raise your right hand, and make a wish.
27. You can wish on a wishbone or on a falling star.

Cures

28. If you rub a wart with a new penny, the wart will go away.
29. If you rub a wart with an uncooked potato peel, the wart will go away.
30. If you wrap some of your own hair around a wart, in a few days it will die and go away.
31. To cure a headache, stand on your head.
32. A cup of whiskey and lemon juice will cure a cold.
33. To cure hiccups, drink water while bending over or standing on your head.

34. To cure hiccups, take twelve sips of water and hold your breath.
35. A teaspoonful of sugar will cure hiccups.

WEATHER LORE

36. If you kill a daddy longlegs spider, it will rain.
37. If you cut your hair during a full moon, it will grow fast.
38. When it rains, say, "Rain, rain, go away; little *Donald* wants to play."
39. When it rains, say, "It's raining, it's pouring, the old man is snoring,/Hit his head when he went to bed and couldn't get up in the morning."

SIGNS

40. If you hiccup, you've told a lie.
41. If your foot itches, you're going on a trip.
42. If your ear rings, someone is talking about you.
43. If your hand itches, you will get money.
44. If you are walking with a friend and you each walk on a different side of a telephone pole or a street-sign pole, you will soon quarrel. (The children we talked to didn't know the traditional charm for this occasion—saying, "Bread and butter" or "Salt and pepper" to stave off the consequences.
45. White spots on your fingernails means you lie a lot.
46. If you drop a knife, a boy will come visit; if you drop a fork, a girl will come.
47. One sneeze means a kiss is on the way, two means a wish, three a disappointment, four a letter, five something better.
48. A rainbow shows where gold is buried.

CAUTIONS

49. Don't make faces at a clock when it's striking twelve or your face will grow funny.

50. Don't kiss your elbow or you'll turn into a person of the opposite sex.
51. Don't pick up a toad or you'll get warts.
52. If a toad spits or pees on you, you'll get warts.

Scaries

Being scared—but not really—is a feeling children love. A child may overindulge in fear, just as he may overindulge in ice cream, and as a result may weep hysterically or wake up with nightmares. But children soon learn their capacity. One girl told us she was always too chicken to summon Mary Worth. She said, "I knew I'd really be scared." And really being scared is no fun.

A child summons Mary Worth, alias Bloody Mary, alias Mary Jane, by going into the bathroom alone at night, turning out the lights, staring into the mirror, and repeating "Mary Worth," softly but distinctly, forty-seven times. She comes at you out of the mirror, with a knife in her hand and a wart on her nose. Never when we read Mary Worth comic strips did we dream that the respectable busybody was moonlighting as a mirror witch!

Children, though they don't know it, have many good, practical reasons for scaring themselves. Obviously, flirting with fear is a way of learning to control it, a way of learning to empathize with others who are frightened, and a way of embellishing one's life with a little dramatic fiction. There are also other, less obvious benefits.

In all societies, the storyteller holds a position of respect. By listening to scary stories, a child learns to tell them, and by telling them, he gains prestige. He also learns confidence in his ability to control and direct others. At Girl Scout camp (a real testing and training ground for the tellers of scary stories), at slumber parties, in a tent set up in the backyard for an adventurous all-night sleep-out, or just sitting on a curb at night, after most of the gang have been called inside, the storyteller does his work. He may tell a widely known traditional tale like this one:

> Once there was this little girl who lived on a farm that was way, way, away from anything. And her parents had to go to town. So they left the little girl with this big collie dog to protect her. The mother said, "Now be sure to lock all the windows and doors." So when the mother and father were gone, the little girl and the collie went around to all the windows and locked them. Down in the basement there was this one little window that wouldn't shut tight, but the little girl thought, "Oh well, I've got the collie dog to protect me." So she went to bed. In the middle of the night, she heard this drip-drip sound and it woke her up and she was really scared, but she put her hand down beside her bed and the collie licked her hand so she felt better and went back to sleep. Then she heard this drip-drip-drip again, but she put her hand down and the dog licked it and she went to sleep. It happened again! Then in the morning she went into the bathroom and there was the collie dog hung up on the shower with its throat cut and all the blood had run out of it. The little girl screamed and screamed. When her parents came home, they found a note under the bed, and do you know what it said? It said, "Humans can lick, too, you know."

This is a cautionary tale—a modern fairy tale—reminding little girls to lock the house up tight. Similar tales about the perils of parking in lovers' lanes, visiting graveyards, taking drugs, and baby-sitting are widely known to grade school-girls. The favorite of those we talked to was "Drip-drip, Scratch-scratch": A couple in a lovers' lane heard on the car radio that a maniac had escaped from the asylum. The boy tried to start the car. Out of gas. He left to get some. The girl locked herself in. The boy didn't return. All night, she heard *drip-drip, scratch-scratch*. In the morning, she got out of the car and saw her boy friend hanging upside down in a tree. His throat was cut—*drip-drip*. And his fingernails were scraping the car's roof—*scratch-scratch*.

Another couple—the story goes—drove away from a lovers lane just in time. The maniac had only one good arm. When they got home, they found his hook wedged into the door handle.

A boy told us about the time when some boys were sitting around telling scary stories and one boy dared another to go to the graveyard and stick a knife into the grave of a man who had just died. And the boy did. And do you know what? When he got up to run, he couldn't, because he'd stuck the knife through his foot.

Girls tell us that baby-sitter stories are the scariest. One of the best is about the sitter who is on LSD. She bakes the baby instead of the turkey and eats it herself or feeds it to the other children. Another good one is about a sitter who receives several phone calls from a man who says that if she doesn't kill one of the children, he will. She finally asks the operator or the police to trace the call, and they discover he's on the upstairs extension! Somewhat less popular is the one about a sitter who is in charge of a two-year-old and a six-year-old. The six-year-old decides to go down to the basement, and after he is gone, the baby-sitter hears *thump, thump, thump.* . . . (These stories are big on thumps.) When she opens the basement door she sees the boy trying to climb the stairs with his legs cut off. "He was in shock." All the police find is a bloody hatchet.

Children want to explore their deep-seated fears of murder, mutilation, and cannibalism—the worst things they can imagine; therefore, they often insist that these stories are true. If the stories were fiction, the events they describe would be less horrible and hearing about them would therefore not provide as much vicarious satisfaction.

Baby-sitters tell tales of vampires or Frankenstein to children more often than we suspected before we began looking for scary stories. One baby-sitter, we learned, would take her four charges into a dark bedroom, tell a vampire story, then use a flashlight to single out the vampire's next victim. The chosen one would have to bend his head so that the sitter could bite him on the neck. When each of the children had been bitten, the sitter tucked them in and said good night. We asked, "Weren't you scared?"

"Oh, no! She was our favorite sitter."

A more light-hearted kind of scary story is meant to encourage the listeners to be brave: A ghost with a bloody finger lives in a room in the house. One after another, each member of the family enters the room, only to come running out when the ghost announces, "I am the ghost of the bloody finger." Finally, the baby of the family goes into the room and asks the ghost, "Well, why don't you put on a Band-Aid?" whereupon the ghost disappears. In a similar story, each member of a family goes down to the basement and is frightened by a ghost that says, "Bloody bones and gooey diapers." Finally the baby tells it off: "You take care of your bloody bones, and I'll take care of my gooey diapers."

Some children try to model themselves on these tough babies. In Wisconsin, and perhaps elsewhere, children recite a charm that shows ghosts and monsters who's boss:

> Crisscross, double-cross,
> Tell the monster to get lost!

This is derived from the popular locking rhyme that begins, "Crisscross, double-cross,/Nobody else can play."

Besides stories about tough babies, children tell stories about tough hotel guests:

> There's this spooky hotel where this hippie registers and he gets a haunted room where everybody who has slept there has been driven crazy, but when the hippie hears the chains rattling, he just opens up the door and says, "Cool it, daddy," and the ghost looks at him and runs away.

ONE POTATO, TWO POTATO...

The hippie is both the hero, who isn't afraid, and a kind of monster himself, who scares even the ghost.

Here is another hotel story:

> There is this big movie in town and all the hotels are full up. Except this one. And there's just one room left in it. But this man says he'll take it. The clerk says, "I wouldn't take it if I were you. I wouldn't sleep in it myself." But the man says he'll take it.
>
> So at midnight the man hears chains rattling and howling and all that and gets up. There's a ghost who says, "I am the ghost of the three red eyes."
>
> The man says, "Shut up or you're going to be the ghost of the three black eyes," and he goes back to bed and goes to sleep.

A story that encourages a rational approach to the mysterious is about a house that is haunted by a man who cut his throat. He drives everyone out by whispering, "Want a shave?" Finally, two brave men discover that the whisper is just the noise of a branch scraping against a window.

Some stories distance fear and achieve a kind of humor not by puns or anticlimax, but by exaggeration. The ever popular tale of the young lady who wears a mysterious black ribbon around her neck probably belongs in this group. When her curious husband finally snips the ribbon, she just has time to say, "You'll be sorry," as her head falls off. But this story is pretty tame compared to the one about the man who loves mayonnaise. He loves it so much that he uses a jar of it every day. One day he wakes up to find a new jar in his refrigerator. This happens again and again. Finally, he decides to stay up and see who's putting a new jar of mayonnaise in his refrigerator every night. At midnight, he sees a one-armed man come into his house and squeeze pus from the stump of his arm into the mayonnaise jar.

Then there is the woman who is accidentally locked in a house for a month. She survives by eating corn chips or potato chips. When the owner returns he learns what she has been eating and gasps, "Those boxes weren't filled with corn chips! Those were pieces of my dead skin from when I had leprosy!"

The gory story shades into the trick story. An example is the one about a boy sent to buy some liver. He loses the money, and in order not to come home empty-handed, goes to the graveyard, digs up a corpse, and takes out its liver. One night the body from the graveyard comes to the house seeking its liver. It climbs the stairs one at a time. (There's an abundance of stair-climbing in scaries.) "Where is my liver? Now I'm on the second step; who's got my liver? Now I'm on the third step . . ." At the climax of the story, the teller shouts, "*You've* got it!" and grabs someone.

Another famous trick story is about the gambler who buys his one-armed wife a golden arm. After she dies he digs it up and takes it to bed, and soon he hears her climbing the stairs, moaning, "Where is my golden arm?" At the right moment, the teller grabs a listener's arm and utters a blood-curdling "Here it is!"

Some stories verge on straight jokes. The green ghost with the purple fingers and the blue tongue scares a little girl in bed for three nights. When she asks him why he is doing that to her, he gives her the raspberries. There are dozens of stories of this type. A man calls up a woman on the phone and tells her he's coming up to her apartment. She asks him who he is, and he says, "The Widow Viper." He telephones her from every floor as he approaches her apartment. The woman calls the police. When she hears a knock on the door, she says, "Oh, thank heaven," and opens it. And there stands . . . a little old man who says, "I'm the widow viper. Do you want your widows vashed?" Here is another example:

> A girl lived out in the country. One night there was a knock on the door, so she opened it and there was a coffin. It came toward her, closer and closer. She ran into the living room. It came after her. She ran into the dining room. It came after her. She ran up the stairs, but it

247

came up the stairs, one, two, . . . until it reached the top. She ran into her room and shut the door, but the coffin opened the door and came closer and closer and closer, until she was up against the wall. At the last minute, she pulled out a box of Smith Brothers cough drops, and stopped the coffin.

The chase is an element in many stories. Just as the coffin chases a girl through the house, so does the pink gorilla. In fact, the pink gorilla chases the poor girl out of the house and through the streets for as long as the storyteller can keep inventing incidents. When the terrible gorilla finally catches up with his victim, he announces, "Tag, you're It."

Scary stories are sometimes merely retold versions of television horror shows or movies. (In the thirties and forties, we retold stories that we had heard on radio programs like "Inner Sanctum" and "I Love a Mystery.") Stories are also borrowed from books. Versions of "The Monkey's Paw" and "The Legend of Sleepy Hollow" are sometimes told by children who have never read them.

> Once upon a time, there was an old man who was invited to a party. In those days there was a tale about a headless horseman who would chop off the heads of people who rode at midnight. At the party, the old man fell asleep. When he woke up it was midnight. He tried to hurry to his house as quick as he could. But on a bridge the headless horseman appeared and chopped off his head. The next day people saw a pumpkin head beside the bridge.

Usually the more complicated stories are told by older children to younger ones. The older child gets to demonstrate his superiority, and the younger ones get to crowd close together and enjoy the luscious camaraderie that comes from being scared together.

A different kind of scary story is the neighborhood story,

which gives a certain glamour—some literary resonance—to the otherwise unremarkable places where children grow up. Children in Kokomo, Indiana, in the fifties told each other about an old man dressed in white who had a white dog. He and his dog walked up and down the alleys of Kokomo late at night. Children tried to catch him but never could. He would always appear when least expected and was never seen by a group but always by one child alone. When the kids were together and heard a dog bark, they knew he was in the neighborhood. One day they saw a white dog running down the street, dragging a leash. They figured the old man had died.

A mysterious old man dressed in white is a more believable figure in this rational age than a ghost would be, but this man's ghostly characteristics are obvious.

Often, neighborhood stories are centered on legendary residents who are reputed to chase children who cut across their lawns and to wave pitchforks or shotguns. One boy from Kansas City told us that at his school the little kids believed that the former principal was buried under the mound at the base of the flagpole, which came right up out of her grave. Other children told us of a teacher who looked like a witch; if she touched you, you would get warts.

Most local stories are of pretty standard types. In El Paso children speak of a real woman in their neighborhood who is known as *La Llorona* ("The Crier"). According to the story, her son was killed by a boy playing with a slingshot. Every night at eight she weeps, and if you speak while passing her house, she will put a curse on you. Similar stories are told in many places.

In Selma, Alabama, children tell of the Cat Man, a restaurateur who made the best hamburgers in town—from, as it turned out, cats. "You used to be able to see him around town after he got out of jail, but he died about five years ago."

And a girl told us of a black ragpicker who actually worked

249

for her grandmother. His name was Old Moe, and he would carry off in his bag the bad children who didn't mind their parents. The girl admitted this was "just a story" but insisted Moe was real. He probably was, but stories about bogeymen who bag bad children are common.

Another way children give local color to their neighborhoods is by assigning names to their particular landmarks. These names aren't always scary, though they may be. While adults are finding their way from house number to house number, children range between Skull Rock, The Fort, Clay Hill, The Burma Road, The Woods, and The Ghost House or The Castle.

Besides stories, scaries include games, songs, and various versions of a kind of ceremony that is also a trick. In the latter, a child may, for example, "draw" with his finger a daddy snake, a mama snake, and a baby snake on a friend's back. Saying, "Sometimes they crawl up," he traces the snakes' movements with his hand. "Sometimes they crawl down"—he traces the snakes' trails. "Sometimes they even bite!"—he squeezes his friend's neck. Or he may announce in a mysterious voice, "We are going on a treasure hunt," and draw a figure eight on a friend's back. Then he says, "X marks the spot," and draws an X. "Two black lines"—he draws parallel horizontal lines. "And a question mark"—he draws a question mark and adds a punch in the small of the back for the period. "A pinch"—he pinches an ear lobe. "A squeeze" —he squeezes his friend's shoulders. "An African breeze"— he blows on the back of his friend's neck. "Blood running down"—he runs his index fingers in wiggly lines down his friend's back, then says, "Gotcha!" as he pokes him in the waist. Another version goes: "X marks the spot. A dash and a dot. Two bullet holes. Blood running down. A cool fresh wind. And chills."

Games that enable children to play with fear include Gray Ghost (sometimes called Ghost in the Graveyard), Colored

Bunnies (or Colored Eggs), Old Witch, and Pray for the Dead. In Gray Ghost, the ghost hides; the other players count: "One o'clock rock, two o'clock rock . . ." up to twelve o'clock. Then they go looking for the ghost.

> Starlight, star bright,
> Hope I see a ghost tonight.

A player who sees the ghost shouts, "Gray Ghost!" (or "Ghost in the Graveyard!") and everyone hightails it for the base. Those tagged become ghosts.

In Colored Bunnies, one player is the mother, and secretly informs each of her bunnies what color she is naming him. The wolf comes to the door.

"Knock, knock."

"Who's there?"

"The wolf."

"What do you want?"

"Some bunnies."

The mother may put him off by telling him that he's not clean enough or that the bunnies are asleep, but soon the wolf demands prey of a particular color, crying, for example, "I want some red ones." The bunny of that color runs for a distant base. If the bunny is caught, he takes the wolf's place. If he is not caught, the wolf repeats his demand, substituting another color. Tricky mothers may name all their bunnies the same color. When the wolf finally mentions it, all the children run.

The players in Old Witch edge closer and closer to the Witch. At each step, they ask, "Hey, Witch, you coming out tonight?"

"No."

"Why?"

"I'm combing my hair," or "I'm drying my panty hose."

When the questioners are close enough to suit her—and as jittery as can be—the Witch suddenly answers, "Yes!" and chases after them. The one she catches takes her place or goes to the dungeon.

Pray for the Dead is played in the fall. A child is buried in leaves. The others kneel beside the "grave" and chant, "Pray for the dead, and the dead will pray for you." The chant goes on for an indeterminate period. The buried child slowly stirs, then suddenly explodes from the leaves. The others run away screaming. Whoever the ghost catches is It next time.

Children's interest in the scary supernatural expands in the fifth and sixth grades. Stories, jokes, tricks, and games aren't enough any more. In almost every sixth-grade class there is some would-be master of the occult who organizes séances or tries to hypnotize his friends. Sometimes the craze for "knocking yourself out" by hyperventilating flourishes briefly. At slumber parties, girls try to lift up a prone classmate, using only two fingers each. The procedure takes about a dozen girls, and is regarded as magical. Girls also try to make each other faint, by squeezing each other's midriffs.

At slumber parties, girls may also play a game called Trance. A girl lies down on the floor, and the master sits behind her head. The others form a circle around them and hold hands. The master presses her index fingers against the temples of her subject. The subject closes her eyes. The master moves her fingers in small circles, saying things like "Sleep," and "Now you are in my power." Eventually the subject—the "monster" —stands. The master controls her by clapping. One clap means *go*; two, *faster*; three, *stop*. The master also gives instructions, things like "Walk into the wall," or "Strangle Suzy."

Our informants were cagey when we asked them if the monster was really in the master's power. "Of course not," they said, and shrugged. But clearly they liked the idea that to some degree the monster really had abdicated her control over herself to the master. They liked the idea of temporarily not being themselves.

When their party settles down, the girls may sing songs, among them this version of "Allouette":

Suffocation, we love suffocation,
Suffocation, so much fun to play.
First you take a plastic bag,
Then you put it on your head.
Go to bed,
Wake up dead,
Oh, oh, oh, oh.
[Repeat.]

Because death is a frightening subject, it inspires flippant songs like this one, which are traditionally sung in unison by laughing, self-confident friends. However, not all children's rhymes about death are so ghoulish. An old jump-rope rhyme still used in Texas has a tone of stoic dignity:

Grandma, Grandma, I am ill.
Send for the doctor to give me a pill.
Doctor, Doctor, shall I die?
Yes, you will and so will I.
How many carriages shall I have?
Ten, twenty, thirty, forty, . . .

Cartomancy, Chartomancy, Onomancy, Sortilege, and Other Methods of Divination

Girls like to play with the idea of having boy friends. Traditional practices help them to do so. And the girl who pinches soda straws or pulls the petals off a flower while muttering, "Loves me, loves me not," knows that she is following ancient custom and that she is not unusual because she is wondering about this question.

A popular way to discover who loves you is to recite the alphabet while twisting the stem from an apple. When the stem comes off, the initial of your lover is revealed. A less popular but by no means extinct custom is to peel an apple in one long strip, which you throw over your left shoulder. The shape it takes when it falls reveals your lover's initial.

ONE POTATO, TWO POTATO...

Years ago, apple seeds were used in a more elaborate ceremony. A girl counted the seeds from her apple as she chanted:

> One I love, two I love, three I love, I say.
> Four I love with all my heart,
> Five I'll cast away.
> Six he loves, seven she loves,
> Eight they both love.
> Nine he comes, ten he tarries,
> Eleven he courts, twelve he marries.
> (Mississippi, 1919)

If there were more than twelve seeds, she started over.

Another way of learning the name of a secret admirer is,
as we have seen in an earlier chapter, to jump rope while
reciting a rhyme like:

> Ice-cream soda, cream on top,
> Tell me the name of my sweetheart.
> A, B, C, D, ...

The letter the jumper misses on is the initial of her admirer's
name.

A longer version from Texas requires the jumper to continue jumping after she misses, inserting the name of her
admirer, and her own name, as she chants:

> *David* and *Ann*
> Went on a ride.
> *David* asked *Ann*
> To be his bride.
> Yes, no, may-be-so,
> Yes, no, ...

Ann's answer will be revealed when she misses.

Counting buttons is still a popular way of finding out what
kind of job a future husband will hold:

Rich man, poor man, beggarman, thief,
Doctor, lawyer, merchant chief,
Tinker, tailor, cowboy, sailor.

Names are always significant. If a girl's and a boy's first or last names start with the same letter, that's an obvious sign. Usually, names must be made to yield a hidden meaning. In one of the ways to make them do this, you begin by writing a couple's names side by side. You cross out the letters they have in common. Then you count the remaining letters as you say, "Friendship, courtship, love, hatred, marriage." It works out like this: Sally Brown—John Smith = Love. Or you can count the remaining letters as you say, "Loves me, loves me not." With these two names, the answer comes out "Loves me," confirming the first prediction.

Another method of divination that requires crossing out begins with the creation of a chart. You ask a girl to name four cars, colors, boys, houses, states, and anything else you can think of. Arrange her replies thus:

Pinto	Mustang	Cadillac	Mercedes
Red	Blue	Green	White
Bill	Tom	Jerry	Al
Cabin	Tent	Colonial	Split-level
Kansas	Texas	Oregon	Maine

Then you ask her at what age she'll marry. If she answers, let us say, "At twenty," you count the squares and cross out the twentieth. Then you keep counting to twenty and crossing out, skipping the eliminated squares and the last remaining square in each row, until there is just one item left for each category. Now you know what kind of car she'll drive, what color dress she'll wear at her wedding, whom she will marry, and so on.

Another count and cross-out system is based on this pattern:

ONE POTATO, TWO POTATO...

```
L   M   D   H   E
O   A   I   A   N
V   R   V   T   G
E   R   O   E   A
    Y   R       G
        C       E
        E
```

A girl asks a friend to choose a number. If, say, she chooses 4, they go through the words, one by one, crossing out every fourth letter, and on subsequent rounds skipping the letters that have already been crossed out. The first word to be completely crossed out indicates the first thing that's going to happen to the person who chose the number. In this instance, the first thing that will happen to the girl will be a divorce; that will be difficult, since presumably she will not yet have married, but then the pronouncements of the oracles are notoriously enigmatic.

Oracles also consult the gods by means of a string tied around a pencil, a needle, or a ring. You hold this contraption over a person's hand. If it swings in a circle, the person will soon be married; if it swings from side to side, she will lose her boy friend. The interpretations vary. The self-appointed oracle consciously changes the interpretation to fit the person whose future is being told. Older children become very clever at prognosticating. One junior-high-school boy told us he would read his classmates' palms and somewhere in his interpretation include, "Not too long ago you had a fight with your mother."

"They're really impressed," he sneered.

"Does it always work?" we asked.

He looked at us in disbelief. "Everyone just had a fight with his mother," he said.

One method of predicting whether or not a couple will get along resembles something done by a computer. You translate the names of the boy and girl in question into numbers determined by the vowels each name contains. For example, using as a guide the pattern *a-e-i-o-u,* you would denote John Wolf by 00020, since the number of *a*'s, *e*'s, and *i*'s in his name is 0, the number of *o*'s is 2, and the number of *u*'s is 0. Betty Ward would be 11000. Added together, these names total 11020. Since the same digit appears twice in a row, we know that John and Betty love each other.

Perhaps the best-known fortune-telling device is the wiggle-waggle paper predictor. We call it that; the children don't have a name for it. Take a sheet of paper and fold it as directed here.

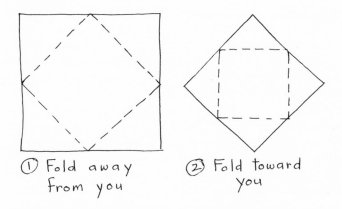

① Fold away from you   ② Fold toward you

When you've reached Position 5, open the paper back up to Position 3 and write a number between 1 and 20 on each of the eight outside triangles. On the underside of each tri-angle, write a "fortune"—something like, "You love yourself," "You are a nice person," or "You love a boy with blue eyes." Then turn the paper over and write the name of a color on each of the squares.

Slip the first two fingers of your left hand under the square farther from you on the left side, and your left thumb under the square nearer you. Arrange the fingers and thumb of your right hand under the right-side squares in the same way.

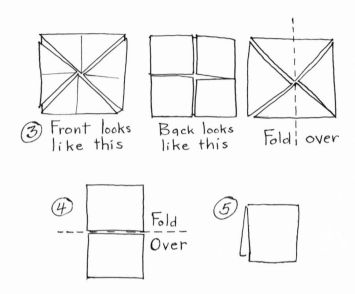

③ Front looks
like this

Back looks
like this

Fold over

④ Fold
Over

⑤

Pinch together the fingers and thumb of each hand so that
they grasp the fold of paper between them. Then push the
pinched fingers of each hand toward each other, closing the
predictor and revealing the names of the colors. Ask a friend
to choose a color. Let us say she picks blue. Blue has four
letters. *One:* You open your fingers, revealing one set of
numbers. *Two:* Closing your fingers, you pull your hands
slightly apart, revealing another set of numbers. *Three:* Moving your hands back together, you open your fingers and
return to the first set of numbers. (If this sequence of movements is too hard for you, get a little girl to show you how.)
Four: You close your fingers and move your hands slightly
apart. Now ask your friend to pick one of the numbers that
is exposed. If she chooses 6, you blink and wink your predictor
six times. Repeat this operation four times in all. The fifth
time your friend picks a number, you turn up the sibylline
pronouncement on the underside of the flap, and she reads,

"You love yourself," or whatever. Girls carry these gadgets in their purses, ever ready to prognosticate.

Girls also fold a love charm that looks like this:

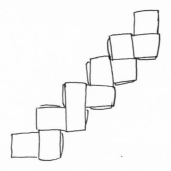

Often they use gum wrappers, tearing them in half lengthwise and using one half for each link. It is commonly believed that the longer the charm is, the greater its potency. If you can make one the height of your boy friend, it's a sure sign that he loves you—or that you love him. However, girls often stop extending the charm when they have made one that is long enough to wear as a bracelet.

Children so enjoy the feeling that predicting gives them that they preserve rituals that seem pretty pointless. For instance, holding a dandelion or a buttercup under the chin of a friend, a girl will note the yellow reflection on her friend's skin and announce with satisfaction, "You like butter." Few children wonder about the utility of this revelation. They value revelation for its own sake.

Pursuing revelations, children will play with cards for hours, laughing over the way the cards contradict themselves but eager, nevertheless, to see what the next hand will say. For some children, hearts mean good luck, spades mean hard work, diamonds mean that someone will give you money, and clubs mean that you will be sick. Other children associate the suits with various types of boys: hearts indicate a blond athlete; spades, a dark sarcastic person; clubs, a dark, nice person; and diamonds, a pale intellectual.

There are different ways of reading the cards. One is to ask them a question that can be answered by Yes or No, then turn over three cards. If two of the three are red, the answer is "Yes." If all three are red, it's "Absolutely!" Some girls remove the jacks from a deck and name them after boys. Usually, one is named after a boy whom the girls consider "gross." Then three other cards are selected, to stand for "going steady," "engaged," and "married," and one of the girls asks a question like, "Who will I marry?" The dealer deals a card to each jack, repeating until the "marriage" card shows up. For the answer to a question like, "Who will marry the fat lady in the circus?" the dealer need turn over only a single card. If it is a spade, and the jack of spades stands for Jeff, Jeff is the boy who will marry the fat lady. Common questions are, "Who will be divorced eight times?" and "Who likes Jane [or Alison or whomever]?" Another common question is, "Who will die very young?" Children don't seek revelations about death as often as they do those about boy friends and weddings, but death, too, they know, is part of the future.

Children don't really think this sort of magic works. They know that they are playing games and that the next prediction will contradict the last. However, games that predict the future give them a traditional framework that encourages them to think about the future. These games also give children a feeling of power and control. The feeling is real, even if the power and control are fictitious.

NOTES

Superstitions

The anecdote about the safety jingle is reported by Beverly Schanzer, "Accidents That Don't Have to Happen—What Parents Should Know," *Redbook*, 137 (July 1971), 155.

6 | Conclusion

Linking the Generations

Childlore is part of the web of common reference—sorely tattered in this age of specialists—that gives us all some sense of belonging to the same club. In an age when few people read the same books or recognize a wide range of literary allusions, almost everybody still recognizes allusions to the oral tradition of childhood, things like, "Cross my heart," "Here I come, ready or not," "Twinkle, twinkle, little star," "Eeny, meeny, miney, moe," "Sticks and stones," and so on. Popular songs include fragments of autograph rhymes, such as "Roses are red"; of superstitions, such as "Loves me, loves me not"; and of jeers, such as "Sarah, bum bara, fee fi banana, fanana, fo farah." Literary poets allude to "Kings X," Prisoner's Base, Hide and Seek, and other lore.

Sometimes adults do more than merely allude to childlore; they imitate and share it. A newly hired computer technician told us that one of the first things she learned on her new job was:

IBM, UBM,
We all BM
For IBM.

261

ONE POTATO, TWO POTATO...

This echoes the children's cheer:

> I scream, you scream,
> We all scream
> For ice cream.

Children and teachers share verses, folk wisdom, even games. Faced with a noisy class, many a teacher has imitated Circe and intoned, "First one to speak is a monkey for a week." Poor spellers are taught traditional mnemonic devices that have been passed on for generations: "A rat in the house may eat the ice cream," to help them spell "arithmetic," and the Mexican girl's reply to the red-headed cowboy—"Oh, *si, si,* you are red"—to help them spell "occurred." And in schools across the nation, a weary teacher who needs a time out has the class play Seven-up, a game with an ancestry that is ancient indeed.

Seven students stand. The rest put their heads down on their desks and shut their eyes. The seven go through the aisles, tapping students on their backs. At a signal, everyone sits up and tries to guess who touched him.

A similar game is described in the Bible. Matthew, Mark, and Luke all mention Roman soldiers blindfolding Jesus, then striking him and demanding, "Prophesy unto us, thou Christ, Who is he that smote thee?" In this scene, the soldiers seem to be playing the Roman game called Bucca. Michael Heseltine notes that Bucca was a child's game in which a blindfolded player was tapped on the cheek by friends, who then asked him how many people, or how many fingers, had touched him. In Latin, the term *bucca* means "cheek"; it was used especially in reference to a puffed-out cheek. The parallel between this game and Seven-up is obvious; less so is its relationship to the leaping game Buck-buck, also known as Johnny on a Pony. This game is particularly popular between New York City and Washington, D.C. There is no guessing involved. Teams are chosen. One team forms a line, and its members bend over, forming a many-legged "pony." One

player from this team braces his back against a wall and cush-
ions in his stomach the head of the first player in the pony
line. The players on the other team leapfrog one at a time onto
the pony. "Buck-buck number one!" shouts the first leaper
as he takes his turn. The leapers' goal is to concentrate their
weight on the weakest part of the pony. If it collapses, the
leapers win. If the pony remains standing, the leapers shout,
"Johnny on a pony, one, two, three; Johnny on a pony, one,
two, three; Johnny on a pony, one, two, three," and the two
teams changes roles.

Some versions of the old Roman guessing game Bucca combined leaping with the guessing. Petronius describes such a
game in the *Satyricon*. One player leaped piggyback upon
another, slapped him on the shoulder, and cried, *Bucca, bucca,
quot sunt hic?"* The other player was evidently meant to guess
how many fingers his friend was holding up. This game may
have been ancient even in the time of Petronius, borrowed by
the Romans from the Greeks, Egyptians, or possibly the Chinese.

This combination of leaping and guessing survives in the
north of England in a game that goes by various names but
is often called Husky-bum, Finger or Thumb? In some places
it is played by only two players, just as it was in ancient Rome,
except that the questioner asks, "How many bugs?" instead of
"Bucca bucca, quot sunt hic?" In other places, the game is
played by teams and resembles the American game Buck-
buck. However, in this particular English version of the game,
if the pony team bears up under the weight of the leapers, the
captain of the leaping team holds up one hand and shouts,
"Finger, thumb, or dumb [fist]?" or something similar. If the
captain of the pony team does not answer correctly, his team
must serve as the pony again. Until at least the late twenties
an American version of this game involving both guessing
and leaping was played in the United States at Bath Beach,
Brooklyn. However, in recent years in the United States the
version combining guessing and leaping has given way to

ONE POTATO, TWO POTATO...

Buck-buck, which is purely a leaping game and a test of strength. In parts of England, Husky-bum, Finger or Thumb? has also given way to the British equivalent of Buck-buck, called Hi Jimmy Knacker.

However, the guessing aspect of the old Roman game survived into this century in other games, characteristically played by an adult and a child. In one version, after covering the child's eyes, the adult pats out the beat while saying:

> Hurly Burly trump a tray,
> The cow was sold on market day,
> Simon, Nally hunt the buck.
> How many horns stand up?

The child guesses the number of fingers. If he is wrong, the other player may say, "*Two* you said and *four* it was,/Hurly Burly . . ." and the game is repeated. If the child is correct, the players change roles.

The preservation of the sound "buck" in this game from Roman times to the present is the result of the accidental congruence of several elements. To leap on another's back is to ride him as if he were a pony or horse. (In a Scottish version of this game called Skin the Cuddy, the leaper is known as a "bronco buster.") Bucking is associated with horses, and the Latin *bucca* sounds like the English "buck." The folk are not respecters of etymologies. They order words around like Humpty Dumpty in *Alice Through the Looking Glass*. In twentieth-century guessing games derived from Bucca, a player asks, "How many horns has the buck?" meaning "stag"; here is still another transformation that both disguises and preserves our links with the classical world.

Adults and children also share moralistic folk rhymes—"If you're strong and if you're able,/Get your elbows off the table!"—nursery rhymes, lullabies, and favorite storybooks. Though these are not usually regarded as childlore, we certainly all learn them when we are children. It's just that we wait fifteen or twenty years before we hand them on to another child. The act of transmitting this kind of folklore links a woman to her child and also, in a new way, to her own mother, as she finds herself passing on to the next generation the favorite lullabies and stories that were once passed on by her mother to her.

The Future of Childlore

The belief that children's folklore is a thing of the past—like galoshes, mustard plasters, and the British Empire—is incorrect. Childlore has survived, however, in an increasingly inhospitable atmosphere since the last world war.

In the early fifties, television lured many children away from the games they traditionally played after school and between dinner and dark. It also focused increasing attention on professional sports, and this emphasis, along with the women's magazines' stress on "togetherness" abetted the proliferation of organized athletic leagues for grade-school and junior-high-school boys—and their families.

The promotion of "togetherness" was part of a successful campaign to put women back behind the picture window. Once there, mothers looked around for something to do, and many of them began monitoring their children's lives with unusual intensity. A child just trying to grow up found himself on a schedule of lessons and activities tighter than that of a competitive swimmer preparing for the Olympics.

As if that weren't enough, the booming economy of the fifties and sixties encouraged the schools to hire more specialists, among them teachers with M.A.'s and Ph.D.'s in physical education. (Gym teachers have, of course, worked in the schools for many years, but during the Depression and the years of World War II, several grade schools shared the same gym teacher, who only afflicted any particular class once a month or so. We vividly remember the gloom that settled over our classrooms in the early forties when it was announced that we would be having gym that day instead of recess. We knew what that meant—having to learn some new game or standing around, waiting to climb ropes.)

Moreover, by the late fifties, the physical-education specialists had a cause. Tests had supposedly shown that American children were less fit than their European counterparts. It was clearly the job of the schools to improve the physical condition of American children. To motivate children, Presidential Fitness Certificates were awarded to those who met certain standards. Recess gave way more and more frequently to physical education periods.

But childlore endured, if it didn't exactly flourish. And many of the anti-childlore trends of the last twenty years now seem to be waning. Many women have found better things to do than to try to be supermommies, and in liberating themselves, they have freed their children. The declining economy has also forced cutbacks in the number of teachers, and recess has reappeared in some parts of the land.

There are, however, new threats to some aspects of childlore, the bussing of grade-school children, for instance. Bussing needn't weaken a play group; if all the children in one neighborhood ride the same bus for a short period, it may even have a strengthening effect. But because the time children spend being bussed is deducted from their playtime, they do much of their playing as they ride, and a bus is no place for the traditional games that help them learn about rule-making and that have always held a central place in childlore. Rather, it is a good place for bawdy songs, jeers, tricks, Cooties, ambush games, and scapegoating versions of Keepaway (a spontaneous game in which a glove, shoe, or other object belonging to the victim is tossed from child to child, just out of its owner's reach).

And proposals are being made to keep the schools open the year round, in the name of economy. This change too would interfere with the development of play groups, since within one neighborhood different children would likely be assigned different vacation periods.

Conclusion

Children are also still beset by those who believe that the discipline and narrow focus of organized sports will prevent juvenile delinquency, build character, and add to the prestige of the United States of America.

They may build character; no one can say how playing a particular game will affect a particular child. But often supervised sports produce only obedient specialists. A group in New York is advocating a national jump-rope league, for example, which would have tournaments and produce better jumpers than the street game. It would reduce the complex verbal, physical, and social interplay of traditional jump-rope to mere jumping. Worse, when adults take over, they immediately announce, "There's a right way and a wrong way," and begin demanding that children play "right." We know a boy who grew to hate going to school while his gym teacher was "teaching" jump-rope. She said he was "galloping" instead of "jumping." He was convinced that he couldn't even pass playtime.

This tendency to see games in terms of results is also evident in the remarks of an American Olympics official who spoke enviously of the way the East Germans analyze their children's physical abilities in kindergarten, put them into the sports that the experts deem most suitable, then transfer those who excel to special schools where more experts monitor each student's diet and training program—all in order to turn each athlete into a superspecialist.

But there's more to sports than victories and records that are supposed to make some pseudo-Darwinian point about a player's or a nation's fitness.

We aren't suggesting that supervised sports aren't beneficial to children. Of course they are. But supervised sports are often overemphasized. When adults suppose that *only* supervised sports are good for children, they are mistaken. It is in playing traditional, not supervised games, that children learn how to make rules, how to experiment with their feelings, and how to use language with a flair and an appreciation of its trickiness. They are guided, not supervised, by their traditional childlore, which by its existence helps create a sense of community, of neighborhood—at least among children.

We would like to see children's folklore play a larger role in their lives, but there is nothing that we can do directly to promote it. Its whole value lies in the fact that it is not ours to promote. It is our children's lore. All we can do is recognize its virtues and give children the time and freedom they need to make it flourish.

NOTES

Linking the Generations

The guessing game from the Bible is discussed in E. B. Tylor, "The History of Games," in *The Study of Games,* edited by *Elliott M. Avedon and Brian Sutton-Smith* (New York: John Wiley & Sons, 1971), p. 65. Michael Heseltine's comment on Bucca is in Paul G. Brewster, "Some Notes on the Guessing Game, How Many Horns Has the Buck?" in *The Study of Folklore,* edited by Alan Dundes (Englewood Cliffs, N.J.: Prentice-Hall, 1965), p. 341n. The version of the finger guessing game that we use is from Eugenia L. Millard, "Guessing Games," *New York Folklore Quarterly,* 13 (1957), pp. 135–41. Iona and Peter Opie discuss Husky-bum, Finger or Thumb? and Skin the Cuddy in *Children's Games in Street and Playground* (Oxford: Clarendon Press, 1969), pp. 294–301; 261–62.

Sources of Data

Central to our material are the 379 questionnaires that we collected from fifth-graders in Indiana in 1971, some of which we followed up with interviews. We also collected 205 essays and questionnaires during 1975 from children in Texas, Kansas, Nebraska, Montana, Wisconsin, and New Jersey. Traveling about the country in 1973 and again in 1975, we interviewed children and observed play groups in Kansas City, Missouri; Bloomington, Indiana; Seattle, Washington; and Austin, Texas. In the Canal Zone, we have interviewed 500 high-school students and 400 college freshmen, who were asked mainly to provide variations and explanations of material collected first from grade-school children. Our students were very helpful in securing information from younger brothers and sisters. Some college students interviewed their own children for us. Also, we interviewed the girls from three Girl Scout troops and observed their play activities after their formal meetings; we interviewed 60 sixth-graders; and we regularly observed five local play groups.

The Canal Zone is a good place to study the distribution of children's lore, for both the military families and the employees of the Panama Canal Company—indeed, almost everybody here—came from somewhere else.

In addition to the material gathered by ourselves, we have drawn upon material gathered by others. Our debts to folklorists who have studied particular aspects of childlore are

269

acknowledged after each chapter. However, here we would like to mention three sources that were particularly useful but that there has been no occasion to cite earlier: Edith Fowke, *Sally Go Round the Sun* (Garden City, N.Y.: Doubleday, 1969); Nancy C. Leventhal and Ed Cray, "Depth-Collecting from a Sixth-Grade Class," *Western Folklore*, 22 (1963), 159–63; and the material gathered in Eugene, Oregon by our daughter Eleanor, who also did hours of research for us.

All in all, we have made use of material from forty-three states, the Virgin Islands, the Canal Zone, and American military bases abroad. We have also used material gathered from foreign students from India, England, Germany, Taiwan, Iran, and Panama.

Index

INDEX

INDEX